GREAT PREACHING ON

THANKSGIVING

GREAT PREACHING ON

THANKSGIVING

COMPILED BY
CURTIS HUTSON

SWORD of the LORD
PUBLISHERS
P.O. BOX 1099, MURFREESBORO, TN 37133

Printed and Bound in the United States of America

Preface

The word "thanks" in one form or another is found some 140 times in the Bible.

David probably used it more times than any other Bible character. Paul, who lived continually in the spirit of thanksgiving, runs him a close second, for praise was as natural to him as breathing.

Paul was ever on the lookout to find some cause for gratitude. He sang in prison, his feet in the stocks, his wrists in chains. He sang in the storm, when the fierce Euroclydon tossed the little ship on mountainous waves and every moment threatened disaster. When criticism and contempt were heaped upon him, and the cold shoulder was offered to his loving approaches, the spirit of praise and rejoicing never left him.

And Paul exhorted the churches not merely to give thanks sometimes but at all times—and for all things.

Daniel, whose life was threatened, "prayed and gave thanks before his God."

Jonah, being chastened of the Lord, voiced his thanks: "I will sacrifice unto thee with the voice of thanksgiving."

And Christ is the personification of praise and thanks. He gave thanks for the bread and cup used in the Lord's Supper. On another occasion He prayed, "I thank thee, O Father . . . because thou hast hidden these things from the wise and prudent, and hast revealed them unto babes." At the tomb of Lazarus, Jesus prayed, "Father, I thank thee that thou hast heard me." When Jesus took the five barley loaves and two fishes from the little boy in order to feed the multitude, He first gave thanks.

So giving thanks is not only taught by precept but also taught many times by the matchless example of Jesus.

We, too, must learn to give "thanks always for all things. . . ." For accelerating inflation? for physical ills? for lack of a job? for an automobile accident? Apparently, for in requesting help out of our troubles, we are to let our requests, by prayer and supplication, be made known unto God WITH THANKSGIVING. It is not to the honor of our gracious Master that we should 'sit under juniper trees and hang our harps upon willows.' "I won't be unhappy," vowed a fine old saint; "It is all I have to give to God and I will praise and thank and glorify Him by a happy face and a radiant life."

Thankfulness, or its opposite, is the thermometer by which our spiritual temperature is gauged, the "oil of gladness" that lubricates life's activities.

Here you will find incorporated into one book a broad scope of thanksgiving messages formerly found only by looking from book to book, or not found in print at all. Our prayer is that this collection by varied Spirit-filled authors of the past and present, messages chosen from the pages of THE SWORD OF THE LORD over the past 52 years—the best to be found on thanksgiving—will prove medicine for your heart in times of grief, comfort for your times of distress, encouragement in your times of trial.

As this book goes out on its mission, we pray that God will richly bless it. Many of these sermons have led souls to Christ when preached, and afterward when put in print. That they may still be so blessed is our prayer.

Curtis Hutson, Editor
SWORD OF THE LORD

Table of Contents

CURTIS HUTSON
1934-

ABOUT THE MAN:

In 1961 a mail carrier and pastor of a very small church attended a Sword of the Lord conference, got on fire, gave up his route and set out to build a great soul-winning work for God. Forrest Hills Baptist Church of Decatur, Georgia, grew from 40 people into a membership of 7,900. The last four years of his pastorate there, the Sunday school was recognized as the largest one in Georgia.

After pastoring for 21 years, Dr. Hutson—the great soul winner that he is—became so burdened for the whole nation that he entered full-time evangelism, holding great citywide-areawide-cooperative revivals in some of America's greatest churches. As many as 625 precious souls have trusted Christ in a single service. In one eight-day meeting, 1,502 salvation decisions were recorded.

As an evangelist, he is in great demand.

At the request of Dr. John R. Rice, Dr. Hutson became Associate Editor of THE SWORD OF THE LORD in 1978, serving in that capacity until the death of Dr. Rice before becoming Editor, President of Sword of the Lord Foundation, and Director of Sword of the Lord conferences.

All these ministries are literally changing the lives of thousands of preachers and laymen alike, as well as winning many more thousands to Christ.

Dr. Hutson is the author of many fine books and booklets.

I.

On Being Thankful

CURTIS HUTSON

(Preached in 1972)

"Enter into his gates with thanksgiving, and into his courts with praise: be thankful unto him, and bless his name."—Ps. 100:4.

Dr. Bob Jones, Sr., said, "The loveliest flower that blooms in the garden of the heart is the flower of gratitude; and when gratitude dies on the altar of a man's heart, he's well nigh gone." That's a tremendous statement! "When gratitude dies on the altar of a man's heart, he's well nigh gone."

We read in Romans 1:21-28 where ". . .when they knew God, they glorified him not as God, neither were thankful: but became vain in their imaginations. . .and even as they did not like to retain God in their knowledge, God gave them over to a reprobate mind, to do those things which are not convenient."

It all started when they were not thankful. Because they were not thankful, God gave them up. A lot of sins committed today are a result of a lack of genuine gratitude in the heart.

I. MEN ARE NOT THANKFUL BY NATURE

Gratitude is not a part of our nature. Let me illustrate. Anything you have to be taught to do is not a part of your nature; and anything you do without being taught is a part of your nature.

For instance, it is a duck's nature to swim. When you throw him into the water, he swims automatically. He doesn't have to have a swimming lesson. But it is not a cat's nature to swim. If you throw him in the water, he will drown. It is not a baby's nature to swim. If you throw an infant in the water, he will drown. But an infant can be taught to swim, though it is not a part of his nature. Anything you have to be taught to do is not a part of your nature.

Things that come naturally are a part of your nature. That is why we say that by nature man is a sinner. He doesn't have to be taught to sin. Sin comes naturally.

Now it is the natural thing to be ungrateful, but it is the unnatural thing to be grateful. No child was ever born with gratitude in his heart. Most children are born with their fists clenched as if to say "mine." They have to be taught to say "thank you," and sometimes it takes a lot of repetition to get the lesson over.

Remember when your child was small and you began trying to teach him gratitude? When someone gave him something, you would say, "Now, Billy, what do you say?"

Billy would drop his head. "M-m-m-m . . . ."

"Come on, Billy. Now you know what to say."

"M-m-m-m . . . ."

"Ah, Billy, come on now. If you don't say it, I'll make you give it back." Reluctantly Billy said, "Thank you."

But there was no real gratitude. He just said it because you made him say it. He wasn't born with gratitude. You have to repeat it over and over and over again until finally he learns to say, "Thank you."

A lady gave a little boy a piece of cake. He said, "Oh, thank you, ma'am."

She replied, "I like to hear little boys say, 'Thank you.'"

Right away he said, "If you'll put some ice cream on top, I'll say it again."

Some may say it for its reward, but it's not a part of our nature to be thankful.

A soldier in the third army was sent to a rest camp after a period of active service. When he returned to his outfit, he wrote a letter to General Patton, thanking him for the splendid care he had received. General Patton wrote back that for thirty-five years he had sought to give all the comfort and conveniences he could to his men and added that this was the first letter of thanks he had received in all of his years in the army.

That is just a little indication of our ungrateful nature. But we ought to be thankful.

II. HOW TO HAVE A THANKFUL HEART

A man can never be genuinely thankful until he recognizes where the things he possesses came from. You don't thank someone for something unless you know he is responsible for your having it. My wife gave me this watch several years ago. Of course I thanked her because I knew I wouldn't have it had it not been for her. And a man is not thankful in his heart until he realizes that everything he has came from God.

James 1:17 says, "Every good gift and every perfect gift is from above, and cometh down from the Father of lights, with whom is no variableness, neither shadow of turning." When you realize that everything you have comes from God, then you should feel real gratitude in your heart.

Our first five-room home didn't have carpet on the floor. We had linoleum. I remember it so well. But when Gerri and I bought our second home, it was carpeted. I had never lived in a home with carpet, so I would take off my shoes and walk barefoot. I thought, *That's the most wonderful thing in the world: I, just a dirty old bum, don't deserve this.* I would lie down on that carpet, pull the loop up, run my finger down the loop and thank God for each loop in the carpet. I really felt gratitude in my heart for such luxury.

God wants us to feel that way. We shouldn't take His blessings for granted. We have more than we've ever had. God has blessed us tremendously. The most wicked, sinful person is one who thinks he is a self-made individual and fails to recognize that "every good gift and every perfect gift is from above, and cometh down from the Father. . . ."

When I was in Haiti several years ago, I saw little children with swollen stomachs, not from an overabundance of food but from a lack of it—little children dying of malnutrition. I've seen them buy a little cake made from the root of a plant, which looked almost like rubber and would stretch before it would break, and eat little parts of it, then put the rest back in their pockets or in a little piece of paper and keep it until later in the day. Some would eat several days on that one little cake.

Yet God has blessed us with an abundance. In Psalm 103:2 David said, "Bless the Lord, O my soul, and forget not all his benefits." So should we. All the things we enjoy are benefits received from God.

If you are really to be grateful in your heart, then there must be a thorough understanding of where things came from.

My salvation is from the Lord. I owe my existence to the Lord. He holds a twofold right of ownership over me: *The right of creation*—He made me from the dust of the earth and gave me the breath of life. My heart beats at His command; *The right of redemption*—He bought me with His own blood at Calvary. Everything I have is from Him. If

I could only drive that point home to you! All you have and all you are, are because of God.

When I was working at the post office, a man came in one day with some big and beautiful tomatoes.

I asked, "Where did you get those?"

"I raised them," was his reply.

"YOU raised them?"

"Well," he said, "I know God did it, but you should have seen my garden before I started helping the Lord with the weeds!"

A man had just been saved. He used to gamble a lot before he was saved.

Some friends came to him afterwards and said, "Let's play cards."

He said, "I don't play cards."

"Come on. Let's play some. We know you love to play."

He replied, "I did, but I can't play anymore."

"Why can't you play?"

"I don't have any hands."

They looked down and saw two hands at the end of his coat sleeve and laughed. "You've got hands. There they are—two of them."

"No, I don't."

"Well, if they're not your hands, whose hands are they?"

"They are God's hands."

When I think where God has brought me from and where He has put me, I marvel. Some day I'll pinch myself and realize it is not all true. It all seems like a dream. May I never get to the place where I don't have genuine gratitude in my heart. The basis of thanksgiving is a recognition that everything comes from God. He gave me all that I have.

III. FOR WHAT SHOULD WE BE THANKFUL?

Ephesians 5:20 commands, "Giving thanks always for ALL things unto God and the Father in the name of our Lord Jesus Christ." A big order, isn't it? He said we are to thank God for ALL things—even the bad things in life.

It is easy to thank God when you get a new home. It is easy to thank God when you get a new automobile. It is easy to thank God when you get a raise in salary. It is easy to thank God when you are in good health. But what about when your health breaks? What about when you are put in the ambulance and carried to the hospital, and the doctor says, "I have sad news for you. You have only eight weeks to live"? Can you still thank God, or do you get bitter then?

A man invited a friend to go hear a preacher, saying, "I want you to hear the most thankful preacher I've ever heard."

The two men weathered a storm to hear him preach. On the way they thought nobody would be there; that even the preacher wouldn't come. But when they got to the little country church, there was the preacher seated on the platform.

The stranger said to his friend, "He has nobody to preach to. There's a storm outside. It looks like we will have a flood. He won't have anything to be thankful for tonight."

"Yes, he will. He'll thank God for something."

When the preacher stood up, he bowed his head and prayed, "Dear Lord, it is stormy outside. It looks as if the roads will wash away before we can get out of the church tonight. It's an awful storm. But we're thankful that it's not always this way."

The only way you can thank God for "all things" is to couple the "all things" of Ephesians 5:20 with the "all things" of Romans 8:28: "And we know that ALL THINGS work together for good to them that love God . . . ." If you really believe that, you can thank God even for the bad things in life.

I've lived long enough to see that some of the things I thought were bad were the best things that ever happened to me.

Matthew Henry, the famous Bible expositor, was once accosted by thieves and robbed of his pocketbook. He wrote these lines in his diary:

> Let me be thankful, first, because I was never robbed before; second, because, although they took my purse, they did not take my life; third, because, although they took my all, it was not much; and fourth, because it was I who was robbed, not I who robbed.

There's always something to thank God for.

IV. HOW TO ABOUND IN THANKSGIVING

You can abound in thanksgiving. I like a person who is thankful, don't you? I don't like a complainer. "How are you doing today?"

"Terrible."

Dr. Tom Malone once asked a fellow, "How are you getting along?" His reply was, "Pretty good, under the circumstances." Dr. Malone said, "What are you doing under there?"

Say, we are not supposed to be under the circumstances. We are supposed to be on top of the circumstances.

How can we abound in thanksgiving? Well, by T-H-I-N-K-I-N-G. I'm told that in the old Anglo-Saxon language the word "thankfulness" means "thinkfulness." And the more you think, the more thankful you will be. So, the folks who are not thankful don't think much.

My wife and I were talking last night about our four children. How thankful we are for them! They are the greatest, sweetest and I think the prettiest—especially those who favor me! Not one of our three daughters has ever given us any problems. Our son is now a pastor in Alabama. When we're alone, I tell them I thank God for them and think they are the greatest. I thank God for my family.

Think of the families where they curse and fight each other and where the windows are knocked out by bottles thrown through them. Then think of your own dear family. It would be a good time to express your gratitude to God for each and make some kind expression to them. I know your wife will think you have lost your marbles, but show her your gratitude anyway.

I've been thinking about my wife. The Lord knew exactly what I needed. He gave me a wife. Some folk think a preacher's wife ought to be a preacher, that she ought to teach the Bible in the church, etc. The Lord called ME to be the preacher. If she had the desire to preach that I do, we would be in a fight all the time. She wouldn't want to wash and iron my shirts, nor stay home and cook. She wouldn't want to keep the supper warm for me when I come home late. She would want to be out going, too. But He gave me someone who wants to stay at home and watch the children, someone who enjoys cooking and seeing me eat.

She will watch me eat and say, "Eat that."

"I don't like that."

"Taste it. You'll like it."

"But I've already tasted it."

"Ah, try it. You'll like it. You'll like it. Eat it."

"Well, I don't want any."

She will take a spoon when I'm not looking, come toward my mouth and say, "Open your mouth. I want you to taste this."

He gave me exactly who I needed.

I've been thinking about my health. I used to train with weights. As a matter of fact, I once won third place weightlifting out of thirteen southern states. I didn't know what in the world I was doing; I just wanted to be a show-off. I wore tight T-shirts rolled up to the shoulders. My waist was 28 inches, and I wore tight blue jeans and pulled the belt in as tight as I could, then I would flex my muscles. God was letting me do that because He knew I was going to be a preacher and would need that exercise.

And do you know what? I have only one time been sick enough to have to miss a service. I never appreciated my health so much as when I was sick. I vowed then to try to take better care of myself. Thank God for my health!

I visit people who are dying, those who cannot get their breath, ones who have cancer, people who have heart trouble and can't walk up-stairs, those who can't go to church because they can't climb the three or four steps. Oh, how I thank God for my health! I have preached fourteen or fifteen times this week. I'm not getting weaker but stronger.

I don't know what it is to follow a little casket to the cemetery and see it let down. I followed one family three times to the cemetery and side by side we let down three little white caskets, leaving them with not one child. As I drove away, I thanked God that all of mine were still living.

I thank God for friends. Not many weeks ago I followed a hearse to the cemetery. There were two cars in the funeral procession, mine and one other. The men at the funeral home acted as pallbearers. As I conducted that funeral service with only one fellow attending, I thought, *How sad not to have friends!* As I walked away and looked back I thought, *Thank God for my friends!* You have many acquaintances in this world but few friends. I have an abundance of friends, and I thank God for *every* one of them.

A farmer walked up to the pastor and said, "Our son was killed in the war, and we would like to give $200 as a memorial."

Another man was standing by with his strong and healthy son, who too had served in the same war and had come back without a scratch. He said to his wife, "Honey, write a check for $500."

She asked, "Why? Our son wasn't killed in the war. He's here this morning, strong and healthy."

"That's just the point. If they can give $200 to the church when their boy was killed, we can give $500 because our boy went through the war without a scratch."

Thinking—. Thinking—. That's the way to be thankful.

I am being practical this morning. Our house is not a mansion, but we do have two baths, and they're both inside, and a full shower in both! Hallelujah!

We used to take a bath in a No. 2 washtub. Probably you did, too. We would set the tub where the little eave comes out from the house and when it rained, the rainwater would pour into the tub, then the sun would warm it up. Then when it got dark we'd take our bath. The lucky one would be the first fellow in the tub. Now when I take a shower, I thank God and enjoy it, and let it run and run.

I heard of a fellow who wished to dispose of his home. He called his real estate agent and said, "I want to run an ad in the paper to sell my home. Get rid of it as quickly as you can. I'm tired of this old place."

The agent said, "Tell me something about your home so I can run a good ad."

The man told him how many rooms it had. It had carpet. There were expensive shrubs in the yard. He told about some fruit trees in the back yard and many other advantages. He described the house in detail.

When he finished, the agent said, "I'll read it back to you and you tell me how it sounds."

He read the ad—about this beautiful three-bedroom home with two baths, a good stand of grass, fruit trees in the back yard, new roof, central air-conditioning, a remodeled carport for two cars. He kept on reading until the owner stopped him.

"Wait a minute! Wait a minute! Stop. That house is not for sale. All my life I've been wanting a place like that, but I didn't realize I had one until now!"

If you would sit down and do likewise about your wife and children, you might realize that all your life that is just what you have been looking for.

There are many other things to think about. And remember that thinkfulness produces thankfulness.

"Enter into his gates with thanksgiving, and into his courts with praise: be thankful unto him, and bless his name."—Ps. 100:4.

It is said that in Africa there is a fruit called the "Taste-Berry," so named because it changes a person's taste. For several hours after one eats the Taste-Berry, everything is sweet and delicious, even the sour fruit.

Gratitude is the Taste-Berry of Christianity! When we are truly grateful, even the bitter things in life taste sweet.

In closing, let me say just a word to those who are not saved. What is the best way to express your gratitude to such a wonderful Heavenly Father? The psalmist said, "What shall I render unto the Lord for all his benefits...?" Then he answers his own question: "I will take the cup of salvation and call upon the name of the Lord."

God has been very good to many of you, and yet you are unsaved. Why don't you say today with the psalmist, "Because of all his benefits to me, I will take the cup of salvation and call upon the name of the Lord"? God help you to do it, and to do it now.

GEORGE WASHINGTON TRUETT
1867-1944

ABOUT THE MAN:

North Carolina was George Washington Truett's birthplace. By the time he was 18, he was educated well enough to begin teaching in a one-room public school on Crooked Creek in nearby Towns County, Georgia. It was during that two-year apprenticeship that George was converted. Then he established an academy at Hiawassee, Georgia, in 1887. The student body eventually numbered over 300.

When the Truett family moved to Texas in 1889, George went to college—Baylor University—though not as a student. He was offered the position of financial secretary and was instrumental in saving Baylor from bankruptcy. Afterward he became a student, graduated, and unbelievably was elected to become Baylor's president!

But the same year of his graduation he was called to the First Baptist Church of Dallas, remaining there for 47 years, or until his death in 1944. Under his leadership the church grew into the largest church in the world at that time, with 18,124 additions and 5,337 baptisms.

But Dr. Truett had many pulpits besides the pulpit at First Baptist Church. He instituted the Palace Theatre services, held each noon the week before Easter, with nearly 2,000 attending. He preached out in the country churches all across the South, and the common folk heard him gladly. He preached from the steps of our nation's Capitol, and in world centers in London, Stockholm, Paris, Berlin, Jerusalem, etc. Everywhere Truett's preaching produced souls for Christ.

In 1827 he was elected president of the Southern Baptist Convention, which office he served for three terms.

By any standard, he ranks as one of the most popular and influential preachers in America in the first half of the 20th century. He was a world figure; was on close terms with presidents, senators and governors.

Dr. Truett was a great man, a great leader, and a great preacher of the Gospel. His biographers knew whereof they spoke when they explained the man and his ministry in two well-defined words: *"heart-power."*

II.

Count Your Blessings

GEORGE W. TRUETT

"Thou hast granted me life and favour, and thy visitation hath preserved my spirit." — Job. 10:12.

It is of vast importance that every one of us should stop often and recount God's blessings and mercies. That little song, "Count Your Blessings," has in it much merit, certainly so far as the thought is concerned:

When upon life's billows you are tempest-tossed,
When you are discouraged, thinking all is lost,
Count your many blessings, name them one by one,
And it will surprise you what the Lord hath done.

It is of vast importance that we give ourselves often to the blessed task of enumerating our many mercies, then we shall find that these blessings come to us faster than we can count them.

Ingratitude toward man and God is a sin most heinous. You have indicted a man severely when you say about him that he does not have any sense of gratitude. You have indicted him terribly when in truth you can say of a man that he is ungrateful.

Ingratitude is unmanly when it is toward man, and treason when it is against God.

One of the most blessed of all the exercises to which we can give ourselves is that exercise of calling to mind every day the kindness and mercy of God toward us and ours. That hymn that we have sung from childhood is so appropriate: "Come Thou Fount of Every Blessing."

Come, Thou Fount of ev'ry blessing,
Tune my heart to sing Thy grace;
Streams of mercy, never ceasing,
Call for songs of loudest praise.

We should especially see to it that we find occasion for thinking of our blessings when the dark and cloudy days come, for one of the ways to drive those clouds away is to recall the days of sunshine and mercy and blessing.

The man who spoke this text was in the cloudiest day of his life. To all appearances there was neither sun nor moon nor stars in the whole horizon of his life. Job had lost his property, his children and his friends, for they were fair-weather friends.

Finally, when the terrible physical distresses came upon him, those fair-weather friends deserted him; and it would even seem that his own wife had turned atheist, for she said to him, "Curse God, and die!"

But Job, even in that terrible time, had his colloquy with God. Was there ever another such conversation? If you want your heart to burn, go and read that chapter in Job where he talked with God. Note Job's humility and penitence. Note his straightforwardness, then his gratitude, as right out of the depths of that sea of trouble into which he had been plunged, he cried, "Thou hast granted me life and favour, and thy visitation hath preserved my spirit"! What a wonderful recognition of God's mercies in such a day as that!

Job here mentions three things for which profoundest gratitude should be given by us all: 'Thou hast granted me life, thou hast granted me favor, and thy visitation hath preserved my spirit.'

He singles out three truths, and these three truths are so commanding, so wonderful, that they should make every soul, even out of the deepest sea of trouble, look to God and bless Him. O may we do just that this Lord's Day evening!

"Thou Hast Granted Me Life"

First of all, Job said, "Thou hast granted me *life*. I am yet alive. All has been taken from me, it would seem, except life. But, as long as I have life, I will worship God, its Giver, I will honor God, its Author, and I will bless God, its Sustainer.

"Thou hast granted me life"! Does not your heart kindle this evening at the thought that you are alive, that you are a human being? Oh, the abnormality of the man who wishes to get away from life! Do you ever read Keats? How weak is much of his poetry! As you read it you will find lines like this:

"I am half in love with easeful death!"

That idea runs through much of his verse.

Great it is to live; great it is to be a human being. Do you not feel tonight the deepest thankfulness that God made you a human being? What if He had made you a tree? What if He had made you a rock? What if He had made you a bird, or some beast of the field, or the dog there on the porch, or the serpent there in the grass?

Oh, what reverence, what humility and what thankfulness should be in our hearts because God has made us human beings and clothed us with potential dominion over all the world about us!

Read tonight that 8th Psalm, which says:

"When I consider thy heavens, the work of thy fingers, the moon and the stars, which thou hast ordained; What is man, that thou art mindful of him? and the son of man, that thou visitest him? For thou hast made him a little lower than the angels, and hast crowned him with glory and honour. Thou madest him to have dominion over the works of thy hands."

What a wonderful thing to be a human being; what a great thing is life!

What a story it would be if we could come up here one by one and recount the perils out of which we have been delivered!

There was that great train wreck; but you were spared, and so was I.

There was that automobile crash; but you were spared, and so was I, while others went down to dusty death.

There was that awful peril at sea; but you were spared, and so was I.

There was that scourge of the "flu" and other sicknesses, when men and women fell round us every day; but you were spared, and so was I.

How our hearts ought to be lifted in adoring, wondering and grateful praise to such a God as is our God! He spared us despite the fact that we are sinners.

When I asked a man not long ago why he was cutting down a tree that grew in his yard, he said, "Because its limbs are dead and withered and fruit has ceased to grow on its branches. What do I want with a non-productive and worthless tree?" And the man cut the tree away, saying, "This tree is no longer useful to me, it is not profitable, it is not serviceable; I will be rid of it." And he destroyed the tree.

Yet you and I have been spared, and with all that we have often forgotten our Maker and have played the part of the ingrate!

Oh, the wonder of it! God not only gives us this life, this bodily life, but He gives us life eternal. "He that believeth in me, though he were dead, yet shall he live, and he that liveth and believeth in me shall never die!" Oh, the wonder of the life that never dies!

I was talking this evening with a friend as we drove to the bedsides of several sick ones. He remarked to me: "How wonderful it is that God gives eternal life to those who trust Christ!" Eternal life; not life for to-day, not life for a doubtful length of time—but eternal life.

Christ says, "My sheep hear my voice and I know them, and they follow me, and I give unto them eternal life." Trust God, and you shall never perish. How wonderful is life!

You shall hear some day that the preacher before you is dead. Oh, no! His tongue will be quiet, his pulse will be still, his heart will have ceased its beating, but he will be alive—more alive than he is now, more alive than he has ever been! He will have gone from this life; he will be where the conditions of life are perfect, because God gives those who trust Him eternal life.

"Thou Hast Granted Me Favour"

And Job also said, "Thou hast granted me *favour*." God's favor is expressed in so many ways! We could talk for hours about the mercies of God to the children of men. Let us consider some of them.

God has given you a good, sound body. Is not that a cause for which to be devoutly thankful? Sound bodies—well bodies. There may be some about you who are blind. What deep cause for you to praise God and be thankful to Him that your sight has not been taken away! How thankful you and I should be that we can talk, that we can hear, that we are not crippled or maimed!

Where has gratitude gone? Have we been turned into brutish beasts that we cannot thank God for our health and strength of body?

And then, you have a sound mind. How grateful we should be that our minds are unclouded! Ever and anon some mind will reel, and reason on its throne will stagger, and one whose mind was once joyful and bright will become clouded, because reason has fled and the mind is a blank.

If you would see sights and hear sounds which you can never forget, spend two or three hours in an insane asylum. You will wish for many a day you had not gone to carry away those sights and sounds on your mind and heart. But you have your mind, you have your intellect, you can think and reason, you can put this and that together logically and go your way. What cause you have for thankfulness to God!

You have your road in life, your daily tasks, your living; you have your income, your comfortable sense of competence. You are able to work and you have work to do; you have a sufficient amount coming as the product of your work, as the wages of your work, to keep the wolf from the door and make you and your family comfortable. How wonderful is the kindness and mercy of God to you!

Perhaps you are very successful, your business is growing and expanding day by day, your savings are increasing steadily, and every atom of it is because of the mercy of God! If He were to withhold His mercies from you for one moment, your health would be gone, your mind would totter and your reason would fail you. But for God's favor, your business would disappear like the mists of the morning.

"Thy Visitation Hath Preserved My Spirit"

"Thou hast granted me life and favour, and thy visitation hath preserved my spirit"! God *visits* men. How? Does He visit them as of old? How many times He has visited you! How many times He has paused at the door, even at the very door of your heart! Jesus said, "Behold, I stand at the door and knock: if any man hear my voice and open the door, I will come in to him, and will sup with him, and he with me."

God visits men in many ways. There are men and women in this house who could tell of God's visits to them spiritually.

I was a child of ten or eleven years when the sense of sin was first borne in upon me so strongly that I feared to fall asleep at night in the little country home. I had sinned and knew it. I was wrong with God and knew it. Some have felt the conviction of sin more than others. Some have had their hearts fairly torn to shreds, so terrible, so deep was their conviction of sin.

Oh, the power of the conviction of sin, the tragedy of the heart that is exposed before God and trembles out of its personal sense of sin and separation from God and utter helplessness before the onslaughts of sin!

Perhaps in the quietness of your room it was there settled with you and you said, "Christ is mine and I am His." Or in the church, in the great congregation, while the preacher preached and prayers were offered for you, the light came to you and you said, "I see it! I see it! At last I see it! Never can I save myself. I am a sinner separated from God, already condemned. I cannot save myself, but Christ can save me. I surrender to Him and confess Him, here and now!" How wonderful that hour of conversion!

If I may take the liberty of making a personal reference, I will say a word about my own conversion. I was converted when I was about nineteen years of age. There, before my friends from childhood in the little country church, I confessed, "I am for Christ. I accept Him. I yield to Him."

As I went out of the little church house that night, all the way down the road the very trees seemed to me to be clapping their hands, and the very heavens seemed to be putting on new expressions of joy.

Christ is the Saviour of sinners. All through the earthly life Christ visits us and gives His angels charge over us. He comes Himself; He never leaves us, never forgets us. He will be with us in the dark and cloudy days, just as He was with Job and Paul and all the others of His trusting friends. He will be with us when the shadows are about the home. He will be with us in all the upheavals and losses and disappointments that come as men and women travel the road of earthly life—at every step He will be with us, leading us on.

God has given you life; God has given you favor, favor in body, favor in mind, favor in soul. Your Saviour offers not only to be with you here, not only to save you here, not only to glorify life here, but He offers to be your Pilot when you leave this life behind and embark upon the boundless sea, so that you will be carried safely Home. Christ offers you eternal life if you will trust utterly in Him and surrender completely to Him.

Have you made that surrender? How many here can say, "I have made my surrender to Christ; I have taken Him as my Saviour"? Oh, that is a great company!

Here and there in this press of people this summer night some hands could not be lifted. Some could not say, "I am at peace with God." Is there someone here in this press who says, "I want to be right with God; I want to be saved; I want to have forgiveness of my sins; I want to have life eternal"?

There are some uplifted hands that say, "I am not right with God, but I would be right." Are there not others? Yes, I see yours—and yours—and yours—and yours—and yours. There is a hand lifted in the balcony. You are saying, "I want to be right with God." Are there others here to my right? I see yours—I see yours. Does another hand rise in the balcony? Is there anyone on this side of me who says, "I would be right with Him"? Does your hand lift? Does your hand in the balcony lift? Now yours—and yours.

O soul, soul! Satan does not care that tonight it is in your heart to come, if only you will defer action about coming to Christ! Satan does not care, if only you will delay making your surrender to Christ! Come now, I charge you, I pray you, I summon you! Christ's time is today. Say to Him now, "If ever I am to be saved, Christ must be my Saviour." Make your surrender to Him now.

Perhaps it is already settled with you. Come, then, and give me your hand if you will make honest surrender to Christ. Let those come who say, "I have made my surrender, and I want to take my place in the church with God's people." Come now and give your hand while we sing our hymn of invitation:

> **Jesus is tenderly calling thee home —**
>   **Calling today, calling today;**
> **Why from the sunshine of love wilt thou roam**
>   **Farther and farther away?**
>
> **Jesus is calling the weary to rest —**
>   **Calling today, calling today;**
> **Bring Him thy burden and thou shalt be blest;**
>   **He will not turn thee away.**

ABOUT THE MAN:

William Edwin Robert Sangster was born in London in the year 1900. He was educated at Richmond College (B.A.) and the University of London (M.A., Ph.D.).

Sangster, a Methodist, served for sixteen years as minister of Westminster Central Hall, a noted preaching center in London. He also held pastorates in Liverpool, Leeds and Scarborough.

Dr. Sangster was president of the Methodist Conference in England in the 1950's.

He was one of the most popular Methodist ministers of his day.

His printed sermons bear the marks of superb craftsmanship. They are Christ-centered, fervent, directed to the needs of people and faithful to the Scriptures.

Dr. Sangster died on Wesley Day, 1960.

III.

He Delights in Our Gratitude

WILLIAM E. SANGSTER

"And he took the seven loaves and the fishes, and he gave thanks." — Matt. 15:36.

So far as thanksgiving is concerned, the mass of people can be divided into two classes: those who take things for granted and those who take things with gratitude.

It is my aim today to add to the number of those who take things with gratitude.

Notice, first, that *it is the right thing to do*. To take benefits from God or man without a thought or a word of thanks is mean, contemptible and undermines faith in human nature. Where a man has been treated by a fellow man with ingratitude, the milk of human kindness curdles in him. He says afterwards, "He never so much as said, 'Thank you'! Even a dog would have wagged his tail."

Not only is it the right thing to do; *it is the profitable thing to do*. Oh no, I am not thinking cynically, like Sir Robert Walpole, when he said that "gratitude . . . is a lively sense of future favors." I don't mean "profitable" in the sense that if you thank somebody, you are more likely to get help from him again. I mean "profitable" in the sense that a man who is quick to mark and swift to thank a kindness is in a constant state of happiness and good will. He has a barricade built against depression. He faces life buoyantly and confidently because he is aware of mercy streaming on him from Heaven and from his fellow men as well.

So give thanks!

Jesus is our Example in this as in all things. He was constantly giving thanks.

I admit that it isn't always *easy* to give thanks. "How can you thank God for a cancer?" you might ask. Looked at like that, it is difficult,

I know—though, in fact, the only people with cancer to whom I spoke last week both thanked God fervently for His mercies toward them.

I am going to say this. To a Christian, even this quality of thanksgiving is gloriously possible. To those mature in the Christian faith, mercies can still be found near the heart of tragedy.

Oh, I know that there is a grotesque way of looking at it; a form of thanks which is not really thanks at all.

I heard the other day of a little girl—an unusual little girl in some ways and a naughty little girl as well—who detested milk pudding but who had been made to eat some at her dinner. When she asked if she might get down from the table, she was told to return thanks.

"But I have nothing to be thankful for," she said sulkily.

"Very well," said her mother. "Remain there until you have."

There was silence for a few minutes. Then a little voice said: "Thank God I wasn't sick. *Now* may I get down?"

I need hardly say that such freakishness is not the attitude of mind I am commending. Rather, it is this: If, as the Bible teaches, "the steps of a good man are ordered by the Lord," a mature Christian will thank God even in the heaviest and most desolating trouble that, though God did not "lead" him into sickness, he is not deserted in it; that, though he cannot see it as yet, he has faith to believe that somewhere there is mercy at the heart of it, or good that can come out of it; that it is, indeed, only another of the "all things" that 'work together for good, even to them that love God' (Rom. 8:28).

The prayer of thanksgiving at such a time may, indeed, be what the Scriptures call a sacrifice of thanksgiving; a thanksgiving that almost has blood upon it; an adoring venture of faith—believing in defiance of the God-denying look of things. The mature Christian will be able to offer this—not easily but definitely—and the *sacrifice of thanksgiving* will be precious in God's sight.

Thank God that those times which strain faith so hard come only occasionally in life. For the most part we travel a sunlit road; and when we are unaware of the love of God, it is often because we have not looked for it. To see the evidence of God's mercies, you have only to look.

Let us look at them at this time of harvest festival; let us stare at them.

I. THE COMMON BLESSING — SO COMMONLY OVERLOOKED

Let us thank God for the fecund earth. Not without toil, sweat, foresight and struggle have all these lovely things been drawn from the earth. God did not set us in the world to receive our food merely by wishing for it. It comes only by the sweat of someone's brow, but the sweat alone would be useless without the added blessing of God. Look, I say, at this wonderful display, then for all the kindly fruits of earth be grateful.

Let us thank God for our five senses and for whatever measure of health we enjoy.

When a depressed man one day told me that he had nothing to be thankful for, I said, "I'm going visiting; come with me," and the man did so.

I was going to an institution for the aged who were poor and sick. In the town where I then ministered it was an old-fashioned building, and its management left much to be desired. It was not a public visiting day, but I got him in "on the nod," and he made the rounds of the ward with me.

From bed to bed we went, seeing a great many of these pitiable old people. Some were dim of sight; some were quite blind. Some were hard of hearing; some were quite deaf. Some were imbecile; in some their reason was partly impaired. (They seemed almost the most pitiable cases of all because, in their lucid moments, they knew the truth about themselves, and that was hard to bear.)

I didn't say anything much to my companion. I had come to visit the poor souls themselves; he just followed me around.

When we were outside again, I did not rub the moral in. I just shook hands with him, and he parted from me saying, "I don't think I'll ever grumble again."

It was a simple device; just showing him people less fortunate than himself. I think he went away saying, under his breath, "I can see! I can see the face of my dear ones. I can see the sunshine and the first flowers which come out from the hard, dark earth in the spring.

"I can hear! I can hear the songs of birds; the blackbirds fluting in the orchard, and the carefree laughter of little children.

"I have my reason unimpaired! I can think, plan and pray. I am not well off, but I have enough. I have a roof over my head and on my table food that I have bought. I have at least a little in reserve against a rainy day."

Most of us can see and hear, and most of us have our reason utterly unimpaired. Thank God for the common blessings commonly overlooked. Don't wait till you lose them to be grateful.

Look about you; think of the fruitful earth, the solid structure of the seasons, the framework of the universe shaped in love and given to men. These are common blessings, if you like, and yet, if you lost them and could know your loss, you would give almost all the other things you have to recover them, and marvel, in your deprivation, that when you had them, you did not value them more.

Thank God for common blessings:

for the harvest fully gathered in and the great harvest moon rising above;

for the sudden smile of a friend met unexpectedly in a place where you did not expect to meet anyone you knew;

for home, for birthday anniversaries, for the bulge and mystery of stockings in the dark on Christmas morning;

for the loyalty of the family when they laugh at your old joke, told the fiftieth time but tried out expectantly on the new guest;

for all ordinary things, taken for granted when they ought to be taken with gratitude:

Thank God! Thank God!

First, thanks to God for the common blessings, commonly overlooked.

II. THANKS TO GOD FOR THE SPECIAL BLESSINGS— ALAS, SOON FORGOTTEN

Special blessings? Yes, we have had them. We have all had them. You may not have recognized them as such at the time, but they were. I suppose it is more probable, however, that you did half recognize them, but you forgot them so soon.

God never gives a blessing just for the hour. Every special blessing is not only for the hour itself, but for the future. It is a pledge; it is as though God were to say, "I'll do this for you now, then you will always know that you are the object of My love."

What a sad thing it is, therefore, that we forget so soon. That is why new dangers can startle you with fear and dismay. You have forgotten the past mercies. You would have been calm and confident in the presence of this new trouble had you remembered vividly the old deliverance, had you kept it fresh in mind and been able to say, "The God who delivered me then, didn't deliver me then to desert me now." Yet you are fearful in the presence of this new possibility and might be as ignorant as some savage in the midmost forest.

Remember old John Newton?

His love in time past forbids me to think
He'll leave me at last in trouble to sink.

Make a practice of noting your special blessings. Be as thorough about it as a missionary I read about who was a most diligent man in prayer and a master of "method," too. He used to note carefully in little books the special blessings he received and the answers he got to his prayers. The little books are still preserved, I believe.

On the last day of the year he would assess the answers. There were usually between 87 and 90 per cent of plain, impressive answers to the prayers which he had offered. And even concerning the rest, he would not have admitted that they had not been answered. He would have said about those: "In regard to these things, for some purpose known to my Father, the answer had to be 'Wait' or 'No.'"

Make a practice of thanking God for His goodness to you and thanking those, also, by whose hand the blessing came.

It does people good to be thanked. It is amazing what you will do for others, as well as for your own soul, if you will follow this counsel of saying a sincere "Thank you."

Let me put that last point in a picture for you.

When the business depression in America was at its worst, a group of men sat in a room talking over the sad state of affairs. One was a friend of mine, a Methodist minister, William L. Stidger. The conversation concerned the recession in trade and got more miserable every moment it went on.

But as Thanksgiving Day was near—a great day in America—a minister present said, "I have got to preach on Thanksgiving Day and I want to say something affirmative. What can I say affirmative in a period of world depression like this?"

Stidger began to think of the blessings he had had in life and the things for which he was truly thankful. He remembered the woman who had taught him in school, and of whom he had not heard for many years. Although it was years ago, he still remembered that she had gone out of her way to put a love of verse in him; and Stidger has loved verse all his life. So he wrote a letter of thanks to the old lady.

This is the reply he had. It was written in the feeble scrawl of the old, and it began, "My dear Willie." He was thrilled about that. Stidger was over fifty at the time, bald, a professor; and he didn't think anybody was left in the world who would call him "Willie." It made him feel years younger right off. Here is the letter. I'll give it to you word for word:

> My dear Willie,
>
> I cannot tell you how much your note meant to me. I am in my eighties, living alone in a small room, cooking my own meals, lonely and, like the last leaf of autumn, lingering behind.
>
> You will be interested to know that I taught in school for fifty years and yours is the first note of appreciation I ever received. It came on a blue-cold morning, and it cheered me as nothing has in many years.

Stidger is not sentimental, but he wept over that note.

Stidger thought of other people who had been kind to him. He remembered one of his old bishops who had been most helpful at the beginning of his ministry. The bishop was in retirement and had recently lost his wife. Stidger wrote a belated letter of thanks to the bishop. This was the reply:

> My dear Will,
>
> Your letter was so beautiful, so real, that as I sat reading it in my study, tears fell from my eyes—tears of gratitude. Then, before I realized what I was doing, I rose from my chair and called her name to show it to her—forgetting for a moment that she was gone. You will never know how much your letter has warmed my spirit. I have been walking about in the glow of it all day long.

Need I say more? I want you to make a practice of thanking people, of taking a little trouble to thank them. It will please God. He often sends His special mercies by the hands of other people. He normally does. I think He likes His agent to be thanked, also. Here is a resolution to be made. Give thanks! Give thanks!!

First, the common blessings, commonly overlooked; second, the special blessings, soon forgotten.

III. THE GREATEST BLESSING—TRAGICALLY IGNORED

What is the greatest blessing? Oh, there is no doubt about that. Paul was quite a master of words, and he seldom found that they failed him; but there was a subject on which words fell short, and on one occasion, when it came to his mind, he said, "Thanks be unto God for his unspeakable gift" (II Cor. 9:15).

Note that word *"unspeakable."* Paul was saying, in effect, "It just won't go into words."

What was so wonderful that it wouldn't go into words? What had the Father given for which no thanks were really adequate?

The gift of Jesus Christ! He was the unspeakable gift. Thanks be to God (above everything else), says Paul, for Him.

I have often sat and meditated on what my life would have been without Christ. It is a dark picture. Poor as I know my life still to be, I dare hardly think of it apart from Him.

When Baron von Hugel considered the same question, he said of the religion of Jesus:

> I should not be physically alive at this moment; I should be, were I alive at all, a corrupt or at least an incredibly unhappy, violent, bitter, self-occupied, destructive soul, were it not for religion and for its having come and saved me from myself—it, and nothing else; it, in a sense, against everything else.

All this he felt about the power of Christ in his life. I would phrase it differently, but my own honest witness would be no less emphatic than his. I believe every good thing in my life came from God, and—if any doubter wanted to wipe that aside as nothing but an act of faith—I would go further and say that I can actually trace most of them. My deepening conviction that divine love is the only satisfying motive in life, my life's partner, my blissfully happy home, the love of child and friend, the joy of service—all came as smaller gifts in the hand of the "unspeakable gift"—from Christ Himself.

Nor are the blessings only personal. When I see this dark world through His eyes, I have hope for it. When I feel the pulse of His power remolding my own stubborn nature, I know what He can do with all men. When I see His clear reflection in the saints—in men and women who have given Him the fullest opportunity—I know again that He is the Saviour of the world.

Yet multimillions who know of Him ignore Him, deny His worldwide and all-time significance, assert that this world belongs to us who never called it into being nor understand how it works, spurn the "unspeakable gift" as a figment of our child minds.

Be wiser than they are! At this time of thanksgiving—thanksgiving for the harvest, but much more than the harvest—thank God for His "unspeakable gift" in whose hand every other precious thing comes as well.

One of the worst moments for an atheist is when he feels thankful and has no one to thank!

You are not in that position! You thank the Father for the Son, and both for the Holy Spirit. To trace every "good gift and perfect gift" to its true source—the Father of Light—is a good thing; it keeps one orientated to the Highest; it maintains the concept of reverence in our minds without which every mortal mind is deficient; it reminds us (to borrow the language of children) who is "tops."

I conclude with this:

We are often rebuked in our thanklessness by people less fortunate than we are ourselves, and we are often reminded by them of the number and source of our blessings.

Here is an instance. A ministerial friend of mine used to visit an invalid girl. She was a devout person. One of her several sicknesses was a tendency to curvature of the spine, and she lived in a Phelp's box. Have you ever seen a Phelp's box? It looks like a shallow coffin—a grisly anticipation of the grave. Children with a tendency to curvature of the spine used to be strapped in them, as nearly flat as possible.

Her box was by the window. She said to my friend one day, "In this position I can only look up. On those nights when I can't sleep, I play with the stars."

"Play with the stars? How can you play with stars?" he asked.

"This way," she said. "I pick out the brightest star I can find, and I say, *That's Mummy.* I pick out another bright one and say, *That's Daddy.* I find a twinkling one for my brother, my puppy, my spinal perambulator—" on and on she went. Nothing seemed forgotten. Then she concluded with this: "But there aren't enough stars to go around!"

There aren't enough stars to go around! Go home, you thankless people, and count the stars!

(This sermon is from a book of special day sermons which was the last work of William E. Sangster, who died on Wesley Day, 1960. They were sent to the publishers only a day or two before his death. The last weeks of his life were spent correcting and rewriting these sermons. He was virtually helpless, retaining only a little strength in two fingers of his right hand with which to hold a pen. His voice had long been lost, and his only means of communication left with those he loved and with the world was his pen.)

JACK HYLES
1926-

ABOUT THE MAN:

If we could say but one thing about Dr. Hyles, I guess we would call him MR. SOUL WINNING.

Born in Italy, Texas, he began preaching at age nineteen. He pastored several churches in that state, most notably the Miller Road Baptist Church in Garland that was no doubt the fastest growing church in the world for many years. In seven years it grew to the astounding number of 4,000 members.

Then on to the formal downtown First Baptist Church in the Calumet area of Hammond, Indiana. There, after fighting for separation in the church, he won victory after victory. Now that church is the largest Sunday school in the world. Attendance of over 25,000 is common on a Sunday.

Hammond Baptist Schools, Hyles-Anderson College, Hyles-Anderson Publications, and many other gospel projects have come forth from his fantastic ministry.

His best friend, the late Dr. John R. Rice, said about this giant: *"Jack Hyles is a tornado of zeal. He is pungent in speech, devastating in sarcasm. You will laugh and cry — and repent! Preachers who are not dead will preach differently after hearing him. Thousands point to a message from Jack Hyles as the time of a transformed life. He is simply beyond description, with a unique anointing from God."*

Dr. Hyles is the author of many books, including *The Hyles Church Manual, The Hyles Sunday School Manual, Kisses of Calvary,* and a great series of *How to...* books. He also has a large cassette ministry.

Place Dr. Jack Hyles among the giants of this generation!

IV.

"For His Mercy Endureth For Ever"

JACK HYLES

Twenty-six times in Psalm 136 we find these beautiful words, **"For his mercy endureth for ever."** Eleven other times in the Bible we find the same words regarding the nature of God: **"For his mercy endureth for ever."**

"Surely goodness and mercy shall follow me all the days of my life: and I will dwell in the house of the Lord for ever" (Ps. 23:6). The thought of His mercy overcame me this past week. *"Endureth for ever"* means nothing can stop His mercy.

Are you deep in sin? His mercy goes deeper than your sin.

Are you away from God? Is your life counting for nothing? His mercy goes beyond that. No matter how deep you have fallen, His mercy is sufficient. It matters not how far you have strayed; His mercy goes a little farther.

When Jews meet on the streets of Palestine, their greeting is "Shalom," meaning "peace." Paul used grace with peace. Why? No one has peace until he has grace. First Corinthians begins, "Grace and peace be unto you." So does II Corinthians, Galatians, Ephesians, Philippians, Colossians and both books to the Thessalonians. First Timothy says, "Grace, *mercy* and peace be unto you."

When reading that, I told the Lord, "Lord, I think I know why You said 'mercy.' Romans, Corinthians, Galatians, Ephesians, Philippians, Colossians, and Thessalonians were written to *churches,* but Timothy was written to a *preacher.* Lord, You know a preacher needs more mercy than anyone else."

In II Timothy again Paul said, "Grace, *mercy* and peace be unto you." In Titus he said, "Grace, *mercy* and peace be unto you." When God wrote to a preacher, He knew he had more burdens and heartaches than anybody else.

The Lord said to the church at Galatia, "Grace and peace," but to Timothy, "Grace, *mercy* and peace be unto you." In the epistles to an individual, the Lord included mercy. Why? Individuals need mercy. Not a one here but needs the mercy of God. None deserve Heaven. None deserve the blessing of God. So God gives us mercy.

"The Lord's mercies. . . are new every morning" (Lam. 3:22, 23). Why does the Lord say that? Why didn't He say, "Thy mercies are new every *evening*"? At the end of a hectic day, we need mercy. We need mercy after we have grown impatient and lost our temper. Most of us need mercy at the END of the day when we have to look up to Him and confess, "Lord, I didn't mean to do what I did today. Lord, please forgive me." After He has forgiven us, then we could say, "His mercies are new every *evening*." So why did God say "every morning"? We are mean while we are sleeping, so we need mercy each morning!

I preached in Texas the other day near a church I once pastored. In that church was what Dr. John R. Rice called a "long-horned deacon." For some eighteen years I had not one evil thought in my heart against that deacon. As I drove down the street in front of the church and went past the deacon's place, I thought, *That place belongs to that old long-horned deacon.* I asked if he were still living. Yes, I was told. He is now in his eighties. I thought, *I am glad my heart is clean about that fellow. I hold no bitterness.*

That night I dreamed I punched him in the nose! When I woke up, I was glad I had! So even while asleep, we need God's mercy! Since we are sinners morning and evening, therefore the Word says, "Thy mercies are new every *morning.*"

The psalmist said in Psalm 19, "Cleanse thou me from secret faults." Are "secret faults" those faults others don't know about? This verse is talking about my faults that I myself don't even know about. The psalmist prayed, "Lord, cleanse the sins of which I am not aware, those unholy motives, those tainted purposes, the things I should not do, and the things I leave undone that I should do."

That is why I think Jeremiah, the writer of Lamentations, said, "The Lord's mercies. . . are new every morning: great is thy faithfulness."

I got to thinking recently about the events in the Bible where "his mercy endureth for ever." In II Chronicles 5:13 Solomon has finished building the Temple. It is time to dedicate it. The Ark of the Covenant is brought in, singers begin to sing, instruments begin to play, and when the king stands to pray the dedicatory prayer, he says, "His mercy endureth for ever." God blessed them by giving the Shekinah glory in the Holy of Holies. So bright was it that the priests couldn't minister. They said, "His mercy endureth for ever."

I recall my years here at this church. How good God has been to us! Try to think of a service when God did not suddenly speak to someone in the choir, or when He did not give us an extra special blessing, or when there was not some special conversion or some special blessing. I don't know of any church in the world where God has faithfully blessed more than He has us Sunday after Sunday, week after week, blessing after blessing. Every one of us ought to stand up and exclaim, "Blessed be God! His mercy endureth for ever!"

Somebody who came to our services recently said, "When we want a blessing, we come to First Baptist Church, Hammond, for we know we will always get it there." Praise the Lord! Hallelujah!

In I Chronicles 16:41 we read, "His mercy endureth for ever." The Ark of the Covenant had been removed from Israel; the Philistines had taken it to Gath and Ekron and Ashdod. For years the Ark of the Covenant had been gone; now it returns to Jerusalem. Remember David's happiness when the ark came back? David, king of Israel, danced around it. When his wife Michal looked down and saw her husband, she said, "What a disgrace for a king to dance and make a fool of himself!" But David shouted, "His mercy endureth for ever."

In Ezra 3:1 we find, "His mercy endureth for ever." The Temple was destroyed; the Israelites were led away in captivity to Babylon. The walls had been leveled, their homes destroyed and the Temple desecrated. For seventy homesick, lonely years they lived away from home. The Israelites sat down and wept by the river Chebar in Babylon. They would not play their harps, nor sing the psalms of joy.

One day God burdened Zerubbabel to return and rebuild the Temple. God's people came from far and near and laid the foundation for the rebuilding of God's house. The people were happy. The Bible says the singers sang, played their instruments and shouted, "His mercy endureth for ever."

Stop and think how sinful you were; but the mercy of the Lord forgave you. Stop and think of the attitudes we have had this week. Remember the things we have done that we should not have done. We can't forget those harsh words uttered when we should have been quiet. We are guilty of envy, covetousness, jealousy and impatience; yet the dear Lord looks down from Heaven and—"His mercy endureth for ever."

Psalm 106:1 tells us, "His mercy endureth for ever."
Psalm 107:1 tells us, "His mercy endureth for ever."
Psalm 118:1 tells us, "His mercy endureth for ever."

In these psalms David remembers as he does in Psalm 136: 'The seas were parted, for his mercy endureth for ever. Pharaoh's armies were drowned, for his mercy endureth for ever. He fed us with manna from Heaven, for his mercy endureth for ever. He gave us water from the rock, for his mercy endureth for ever.' Over and over again the psalmist remembers the blessing of the past.

Twenty-five years ago I didn't want to come to Hammond, Indiana. Once when visiting Chicago I thought, *This is the last place in the world I would ever want to live.* But God put me here; now it looks as if this is going to be the last place in the world I will ever live.

I didn't want to come to Hammond. We had battles. For a year it was hell. Yet God gave victories! Oh, the goodness of God!

Think of our preacher boys who stand in pulpits around this country and around the world this morning, proclaiming the same *mercy* that we proclaim from this pulpit.

Think of the churches that have been changed, their ministries transformed and preachers set aflame with the Gospel of Christ.

Think of these twenty-two blessed years.

Oh, we have had some heartaches. Fire destroyed two buildings. We had to put our nurseries in the hallways of the Educational Building and buy a furniture store and remodel it in a week. We had to live in all kinds of inconveniences for a long time. But His mercy has endured forever. Some people have called us "nuts," and some have hated us. One man said, "I have to drive down Sibley Street to work, but I won't drive by your church." When I asked, "Why?" he said, "Every time I see your church, I see my liquor and my dirty sins and the life I live. The very presence of that building is a sermon against me."

Thank God, even our buildings speak out *against* unrighteousness and *for* decency!

We have felt attacks but have tried not to retaliate. One reason I think His mercy has been so good is because we have tried to love, to be gracious and kind to everybody. No word has ever come from this pulpit against any man of God. We have tried to stand for God's men and to call this country back to God. If any church in the whole world ought to say, "His mercy endureth for ever," it is this one, this people. We ought to stand up and shout the blessed praises of God!

As I read Psalm 106:1; 107:1; and 118:1, I want to jump up and down and say, "Praise the Lord! His mercy endureth for ever!" God puts up with people like us. God uses people like us. God forgives people like us. God loves people like us. His mercy endureth forever!

Did you know that God will be merciful to you as long as you live? When you young people get old, the mercy of the Lord will still endure. When you middle-aged people get toward the senior years, the mercy of the Lord will still endure. You dear people in your 70s and 80s and 90s, when most of life is over and you wonder about death and what it is like, the mercy of the Lord will still endure. The mercy of the Lord will be there when you go through the Valley of the Shadow and when somebody sits at the bedside waiting for you to go Home to be with the Lord.

The young lady sang this morning about how she wants to see her father. I thought of her father, Bill Gifford, who helped us up in the baptismal room—a great man of God. When he was dying, I went to his bedside. He looked up at me and said, "Pastor, for to me to live is Christ and to die is gain."

Oh, when you come to the Valley of the Shadow, His mercy endureth forever.

When cancer eats up the body—as it is this morning for some people—His mercy endureth forever.

When you cross the chilly Jordan and go into the presence of our Lord, His mercy endureth forever.

When we see Him, His mercy endures forever.

When we rise to meet Him in the air, His mercy endureth forever.

When we come back to earth with Him, His mercy endureth forever.

When we walk the streets of gold and go through gates of pearl, His mercy endureth forever.

No matter what happens, God's mercy is there and will always be there.

In the future, God may allow squealing brakes, burning rubber on the pavement, crashing of steel, and bodies hurling into the culvert or on the shoulder of the road. It may be that He will let you lie there for awhile wondering if death is near. It may be that God has a wheelchair for you. It may be that He is going to let you be deaf. It may be that you will never hear the voice of a whippoorwill again or the sweet music of the choir. **But His mercy endureth forever!** It may be that God will allow pressures to come in your life. You may fall to the bottom of society and one day stumble into a rescue mission like some of these men here. **But His mercy endureth forever!**

You cannot get outside His mercy. You may go to the depth of the sea, but His mercy is there. You may go higher than man has ever gone, but His mercy is there. You may fly in space with the astronauts, but His mercy is there. You may stumble into a tavern and give up your life and virtue, but His mercy is always there. Why? His mercy endureth forever! God's mercy goes beyond your deepest sin, beyond your most lonely hour. His mercy endureth forever!

Two men came to the Temple to pray. One was a Pharisee and the other was a publican. The Pharisee said, "I am thankful I'm not as he is. I am a good man! I do not commit all the dirty sins he commits, and I do good things he does not do." The publican could not so much as lift up his eyes to God but smote his breast and said, "God be *merciful* to me, a sinner."

Listen to me! Are you here this morning in sin and don't know that if you died you would go to Heaven? His mercy endureth forever! This morning God will save any person in this room who will look up to Him and say, "O God, I know I am a sinner, and I am sorry. Be *merciful* to me, a sinner." The mercy of God would cover every sin of your life. His mercy endureth forever!

You ask, "Are you *sure*?" Yes! Look at Ephesians 2:4, "God, who is rich in mercy. . . ." His mercy reaches out to all this morning.

Forty-four people came to my office for conferences from 3:30 Friday afternoon until 11:00 last night. So many of our folks have needs. What about the many who did not come but who also have needs? For everyone who came to my office, God's mercy endureth forever. For everyone who did not come to my office, His mercy endureth forever.

There is a lady here this morning who wonders if life is worth living. Lady, His mercy endureth forever.

There is a man here this morning with cancer eating up his body; he wonders what the future holds. Sir, His mercy endureth forever.

There is a young lady here this morning who deeply loves the man she married, but he has been unfaithful. Lady, His mercy endureth forever!

"Endure" means "nothing can stop it." It comes from a Greek word meaning "to conquer." So "his mercy conquereth forever."

Do you have heartaches? His mercy conquereth heartaches. Do you have sickness? His mercy conquereth sickness. Have you gone into sin? His mercy conquereth sin. His mercy conquereth forever. You can say with the songwriter, Dr. Weigle:

I would love to tell you what I think of Jesus,
Since I found in Him a friend so strong and true.
I would tell you how He changed my life completely;
He did something that no other friend could do.
No one ever cared for me like Jesus.

In the Weigle Music Center at Tennessee Temple University, they built a little apartment for Dr. Weigle when he was nearing 100 years of age. I preached the dedication message. After everybody had gone, I went to see Dr. Weigle. I started to knock on the door, but I heard some noises. I leaned my ear against the door and I heard a voice say, "Hallelujah! Praise the Lord!" I just listened for awhile. Finally, I knocked. He came to the door with the look of Heaven on his face. I said, "Dr. Weigle, what are you doing?"

He clapped his hands and said, "Just practicing for Heaven!"

We too ought to practice for Heaven. We too ought to praise the Lord. Blessed be God! His mercy endureth forever!

When you go home today and have a meal, shout the praises of God. "His mercy endureth forever." Reach up and touch your eyes. If you can see, say, "Hallelujah! His mercy endureth forever!" If you can hear the sound of this beautiful music, say, "Glory to God! His mercy endureth forever." If you can walk out of this building without being rolled out in a wheelchair, say, "Praise the Lord! His mercy endureth forever." Just jump up and down and say, "Hallelujah! His mercy endureth forever." Say it with me: "His mercy endureth forever." Yes, it endures forever and ever and ever!

When kingdoms have crumbled for the last time, His mercy endureth forever.

When dictators have waged their wicked battles for the last time, His mercy endureth forever.

When the stars have fallen like untimely figs from a tree shaken by the wind, His mercy endureth forever.

When the sun refuses to shine and the moon has turned as black as sackcloth of hair, His mercy endureth forever.

When people shall die no more and cemeteries shall not dot the horizon, His mercy endureth forever.

When shoulders shall never stoop, nor brows wrinkle, nor faces become furrowed, His mercy endureth forever.

When all of us awake in His likeness to live forever around His throne, His mercy endureth forever.

Blessed be God! His mercy endureth forever!

WILLIAM BELL RILEY
1861-1947

ABOUT THE MAN:

Dr. W. B. Riley was for 45 years pastor of First Baptist Church, Minneapolis, and pastor emeritus three years. His ministry there built this church to the largest membership in the Northern Baptist Convention.

But all over America Dr. Riley moved and swayed audiences. Thousands were won to Christ in great campaigns.

Riley's ministry was one of preaching the Gospel as well as fighting foes of the Gospel. He sometimes prefaced what he wrote with: *"As one who has given his life to the defense and propagation of fundamentalism."*

William Jennings Bryan once called him *"the greatest Christian statesman in the American pulpit."*

The teaching of evolution was a hot issue in his day, so his debates became another phase of his ministry. Bryan had died in 1925, so the mantle for fighting evolution passed to Riley.

One can well compare Dr. Riley with Charles Spurgeon in the largeness of his work: 1. Like that prince of preachers in London, the Minneapolis pastor-evangelist-crusader carried on for several decades an effective ministry; his church grew about as large as Spurgeon's. 2. Like Spurgeon, he turned out many books, including a 40-volume sermon-commentary. 3. Even as Spurgeon, he was a prophet to a whole nation of moral decline and infidelity in the church. 4. As Spurgeon withdrew from the Baptist Union, so Riley withdrew from the Northern Baptist Convention. 5. Like Spurgeon, he founded a growing training college and seminary. 6. Like Spurgeon, he was an editor, editing *The Christian Fundamentalist* and *The Northwestern Pilot.*

Truly, in the days of his strength, Dr. Riley was one of America's greatest preachers.

V.

Memorials of Divine Mercy

W. B. RILEY

"Then Samuel took a stone, and set it between Mizpeh and Shen, and called the name of it Eben-ezer, saying, Hitherto hath the Lord helped us." —I Sam. 7:12.

Old Testament history from which I bring our text presents Samuel who was priest and practically king and who had just called back the people of Israel from their wicked ways, had harmonized their dissenting spirits and, around the recovered Ark, had established afresh the worship of the Father Jehovah.

This revival of the national spirit in Israel and of her worship of Jehovah so angered the neighboring Philistines that the text tells us, *"They drew near to battle against Israel."*

The devout priest knew the source of infinite assistance; and, seeing the enemy, made his appeal to God. The further record is:

". . . the Lord thundered with a great thunder on that day upon the Philistines, and discomfited them; and they were smitten before Israel.

"And the men of Israel went out of Mizpeh, and pursued the Philistines, and smote them, until they came under Beth-car.

"Then Samuel took a stone, and set it between Mizpeh and Shen, and called the name of it Eben-ezer, saying, Hitherto hath the Lord helped us." —vss. 10-12.

That stone, like the twelve stones brought up from the bed of the Jordan and builded into a monument on its bank, was a memorial and was set to speak to all passers-by of God's deliverance; to mark the place where Israel had known Divine favor. It was an emphatic recognition of the intervention of Providence on behalf of this people. It was an example worthy the imitation of favored men in all generations.

We build monuments to the memory of great events. They more often commemorate the person than God; more often bring renown to Bethcar, the battlefield, than to the Holy One who gave the victory.

It is my purpose this morning to plead for memorials of Divine mercy, for the proper recognition of that Providence which points out the way and administers to each advantage.

No other day in the year is more suitable to such thought than Thanksgiving. So I ask you to join with me in building out of our thoughts memorials to the intervention of that God whose mercies have characterized another twelve months.

First of all, in

Personal Experiences

Life has not been a dead level these twelve long months. Since last Thanksgiving variations in trial, temptation, fear and suffering; in victory, steadfastness, courage and conquest, have characterized the life of each; and those victories and conquests have come from God.

No greater thing can happen to men than to have a visit from the Holy One, and the event is worthy of memorial. Shall we not think back this morning to see what has happened, and wherein He has helped? Can any one of us recall the multitude of His mercies?

Mark Guy Pierce was walking home from church one night. His little daughter, holding his hand, trudged at his side and tried desperately to keep up. Looking up into his face she said, "Papa, I want to count the stars." "All right, darling," replied Mr. Pierce; so she began—"One, two, three, four, five . . . ." After a while he heard her say, "213, 214, 215," then she let out a great sigh, "O Papa, they are too many! I can't count 'em."

Is it not so of the mercies of my God in the past twelve months? But some of them are stars of such magnitude that we can plainly see them.

The spared life! Surely we will not forget this mercy. The dread archer—Death—has drawn his bow on a multitude, but every arrow has missed you and me.

He has even singled out some from our social circles and struck down some from the sweet family and church circles, yet we have stood unharmed, save for our sorrow. The arrow in this incident or that has passed very near to us and put us in jeopardy for a moment, but we escaped unscathed; or, if it has wounded us and left us on beds of suffering for weeks, by God's grace we have been restored and stand up today in a new lease of life.

Is there not occasion here for a memorial of Divine mercy?

Doubtless some here have fared better than did the servant of Job and need not to say, *"I only am escaped alone,"* but have brought through this past year person, family and friends without the loss of one, and hence are saying, "God has been good." It is well-nigh a pity that we can't appreciate our own preservation until somebody else is stricken at our very side.

Many seasons ago an aunt came from Cincinnati to visit at our Kentucky home. The train she left at the little station was wrecked ten minutes later with a great loss of life. When she heard of the sad circumstance, she poured out her very soul in expression of gratitude to the God who had taken her from the train before it plunged to destruction. Yet, the preservation of that day was no greater than she enjoyed every time she ever traveled on a railroad train.

Every day you spend, every hour I spend in health and prosperity as the special object of God's favor, is occasion for this morning's text, and with the downgoing of the sun we are ingrates indeed if we say not from a heart full to overflowing, "Hitherto hath the Lord helped us."

Personal preservation is an occasion for a memorial of Divine mercy.

The Family Circle

What is its message this morning? If anything in this world is more precious to a man than personal existence, it is the house to which he belongs—the blood of his blood—the bone of his bone—the kinships into which God has bound him. That is especially true of the husband and father and, in most instances, still more true of the wife and mother. Everything that affects that strange, sweet, little circle for weal or woe stirs him or her to song or sob.

What has come to it in the past year? With some of you an increase has come. A little one has been added to the home. Some of us have seen our children saved this year. God never gives better occasion for gratitude, for memorials of Divine mercy, than when that same immortal is born again, born from above, "not of blood, nor of the will of flesh, nor of the will of man, but of God."

In Israel of old, when a child was given, they brought it unto the Lord and offered it in dedication, and the parents laid on the altar of God some gift by which to express their gratitude. When Hannah found her little Samuel come as God's message of mercy, she offered three bullocks, an ephah of flour, and a bottle of wine, as a memorial of the same. There was occasion for even greater gift, occasion for such gratitude as that mother in Israel knew.

It is a great thing when an immortal life is launched on the sea of time and started toward the haven of eternity. It is a great day when life is enriched by the new relation of father or mother, or brother or sister.

The Cunarders are perhaps the most noted line of steamers that sail the high seas. Some reckon their success to business skill and sagacity, but I will opine a truer secret is in the circumstances that Mrs. Cunard used to spend a day in prayer for God's blessing upon every new vessel that went off the ways to the ocean wave, and christened it with her tears.

Oh, young mothers and fathers, have you done less for the immortal crafts who have started this year on the long voyage? And when you have seen them set out in health and happiness, have you not hastened back to the beginning—to the birthday—and set up there a memorial of God's mercy?

Then this year, how has the family fared? Have they had food and clothing and comfortable home? Has health inhabited the house and touched one little blossom into richer beauty, and matured another into the fragrance of fuller life, flowering him or her into youth? or, if sickness has visited the home, has the Son of God come to rebuke the same and raise up those Satan thought to destroy; or, if Death itself has been there to do his destructive work, has his visit caused you to call for Christ, as did Mary and Martha, and have Him come to say, "I am the resurrection, and the life: he that believeth in me, though he were dead, yet shall he live: and whosoever liveth and believeth in me shall never die," and with His word of promise sweep out the sorrow, and start in your bosom a song of hope and joy by showing you that the loved one was not dead but evermore alive?

A friend of mine attended a funeral some time ago and at its close he said to the father, "You have just three children left, have you?" To which the man of faith replied, "Oh, no, I still have four. We have not lost our child. He is even more our own in the arms of Christ than if he were here in his cradle."

> **Nearer, my God, to Thee,**
> **Nearer to Thee!**
> **E'en though it be a cross**
> **That raiseth me;**

Still all my song shall be,
Nearer, my God, to Thee,
  Nearer to Thee!

There let the way appear,
  Steps unto Heaven;
All that Thou sendest me,
  In mercy given;
Angels to beckon me,
Nearer, my God, to Thee,
  Nearer to Thee!

Then with my waking thoughts
  Bright with Thy praise,
Out of my stony griefs
  Bethel I'll raise;
So by my woes to be
Nearer, my God, to Thee,
  Nearer to Thee!

The Sphere of Business!

What can be said of that, in the light of the times and from the lesson of that text? It is said that the times upon which we have fallen are hard and full of trial, and there are few who care to question the statement. Yet I do declare that a man reviewing his experience in the marts of trade for the past twelve months ought to find here and there a place and an experience calling for memorials of God's mercy. For some, that is not difficult.

The man whose business has been prosperous, or who in professional attainments has made progress, or before whom high position has opened, readily consents to the erection of memorials of mercy. He sees that all about him are his fellows in lesser favor—men who have known hard knocks, who have cut in twain their personal privileges, who have curtailed all possible expenses, who have put living at lower points and strained credit almost to a crash, and many of them altogether to bankruptcy. It ought not be difficult, then, for the man who has prospered, when prosperity was the exception, to remember God and say, "Hitherto hath He led me"; to be moved to the erection of monuments in memory of His mercies; to be willing to lay in them his silver and gold that God thereby might be honored.

I have noticed in my own denomination that the richer have borne a larger share in all the missionary and benevolent enterprises of the church these last few years than ever before since I can remember. That means that they have some sense of God's great mercy to them and are willing to lay down their silver and gold in evidence of their gratitude. The Lord pity him who does otherwise. The Lord spare the successful man whose soul is being reduced and whose spirit is subsidized by his very success, until he shall see his mistake and be saved through sacrifice.

The man who has been able to hold his own in the business world this year has occasion for memorials of mercy when such a multitude are sliding backward in business interests and prospects. The man who cannot go forward, but is holding his ground, ought to be grateful.

I appreciate the difficulty, in this money-mad Western world, of our accepting such a statement, but really it has excellent occasion. There are 200,000 people today in this city who would be rendered happy indeed if they could be assured that twelve months hence they would still be in possession of what they now have. All men having that confidence should fall upon the philosophy of the old black man who managed to keep himself happy in every time of trouble by saying, *"Bless de Lawd, it am no wus."*

A favorite story of my teacher, Dr. John A. Broadus, related to President Madison who, it seems, was subject to many diseases in his later years and suffered many things from many physicians but was nothing bettered. Among these physicians was an old friend of the ex-President who sent Mr. Madison some vegetable pills and begged that he try them and let him know the result.

In due time the doctor received a most carefully written and felicitous note in which Mr. Madison said:

> My dear friend,
>   I thank you very much for that box of pills. I have taken them every one, and while I cannot say that I am any better since taking them, it is quite possible I might have been worse if I had not. So I beg you to accept my gratitude."

"Really," argued Dr. Broadus, "that is not a mere pleasantry. There is always something known or unknown but for which our condition would have been worse, and that something constitutes an occasion for gratitude."

Look back over the year! Recall the trials of this time and tell me, would not your affairs and mine have fallen lower but for one fact, namely, "Hitherto hath the Lord helped us"? Then a stone in memory of His mercy!

But there are those who have gone into bankruptcy this year. Is there any comfort for them or occasion for making this day memorials of mercy? Certainly there may be!

In a multitude of instances there is the greatest occasion. The men who have failed in business are by no means the worst off among us. "A man's life consisteth not in the abundance of the things which he possesseth." The loss of earthly gains often means the gain of heavenly graces. I have known men in whom bankruptcy wrought humility; for whom business failure produced a greater sweetness of spirit, a broader sympathy with the poor and suffering, a truer sense of Providence in all our affairs.

In Louisville, Kentucky; in New Albany, Indiana; in Lafayette, Indiana; in Bloomington, Illinois; in Chicago and in Minneapolis— wherever God has set me down to speak the Gospel, I have come to know men who discovered their purest riches in consequence of having lost something of the wealth of this world. Some of the best men in my church today are men on whose character business misfortunes have wrought with beauty. Financial reverses quite often produce spiritual recoveries for which we ought to thank God.

A man who takes inventory at the end of a year and finds his bank account in the First National of his city flat but his credit with God fuller than ever before, is the most prosperous man to be found.

Ah, it is better to be a good man than a millionaire; better to grow in grace than to accumulate gold; better to know and yield to a Divine guidance than discover acres of diamonds; better to feel the Father's love than to fill the coffers with earthly treasure.

It is said that Cyrus gave to one of his generals a cup of gold and to another a kiss. The former complained that he had received the lesser favor, and indeed he was right.

And if, this past year, your gold has gone and your silver has been swept away but you have felt the kiss of the everlasting God upon your brow, stand up today with the Samuels of the land and set up the stone to mark the spot of the Father's visit and sing in joyful note, "Hitherto hath the Lord helped us."

What matters it how much we lose of earth's treasures, if only we know the favor of the Father whose wealth is the world's?

Sometime since, when a certain businessman was in hard straits and some acquaintances were expressing their sympathy for him and fear regarding his future, one who knew him and his answered, "Oh, he's in no danger, for he has a rich father, and that father will come to his relief whenever he is called."

But, beloved, those words were not half so true as he employed them, as they are when we who are God's children use them.

My Father is rich in houses and lands.
He holdeth the wealth of the world in His hands!
Of rubies and diamonds, of silver and gold,
His coffers are full, He has riches untold.

It is said that during the famine in Canaan, Joseph ordered his officers to throw wheat and chaff on the waters of the Nile that the people below might see that there was plenty above.

What if your finances are short; eternity will not exhaust the riches of your Father's grace.

A tent or a cottage, why should I care?
They're building a palace for me over there!
Though exiled from home, yet still I may sing:
All glory to God, I'm a child of the King.

Spiritual Progress

What of that, in the light of this text? Are we any stronger in Christ than twelve months since? Is the Holy Spirit any more to us today than then? Are the fruits of the Spirit more apparent in our lives, or more abundant? If not, weeping becomes us; but if so, stones of memorial and songs of joy!

Many here have been saved since last Thanksgiving. Surely you have occasion of gratitude to God. This past year you will never forget in time or in eternity.

So long as I am sane, I shall remember the day my father set down in the Family Bible to mark my first birth; and so long as eternity runs, I shall rejoice in the hour recorded in the Lamb's Book of Life to mark the second birth.

In the city of Chicago I baptized into my church one winter three men who came out of the deepest darkness and the most damnable lives. But their regeneration was truly the work of the Holy Ghost and after it, they were as godly as before it they had been godless. Sometimes I introduced them about to this Christian and that as new converts, and had occasion to say, "Kenna or Sullivan, how long have you been a Christian now?" Invariably they answered by telling me the number of months, days and hours since they were born of the Spirit. And if you could have seen the shining of their faces when they referred to that wonderful work, you could have understood something of their joy.

O beloved, born of God this year, yours is occasion of gratitude, indeed, and whatever others do, you can set up today a stone in memory of His mercy, saying, "Hitherto hath the Lord helped us."

Then some have grown in grace, in the knowledge of the Word. This year you have offered yourself in consecration; your progress is perceptible. The Holy Ghost has called you to higher ground and you have answered. He has taken the things of Christ and showed them unto you as you never saw them before. He has revealed unto you the affection of the Father, and you have felt it in all its sweetness. The very mountains that seemed obstacles a year since, He has helped you to scale, and they have been turned into points of elevation on which you stand to survey a larger horizon of the Christ life. He has led you out into personal work. He has taught you the great truth that God loveth a cheerful giver. He has given you the joy of seeing souls surrender to your appeal.

And for some He has said, "Come into the gospel ministry and dispense blessing to others while I put threefold mercies upon you." Shall ye not then erect memorials to our God?

As teachers in our Sunday school classes; as many whose testimony is needed in prayer meeting; as the saved who watch for the souls of others; as children of the Father, privileged to put up our petitions to Him; as agents of redemption, called to preach the Gospel at home or abroad; as members of the church of the redeemed, led into experiences richer and sweeter than ever known to any save the saints of God—shall we not remember mercy and establish our memorials by offering labor, love and life?

Henry Ward Beecher tells of visiting the church of the Succoring Virgin in one of the cities of France. He found the whole church filled with tablets. Here was one erected by an officer who had been in the battle of Inkerman and came out of those three terrible days unscathed. He hastened to erect this tablet, TO THE MEMORY OF THE VIRGIN'S MERCY IN PRESERVING MY LIFE.

Here is another which reads, MY CHILD WAS SICK. I CALLED TO MARY, THE MOTHER OF GOD. SHE HELPED ME AND MY CHILD IS ALIVE.

Everywhere he found tablets telling what Mary had done. It was a beautiful thing, and Beecher says, "As I read those inscriptions, tears came from my eyes like drops from a spice-bush when shaken on a dewy morning."

But beloved, shall the children of superstition set up to the saints more memorials of mercy than we raise to the everlasting God who is our Father and the Father of our Lord and Saviour Jesus Christ and who has proven Himself precious to us in our person, in our homes, in the marts of trade and in our spiritual experiences? Shall we not recall today what He hath wrought and make this Thanksgiving time tell of His mercies; and shall we not say that having received, we will give and will offer ourselves and every possession put into our power, to the end of annihilating earth's sorrows, staunching her wounds, destroying her sins and bringing her to the salvation of the everlasting God?

In memory of the unspeakable mercies of the past, is it not in our hearts to sing,

> Come, Thou fount of every blessing,
>   Tune my heart to sing Thy grace;
> Streams of mercy, never ceasing,
>   Call for songs of loudest praise.
> Teach me some melodious sonnet,
>   Sung by flaming tongues above;
> Praise the mount—I'm fixed upon it—
>   Mount of Thy redeeming love.
>
> Here I raise mine Ebenezer;
>   Hither by Thy help I'm come;
> And I hope, by Thy good pleasure,
>   Safely to arrive at home.
> Jesus sought me when a stranger,
>   Wandering from the fold of God;
> He, to rescue me from danger,
>   Interposed His precious blood.
>
> O, to grace how great a debtor
>   Daily I'm constrained to be!
> Let Thy goodness, like a fetter,
>   Bind my wandering heart to Thee:
> Prone to wander, Lord, I feel it,
>   Prone to leave the God I love;
> Here's my heart, O, take and seal it;
>   Seal it for Thy courts above.

JOHN R. RICE
1895-1980

ABOUT THE MAN:

Preacher. . . evangelist. . . revivalist. . . editor. . . counselor to thousands. . . friend to millions—that was Dr. John R. Rice, whose accomplishments were nothing short of miraculous. Known as "America's Dean of Evangelists," Dr. Rice made a mighty impact upon the nation's religious life for some sixty years, in great citywide campaigns and in Sword of the Lord Conferences.

At age nine, after hearing a sermon on "The Prodigal Son," John went forward to claim Christ as Saviour. In 1916, with only $9.35 in his pocket, he rode off on his cowpony toward Decatur Baptist College. He was now on the road to becoming a world-renowned evangelist, although he was then totally unaware of God's will for his life.

There was many a twist and turn before Rice rode through the open door into full-time preaching—the army, marriage, graduate work, more seminary, assistant pastor, pastor—then FINALLY, where God planned to use him most—in full-time evangelism.

Dr. Rice and his ministry were always colorful (born in Cooke county, in Texas, December 11, 1895, and often called "Will Rogers of the Pulpit" because of their likeness and mannerisms)—and controversial. CONTROVERSIAL—and correctly so—because of his intense stand against modernism and infidelity and his fight for the Fundamentals.

Dr. Rice lived and died a man of convictions—intense convictions. But, like many other strong fighters for the Faith, Rice was also marked with a sincere spirit of compassion. Those who knew him best knew a man who loved them. In preaching, in prayer, and in personal life, Rice wept over sinners and with saints. But there is more. . .

Less than seventy-one hours before the dawning of 1981, one of the most prolific pens in all Christendom was stilled. Dr. John R. Rice left behind a legacy in writing of more than 200 titles, with a combined circulation of over 61 million copies. And through October of 1981, a total of 24,058 precious souls reported trusting Christ through his ministries, not counting those saved in his crusades nor in foreign countries where his literature has been translated.

And who but God knows the influence of THE SWORD OF THE LORD magazine which he started and edited for forty-six years!

And while "Twentieth Century's Mightiest Pen"—and man—has been stilled, thank God, the fruit remains! Though dead, he continues to speak.

VI.

Count Your Blessings

JOHN R. RICE

"Bless the Lord, O my soul: and all that is within me, bless his holy name. Bless the Lord, O my soul, and forget not all his benefits: Who forgiveth all thine iniquities; who healeth all thy diseases; Who redeemeth thy life from destruction; who crowneth thee with lovingkindness and tender mercies; Who satisfieth thy mouth with good things; so that thy youth is renewed like the eagle's." —Ps. 103:1-5.

The Pilgrim Fathers who had come to America to make a home in the wilderness where they might have freedom to worship God according to the dictates of their conscience, had the first harvest in 1621.

So at Plymouth, Massachusetts, the little handful of devoted people, hewing homes out of the wilderness amid many perils, set apart a day for thanksgiving to God. On that day they feasted and gave thanks.

President Lincoln appointed the last Thursday of November, 1864, as Thanksgiving Day. Now the Thanksgiving Day tradition is firmly established in America.

Every person who has a grateful heart should devoutly thank God, take stock and count his blessings.

However, Thanksgiving Day should be only one day to make official and public the praise that should resound in our hearts and testimonies throughout the rest of the year.

By divine inspiration, David wrote, "I will bless the Lord at all times: his praise shall continually be in my mouth"! (Ps. 34:1).

Again he said, "And my tongue shall speak of thy righteousness and of thy praise all the day long" (Ps. 35:28).

In Psalm 71:22-24 David declared:

"I will also praise thee with the psaltery, even thy truth, O my God:

unto thee will I sing with the harp, O thou Holy One of Israel. My lips shall greatly rejoice when I sing unto thee; and my soul, which thou hast redeemed. My tongue also shall talk of thy righteousness all the day long: for they are confounded, for they are brought unto shame, that seek my hurt."

In Psalm 103 David, moved by the Spirit, exhorts himself, "Bless the Lord, O my soul: and all that is within me, bless his holy name. Bless the Lord, O my soul, and forget not all his benefits." David set himself to count his blessings and to bless and praise and thank the Lord with all that was within him!

The unseen angels about us praise God, for in this same Psalm the divine Spirit, speaking through David, commanded, "Bless the Lord, ye his angels, that excel in strength, that do his commandments, hearkening unto the voice of his word. Bless ye the Lord, all ye his hosts; ye ministers of his, that do his pleasure." The hearts of angels continually run over with praise! Cherubim and seraphim praise Him with full hearts. No wonder Heaven is full of music and song! The goodness of God is so great that these holy beings cannot but burst forth in continual praise!

Even the inanimate universe praises God. Verse 22 of this Psalm says, "Bless the Lord, all his works in all places of his dominion." We are told in Psalm 19,

"The heavens declare the glory of God; and the firmament sheweth his handywork. Day unto day uttereth speech, and night unto night sheweth knowledge. There is no speech nor language, where their voice is not heard."—Vss. 1-3.

I do not personally ascribe personality to the stars and planets in the limitless skies, yet the glory of God is shouted by every starry constellation, by the flaming atoms of every sun, by the intricate and mathematical perfection of the movements of every solar system, every galaxy of stars.

An inanimate phonograph may play the tremendous praises of the *Hallelujah Chorus*, or a tiny radio may transmit the saving Gospel of God's preacher to a million ears. And as truly as that, God has made His entire creation to shout that there is a mighty, a glorious, powerful, beneficent and holy God. If creation does not preach the Gospel, it at least shows forth the glory of God so that only a fool can deny there is a Creator, a God to whom one must give an account.

I ask you, how can the redeemed child of God keep silence when the whole universe shouts the praises of God!

O Christian, count your blessings! Like David, declare, "Bless the Lord, O my soul: and all that is within me, bless his holy name."

See that the prayer of your lips is praise from the heart. See that your whole being is involved in this holy matter of thanksgiving and glory to God! Count your blessings. "Forget not all his benefits."

This is a good time to remember the words of Rev. Johnson Oatman:

> **When upon life's billows you are tempest-tossed,**
> **When you are discouraged, thinking all is lost,**
> **Count your many blessings, name them one by one,**
> **And it will surprise you what the Lord hath done.**
>
> **Are you ever burdened with a load of care?**
> **Does the cross seem heavy you are called to bear?**
> **Count your many blessings, ev'ry doubt will fly,**
> **And you will be singing as the days go by.**
>
> **When you look at others with their lands and gold,**
> **Think that Christ has promised you His wealth untold;**
> **Count your many blessings, money cannot buy**
> **Your reward in Heaven, nor your home on high.**
>
> **So, amid the conflict, whether great or small,**
> **Do not be discouraged, God is over all;**
> **Count your many blessings, angels will attend,**
> **Help and comfort give you to your journey's end.**

I. FORGIVENESS OF SIN, GREATEST OF ALL BLESSINGS

In the divinely-given list of blessings for which David was inspired to thank God, the first named is the forgiveness of sins.

"Bless the Lord, O my soul, and forget not all his benefits: Who forgiveth all thine iniquities. . . ."

Forgiveness of sins is the greatest blessing God has ever done for a mortal being. It was this for which God gave His Son—to forgive our sins and save our soul. It is this for which Jesus came into the world— "Christ Jesus came into the world to save sinners..." (I Tim. 1:15). Jesus said, "For the Son of man is come to seek and to save that which was lost" (Luke 19:10).

In all of God's plan, nothing else in the universe is as important as forgiving, saving, restoring to God's fellowship those who are estranged from Him, who are fallen from His holiness, who are become His enemies, who have been captured and ruined by sin! Forgiveness of sin is the highest aim of God.

A woman wrote to differ with me when in THE SWORD OF THE LORD I had published the statement that soul winning was the one thing dearest to the heart of God, the one main duty for every Christian. "Soul winning is all right, but it seems to me the main thing is to honor Jesus Christ," she stated.

She meant well, but she had wholly misunderstood the Lord. The best way to honor Jesus Christ is for us to take upon ourselves the same burden He has for dying sinners.

I reminded this woman that God was willing to turn His back on His Son and let Jesus die a criminal's death, in public shame, between two thieves, and be the victim of every indignity that wicked hearts could devise, in order that sinners could be saved!

How God longs to forgive sinners! The forgiveness and salvation of sinners is first in His plan.

Just so, every Christian ought to rejoice over this blessing—that his sins are forgiven, that he is saved, that he is redeemed, that he is restored to fellowship with God—above all others!

Jesus gave mighty power to the seventy whom He sent out to witness in villages and towns whither He Himself would come, "power to tread on serpents and scorpions, and over all the power of the enemy: and nothing shall by any means hurt you" (Luke 10:19). God has never given to anyone else such blanket power for more than a short season of time. These disciples returned to tell how devils had been subject to them.

But did Jesus encourage them to rejoice over miracles done, over devils cast out, over a mighty ministry? To the contrary. "Notwithstanding in this rejoice not, that the spirits are subject unto you; but rather rejoice, because your names are written in heaven" (vs. 20).

Thoughtless Christian, do you lament for not having the great things of the earth? How foolish you are! Queen Victoria, monarch of Great Britain and Empress of India when the sun never set on British possessions at the highest point of England's career, yet stood to her feet during the singing of the *Hallelujah Chorus* to bear homage to the Saviour. That true soul was glad to be only a subject before Jesus Christ.

A few years ago when the king and queen of England were being entertained at the White House, Chief White Feather, an American Indian Christian, was invited to sing. He chose "I'd Rather Have Jesus."

Later the king of England said to Chief White Feather, "I too had rather have Jesus!"

What did J. P. Morgan, multi-millionaire financier, rejoice about in his Will? Not in his stocks and bonds, not in railroads, steamships and banks, but in the blessed truth that he had found peace and forgiveness through the blood of Jesus Christ and could safely risk his soul in the mercy of such a Saviour!

Oh, what a blessing to have our sins forgiven!

David knew this blessing full well. Read Psalm 55 again. David knew what sin was and how it burned, hurt and damned. He could say, "My sin is ever before me." With a broken heart, he could plead for purging with hyssop, for the cleansing of his heart, for the renewal of a right spirit. David, who knew what it was to confess his sin, knew also what it was to praise God for forgiveness!

The Christian can praise God not only that he has been born again, not only that all his sins are laid on Christ and that he is counted just and thus guaranteed an entrance to Heaven, but he can also thank God for that daily cleansing, that daily taking of sin out of the way so that his fellowship can be renewed and he can daily walk in the light and joy of the Lord.

I would have every Christian at this Thanksgiving season stop and remind himself how great is the blessing of forgiveness and salvation, then praise the Lord!

I wonder if you find your heart cold, unresponsive? Then you have lost your first love, as had some in the church of Ephesus. You have forgotten the pit from whence you were dug.

How wicked, how ungrateful not to have a heart running over with praise for such a Saviour, for such a salvation, for such an everlasting life as the believer has in Christ!

When we praise God, let us not fail to praise Him for the forgiveness of our sins. And at Thanksgiving, let the most profound gratitude go out from grateful hearts to a forgiving God whose mercy is everlasting. When we name the benefits of God, remember Him "who forgiveth all thine iniquities."

II. IT IS GOD "WHO HEALETH ALL THY DISEASES"

Second in David's list of blessings is the healing of body. He cried out for all within him to praise God for this benefit, and to bless the Lord "who healeth all thy diseases."

Do I believe in divine healing? Certainly I do! I believe that all true healing is from God.

God heals through doctors, and He heals without doctors. God uses means, and sometimes He heals without perceptible means. Sometimes God heals through medicine and treatment of doctors; and sometimes He heals in spite of medicine and doctors.

Sometimes God heals by simple faith, inspired by true teaching of the Word of God. And sometimes He heals through faith, though the faith may be inspired by the preaching of some quack "healer." Yes, I believe in divine healing.

But while I believe in divine healing, I do not believe always in divine healers, nor the methods usually employed by so-called healing evangelists.

I do not believe in the doctrines often taught by quacks and charlatans or by some sincere but misguided souls in divine healing meetings. I am sure it is not always God's will to heal the sick. Sometimes He wants us sick for His glory, or for our good. Sometimes God wants a saint in Heaven.

The Bible does not teach that one should always ask for healing of body, whether it be God's will or not. Neither does it teach that the use of medicine or doctors is wrong.

Again, it is certainly wrong to suppose that healing is the greatest boon that can come to a person. Those "healing evangelists" who make healing the main thing do not have the Bible emphasis. Salvation ought to be first in our preaching and advertising.

So one must not ask for healing first and must not first thank God for healing. But let everyone rejoice first in that blessing of all blessings— the forgiveness of his sins. Then let him thank God for the secondary blessing of healing, if God sees fit to give that.

The above was necessary to be said, because I would not be a party to false doctrine and fanatical practice. Yet I thank God that He heals the sick. Among my readers are countless thousands who know that God has heard their cry and lifted them up from beds of sickness. And countless others know that the baby for whom they first despaired, after prayer is now well. Or the mother or father or companion, who was once so low, was lifted up by the hand of God in answer to prayer.

While on earth, in His loving compassion, Jesus often healed the sick. He does not have less compassion now. When people trusted Christ for healing in New Testament times, He lifted them up, as the paralytic borne of four and let down through the roof (Mark 2). Do you believe that God doesn't still answer the prayer, uttered in simple faith, for healing of the body? In James 5:13-16, we read simple instructions and blessed promises about healing:

"Is any among you afflicted? let him pray. Is any merry? let him sing psalms. Is any sick among you? let him call for the elders of the church; and let them pray over him, anointing him with oil in the name of the Lord: And the prayer of faith shall save the sick, and the Lord shall raise him up; and if he have committed sins, they shall be forgiven him. Confess your faults one to another, and pray one for another, that ye may be healed. The effectual fervent prayer of a righteous man availeth much."

Make sure you understand this passage. A sick person should call for the elders of his own church, not necessarily call for a traveling evangelist. Those who know the one sick will have some impression about what would glorify God and will be able to pray more nearly in the will of God, than will a stranger.

Notice, too, that it is "the prayer of faith" that saves the sick, not the oil. Oil may be a fitting symbol of the Holy Spirit, who raised Christ up from the dead and who dwells in the body of every Christian and can heal the body, but oil does not heal. The prayer of faith heals. If God gives the faith, one may expect the healing. If God does not give the faith, as sometimes He certainly does not, then one need not expect healing.

Since it is not always God's will to heal, then God does not always give faith. Sometimes there is sin in the life, and until the sin is confessed and forsaken, God will not give faith. But in many cases no unconfessed sin hinders, yet it is simply not God's will to heal the sick.

Face the blessed truth that ofttimes God has something far better for you than healing.

It is better to be sick in the will of God than well out of the will of God. It is better to glorify God in trouble than never to have trouble. It is even better for a Christian to die and be with the Lord than to remain here well and strong.

So a Bible-believing Christian must pray, willing to have the will of God. This Scripture does not teach, and no preacher ought ever teach, that a Christian has a right to demand healing in every case. God has not promised that, and it is presumptuous to demand what He has not promised. One may ask with a willing, submissive heart. If God gives the faith, then one may claim the blessing. But if He withholds faith for healing, then the Christian must ask for the blessed will of God, which is better than healing.

One should notice also that it is unconfessed sin which often brings ill health. Christians should confess their faults one to another and pray one for another "that ye may be healed."

In Corinth some Christians were weak and sickly, and some had already fallen asleep, that is, died, because of their sin (I Cor. 11:30).

It is not always God's will to heal the sick, but it sometimes is. That is easy to see when you count how many times a person may be ill and then restored to health before he dies. Surely it is usually God's will to heal the sick, and it is always His will for us to bring the matter to our loving and wise Father.

I cherish in my heart and thank God for many memories of answered prayer, many healings of the body. God has many times healed me and my loved ones and others. Like David I can say, "Bless the Lord, O my soul. . . who healeth all thy diseases."

But some of you have seldom been sick. You are in the strong health of young manhood or womanhood. In fact, you hardly need to think of any human frailty since you are so strong and well. Then all the more you ought to thank God. He who made you, who preserves you, who hedges you about with His mercy and power so that you are rarely sick, deserves all the praise for your good health.

I say to my soul today, "Bless the Lord, O my soul, and forget not all his benefits. . . who healeth all thy diseases." As you count your blessings, be sure to thank Him for His sustaining care, His overshadowing wings of protection.

III. GOD PRESERVES OUR LIVES

The third blessing of which David is reminding his soul, the benefit for which he blessed the Lord continually, was this: "who redeemeth thy life from destruction. . . ." God preserves our lives day by day.

We make it too much a matter of course and not a blessing from God that we are not cut down this day by death!

The blessed teaching of Scripture is that "the angel of the Lord encampeth round about them that fear him, and delivereth them" (Ps. 34:7).

God's guardian angels continually protect Christians. Of the angels we are told, "Are they not all ministering spirits, sent forth to minister for them who shall be heirs of salvation?" (Heb. 1:14).

It is true of Jesus, and certainly somewhat true of every believing child of God, that "he shall give his angels charge over thee, to keep thee in all thy ways. They shall bear thee up in their hands, lest thou dash thy foot against a stone" (Ps. 91:11, 12).

I found that promise and other wonderful promises of protection in Psalm 91 when I was called into the army in World War I. What a comfort was Psalm 91:1, "He that dwelleth in the secret place of the most High shall abide under the shadow of the Almighty."

And again, "He shall cover thee with his feathers, and under his wings shalt thou trust: his truth shall be thy shield and buckler. Thou shalt not be afraid for the terror by night; nor for the arrow that flieth by day; Nor for the pestilence that walketh in darkness; nor for the destruction that wasteth at noonday" (Ps. 91:4-6).

True, God has a time for Christians to die. It is equally true that Satan cannot bring one of God's children to death without God's consent. God allowed Satan to bring great trouble to Job, but Satan could not touch his life. God preserves the lives of His saints.

We may well believe that Satan so hates us that he would destroy every Christian if he could. Did he not hate Jesus? Did he not put it into the heart of Herod to kill all the babes of Bethlehem under two years old? Did he not put it into the heart of Pharisees again and again to almost stone Jesus? Did not Satan stir His own townsmen at Nazareth to try to hurl Jesus over the brow of a cliff to kill Him?

And in the Garden of Gethsemane, Jesus was sorrowful in soul, "even unto death." I believe Satan would have had Him die there at the wrong time and in the wrong place, had not Jesus prayed and His prayer been answered. His life was spared until the morrow when He could die in the will of God (Heb. 5:7).

Satan, who hated Jesus, hates every one of us who love the Lord.

Satan would delight to have an epidemic of smallpox or bubonic plague or influenza or some other disease sweep away thousands. He would delight to have a nuclear bomb drop that would blot out millions, including saints of God.

Every out-and-out Christian wrestles not against flesh and blood, but against principalities and powers and the rulers of darkness. Satan would want demons to possess us. He would want to cut us down by insanity, by evil habits, through evil men, or by dire accidents. But God "redeemeth thy life from destruction. . . ."

January 1, 1940, I was led of God to leave the pastorate of my beloved church in Dallas, Texas, to enter full-time, nationwide evangelism. With holy dedication I gave myself completely to Him. I pledged myself at any cost to help bring back citywide revival campaigns, mass evangelism, in America. I believe that God accepted the little I had to offer but which was offered with such love and prayer. I believe also that Satan hated my decision and would have gladly killed me if he could have.

At that time I was speaking in Chicago, in the Grand Opera House in noon services. These were broadcast daily. God saved a good many souls and reached hundreds of thousands in those grand early days of the Christian Businessmen's Committee of Chicago.

One day I drove north on LaSalle Street. As I crossed Division Street, a Power & Light truck with a large pump mounted in front of the radiator, like a battering ram or a deadly weapon, ran around a horse-drawn milk wagon and plunged into the side of my car. It seemed like an engine of destruction aimed by Satan to take away my life. That heavy pump crashed into the left front door of the car, crushing it in until it rested against my side. The car spun around on the icy street. It was badly damaged.

But, thank God, the impact which crushed the door in until it rested against my side, left not a scratch, not a blue mark, not a bruise! I was perfectly protected. I felt then and feel now that the angel of God said to Satan, "Thus far and no farther!"

Another time Dr. and Mrs. Sam Morris, Mrs. Rice and I took three days off to visit Carlsbad Cavern in New Mexico. As I drove from Dallas to Stamford, Texas, where Dr. Morris was then pastor, I bought a watermelon at Weatherford, Texas.

The next day it showered from time to time. When at last we decided we would eat the melon, the roadside was muddy. So we four sat on the tracks of the Texas Pacific Railroad (which ran beside the highway) and cut the melon.

As we talked of God's goodness, suddenly I was impelled to look up. Bearing down on us was a train roaring along perhaps at eighty miles an hour. No whistle, no warning. I leaped to my feet and pulled Sam Morris to his feet. Startled, he pulled his wife away. My wife sat on the culvert nearby. The train roared by within inches. A half second more and three of us would have been instantly killed.

All of us felt then that God had delivered us from a malevolent Devil. He hated Sam Morris' fight on the liquor traffic. He hated my fight for the return of old-time revivals, my pressure against modernism and sin. I praised Him then and praise Him now 'that He redeemed our lives from destruction.'

Christians should devoutly thank God that His care never ceases. We sleep, we work, we pray with never a thought that all about us are protecting hosts of God's angels! They were around Elisha at Dothan, the chariots of God and the angels of God. Likewise, they are around all who fear the Lord today.

So when you count your blessings, be sure to remember with grateful heart the God who redeems your life from destruction and keeps you every day.

IV. IT IS GOD WHO CROWNS US WITH LOVINGKINDNESS AND TENDER MERCIES

The fourth blessing about which David reminded his soul and for which, with all that was within him, he blessed God, was the crown of lovingkindness and tender mercies: "Bless the Lord, O my soul. . . who crowneth thee with lovingkindness and tender mercies."

It may be here that David was inspired to mention all the various ways that God blesses a Christian out of His lovingkindness. But since in this passage David had already been led to praise God for forgiveness of sins, for healing of the body, and for protection from death, and in the next verse he praises God for food, I judge that David was principally praising God here for the love and kindness of friends and family.

Sold into slavery and then put in prison in Egypt, Joseph found it so. "But the Lord was with Joseph, and shewed him mercy, and gave him favour in the sight of the keeper of the prison" (Gen. 39:21). Soon Joseph was ruler and manager of the prison. It was God who gave Joseph favor in the eyes of Pharaoh and made him ruler of Egypt.

Daniel was a teenager when he was carried captive into far-off Babylon. But God's lovingkindness and mercy did not fail him there, because we read, "Now God had brought Daniel into favour and tender love with the prince of the eunuchs" (1:9).

We read how Nehemiah obtained favor from the king for his expedition to restore Jerusalem.

We read how Esther was given the love and confidence of the king who held out to her the golden scepter when otherwise she would have been put to death.

We read how the same king could not sleep but read in the Chronicles how Mordecai had saved his life and how his heart was turned in favor toward the Jew, hitherto despised.

We read how God knit the heart of Jonathan to David as his own soul, with a love surpassing the love of women.

So all the lovingkindnesses, all the tender mercies which come to one in this life are but the evidences of the loving provision of God.

On the wall of a home I saw a motto,

GOD COULD NOT BE EVERYWHERE AT ONCE, SO HE MADE MOTHERS.

Many mothers are not what they ought to be, but we are right in believing that it is God who puts the instinctive mother-love in a woman's heart.

I missed all too much of the comfort and joy a mother brings, since my beloved mother went to be with the Lord before I was six. But, oh, in the treasured memories of childhood I hold most dear the evidences of my mother's love, of her pride in her son, of her prayers for him.

And everyone who had a pure, good, godly mother who poured out her love as sweet perfume over her family, should thank God for that lovingkindness. When you count your blessings, be sure to remember a mother's love.

And God, who wants Christians to call Him "Our Father," made a father's heart. God wanted some way to manifest His own heart, so He made fathers. He said, "Like as a father pitieth his children, so the Lord pitieth them that fear him" (Ps. 103:13).

As one begins to really count his blessings, it is amazingly clear that all the good ones are beyond price, greater than money can buy. You may thank God for whatever prosperity He has given you, but I assure you that money and much property are not the greater blessings. They are not even named in these five wonderful blessings summed up in our text in Psalm 103:1-5. God has something far better for our happiness and welfare than wealth.

Sometime ago I was thinking about the limited and restricted life of a young farmer I had met. He had little education. He was in a provincial community and would probably never be heard of beyond the small community in which he lived. His house was small and plain. His life included hard work and a boresome routine of chores.

But then I reflected: he had a wife who was not only radiant in face and beautiful in form, but modest, natural and unspoiled. She delighted in her home and children. Her house was spic and span. She loved her husband with a constant outpouring of service, admiration and delight. Her greatest desire was to make him happy. As I looked on the poor young fellow with wife and children, I thought, *How blessed he is!* The richest man in the world could not have a more beautiful wife nor rejoice in a love more pure and unselfish and sweet! No king on a throne could have healthier, happier, more beautiful children, nor better taught and with better manners.

That young farmer was rich beyond expression. God had flooded his life with "lovingkindness and tender mercies."

And at this Thanksgiving season, every man who has the love of a good wife ought to rejoice and praise God for such a crowning joy!

I loved my six daughters passionately when they were little. If possible, I love them even more now. Not one of them but that I sometimes bathed and usually fed when I was at home. I corrected them, entertained them, taught them. The baby's high chair always sat by me at the table. I carefully drilled them so that the first consecutive sentence each could say would be, "I love Daddy." One of them always, when I carried her, held onto my ear. Another always held onto my tie.

Now they are married. That hunger is now partly fulfilled by grandchildren. But I can speak on good authority when I say that any man who has had the tiny hand of a baby gripped around his finger, a little face looking up into Daddy's and asking questions and believing every answer was gospel truth, little feet running to meet Daddy when he came home at night, and little arms around his neck and warm, wet lips kissing his face in greeting, has worn the crown of a king!

Oh, the crowning glory, the lovingkindness, the tender mercy that God gives every man to whom He gives faithful and sweet children!

God has given many friends. But a man who takes a stand plainly, sharply, aggressively for the fundamentals of the Faith, any stand against sin and worldliness and formalism and modernism, is certain to be hated and opposed by some. I thank God also for my enemies. But how I do thank God for friends!

Literally thousands of Christians write me for counsel and follow my advice. More than once I have had letters from those who said, in effect, "I am engaged to a certain person. Here are the circumstances. Should I go through with our marriage plans? I will do exactly what you say." There are multitudes who want to read every book I write, who pray for me, love me, and encourage me. For them I thank God. They are an expression of the loving mercy and kindness of God!

It is said that when God had Saul anointed to be king, "there went with him a band of men, whose hearts God had touched" (I Sam. 10:26). Oh, what agony, defeat and frustration would be the part of any preacher if God called him to preach and called no one to hear! if God called a man to write and called no one to read! if God called a man to warn and called no one to heed his warning!

In counting my blessings, I know that I for one, will count strongly and with profound gratitude the lovingkindness of God who has crowned me with the love and mercy of thousands who have some way been led to love, comfort and encourage me.

O Christian, bless the Lord with all that is within you and forget not all His benefits. Bless the Lord "who crowneth thee with lovingkindness and tender mercies."

V. BLESS THE LORD "WHO SATISFIETH THY MOUTH WITH GOOD THINGS"

Some Christians consider themselves altogether too spiritual, too other-worldly to pay much attention to the simple blessing of food. But David thanked God for this blessing, counting it among the wonderful things to be treasured in heart and for which his whole soul should bless the Lord. And so should we!

It is altogether proper at Thanksgiving to have a feast with turkey and dressing or "stuffing." (The best dressing is made with Southern corn bread, chopped onion and sage!) I believe in the festive cranberry sauce, the pumpkin pie.

The Jews were taught to keep feasts: the feast of tabernacles, the passover feast, for example. When, under Nehemiah's leadership, the walls of Jerusalem were rebuilt and the gates were set up and the law of God read and explained to the people, the people wept over their sins. But we read:

"And Nehemiah, which is the Tirshatha, and Ezra the priest the scribe, and the Levites that taught the people, said unto all the people, This day is holy unto the Lord your God; mourn not, nor weep. For all the people wept, when they heard the words of the law. Then he said unto them, Go your way, eat the fat, and drink the sweet, and send

portions unto them for whom nothing is prepared: for this day is holy unto our Lord: neither be ye sorry; for the joy of the Lord is your strength." — Neh. 8:9, 10.

There is certainly a time for fasting, for mourning and sackcloth, for waiting on God and confessing of sins. Christians do too little of that. But it is equally true that there is a time to "eat the fat, and drink the sweet, and send portions unto them for whom nothing is prepared."

At the blessed time when all the redeemed of all ages will be caught out to meet Christ in the air and assemble in Heaven, we will have a feast, illustrated in Matthew 22:1-10 by the parable which Jesus gave of "a certain king, which made a marriage for his son." Again, when someone sitting with Jesus at a feast said, "Blessed is he that shall eat bread in the kingdom of God" (Luke 14:15), Jesus gave the parable of the great supper to which all are invited.

And the dear Lord Jesus came to enjoy the great feast made for Him in Bethany at the home of Mary, Martha and Lazarus. We are told that He ate with Simon the Pharisee, and again that Matthew the publican made a great supper for Jesus and invited other publicans and sinners to hear Him. And Jesus seemed to enjoy the wedding feast at Cana of Galilee, where He turned the water into wine.

It is true that the Lord was more concerned about soul winning than with food. When the disciples wanted Him to eat after He had won the woman at the well of Sychar in Samaria and waited to preach to others coming to Him, He said, "I have meat to eat that ye know not of" (John 4:32).

The wicked charge that Jesus was a glutton and a winebibber was not true, but Jesus did delight in good food and in fellowship around the table. So we do well to have feasts at Thanksgiving, at Christmas, and at other times, when we can rejoice in the Lord over His goodness!

Consider that the dear Saviour, the Creator, planned every bit of food available on earth. One of the best evidences of the folly of the evolutionary guess as an explanation of the origin and nature of this universe, an evidence for direct creation as the Bible teaches, is the fact that God has supplied the answer to every physical need.

Who but a personal God would make lungs and air for the lungs to breathe? Who but a personal, intelligent and benevolent God could fit the earth so exactly for human habitation, foreseeing the proper temperatures for life, the proper atmosphere for breathing, plants to make oxygen for animals, animals to make carbon dioxide for plants? How could it be accidental that the mass of earth, controlling the weight of all on it, would be matched by the necessary muscles of man and beast?

A thoughtful and loving God prepared sound for ears and ears for sound. He prepared the nose for odors and odors for the nose. He prepared the eyes for color and colors for the eyes.

The infinite variety of fruit was created by the plan of God. He put the color and tang and texture in every fruit and berry and melon. He put the taste and the proteins in the beefsteaks; the amino acids and the calories in the pork chops; the vitamins and the roughage and the tremendous energy of starch in the wheat grain; the health and goodness in every salad.

It seems the dear Lord Jesus, with infinite delight, took pains to make every food good for the body and pleasant in looks, odor and taste. He did not people the fathomless ocean with fish without planning what would be good for man's food. Since "every good gift and every perfect gift is from above, and cometh down from the Father of lights, with whom is no variableness, neither shadow of turning" (James 1:17), we know that food is the love gift of God to His people.

Every Christian should receive every meal with the same delight and gratitude felt by a girl in love who receives an enormous box of chocolates from her sweetheart.

So let everyone who counts his blessings think of the unfailing favor of God who, day after day, has supplied food to satisfy the body and delight the heart.

How fitting that, with bowed heads and reverent hearts, every home should thank God for the food supplied. What wicked ingratitude to eat like pigs, with both feet in the feed trough, without a heartfelt thank-You to the Giver of every good and perfect gift!

The Bible tells us that it is the work of "seducing spirits and doctrines of devils," when cults command people "to abstain from meats, which God hath created to be received with thanksgiving of them which believe and know the truth." God explains, "For every creature of God is good, and nothing to be refused, if it be received with thanksgiving: For it is sanctified by the word of God and prayer" (I Tim. 4:1-5).

The Roman church was wrong in forbidding Catholics to eat meat on Friday or during Lent. How wrong Seventh-Day Adventists are in encouraging people to keep the ceremonial laws of the Jews as to food!

Every creature of God is good, provided it be received with thanksgiving! The Word of God, and prayer at mealtime, sanctify the food and make it suitable, fitting and holy in God's sight!

Every Christian is to thank God for food at every meal. While at a restaurant, Christians may bow their heads together and one softly give thanks to God. If one is alone in a public place, he can, without being unduly conspicuous, bow his head in humble and fervent thanks to the God who gives him every good thing. God is not embarrassed to give you your food in the presence of gainsaying worldlings; then why should we be ashamed to thank Him in their presence?

Little children ought always be thankful for their food. The first prayer my babies ever learned was, "Jesus, we thank You for this breafus' food." Sometimes when a child was late in getting to the table and did not get to bow her head and hear the prayer of thanksgiving, she would break into tears of disappointment.

I suggest that every reverent heart stop now and thank God for all the years He has provided food, drink and other ordinary but necessary comforts of life. Do we thank Him enough?

VI. WHAT SHALL A CHRISTIAN DO ABOUT THESE MANY BLESSINGS?

Now that you have seen in mind your many blessings, what will you do about it? Let me suggest some things.

1. By all means set aside a time when you can pour out praises of thanksgiving to such a good God and wonderful Saviour! Do not be content with a general feeling of gratitude. Be definite as you recount your blessings.

2. The first opportunity available, publicly thank God for all He has done for you. Give Him glory as you speak to individuals. Lead your family in regular, frequent, open praise for His lovingkindness.

3. Since God has been so good, dwell upon His blessings until your heart is happy and content. "Why art thou cast down, O my soul? and why art thou disquieted within me? hope in God: for I shall yet praise him, who is the health of my countenance, and my God" (Ps. 43:5).

To dwell upon your blessings will multiply them. To acknowledge your blessings and your gratefulness will certainly bring happiness and contentment. Every Christian has enough blessings to make him shout the praises of God.

4. That God has been so wonderfully good in the past is evidence

that He is on the giving end. Therefore, past blessings should encourage us to ask for more. David said, "Because he hath inclined his ear to me, therefore will I call upon him as long as I live" (Ps. 116:2). Again we read where David said, "What shall I render unto the Lord for all his benefits toward me? I will take the cup of salvation, and call upon the name of the Lord" (Ps. 116:12, 13).

Counting your blessings will be a tremendous encouragement to pray.

5. Now that you have counted your blessings, 'naming them one by one' and, since it has surprised you what the Lord has done, see that it makes your love and obedience abound. Jesus properly said, "If ye love me, keep my commandments" (John 14:15). Make a holy resolve that, in the light of all God's wonderful blessings, your life will glorify Him.

Years ago a man from Rock Island, Illinois, came to visit me as I conducted revival services in Gary, Indiana. We sat in my hotel room. Some two years before the dear man had heard me preach in Jackson, Michigan. Recently widowed, he was left lonely. The Depression and hard times had robbed him of his cherished job. He heard me preach on "Ye Have Not Because Ye Ask Not." It was the first time he had heard that it was all right to ask God for a job.

As he sat in my hotel room with his hands upon his knees and with tears trickling down his cheeks, he told me his story.

He had earnestly prayed for work. The next day he had gotten a job in the big manufacturing plant where he wanted to work, in the very department he chose, under a foreman whom he greatly admired. Then he had been transferred to Rock Island, Illinois, to a better job. While there he found a little church where he was happy and where he heard the Gospel. When he prayed for God to give him some work to do in the church, he was asked to teach an adult class. The church then elected him assistant pastor. Then he prayed again, and God sent an evangelist and a great revival with many, many souls saved.

He told me how his whole life was transformed and how his empty heart was filled with blessings. "After all He has done for me, Brother Rice . . ." and he broke into sobs, then continued, ". . . after all He has done for me, I will serve Him—I will serve Him 'til I die!"

As I said then, so say I again, "And so will I!"

So, we close as we began, "Bless the Lord, O my soul!"

ROBERT GREENE LEE
1886-1978

ABOUT THE MAN:

R. G. Lee was born November 11, 1886, and died July 20, 1978.

The midwife attending his birth held baby Lee in her black arms while dancing a jig around the room, saying, "Praise Gawd! Glory be! The good Lawd done sont a preacher to dis here house. Yas, sah! Yes, ma'am. Dat's what He's done gone and done."

"God-sent preacher" well describes Dr. Lee. Few in number are the Baptists who have never heard his most famous sermon, "Payday Someday!" If you haven't heard it, or read it, surely you have heard some preacher make a favorable reference to it.

From his humble birth to sharecropper parents, Dr. Lee rose to pastor one of the largest churches in his denomination and head the mammoth Southern Baptist Convention as its president, serving three terms in that office. Dr. John R. Rice said:

"If you have not had the privilege of hearing Dr. Lee in person, I am sorry for you. The scholarly thoroughness, the wizardry of words, the lilt of poetic thought, the exalted idealism, the tender pathos, the practical application, the stern devotion to divine truth, the holy urgency in the preaching of a man called and anointed of God to preach and who must therefore preach, are never to be forgotten. The stately progression of his sermon to its logical end satisfies. The facile language, the alliterative statement, the powerful conviction mark Dr. Lee's sermons. The scholarly gleaning of incident and illustration from the treasures of scholarly memory and library make a rich feast for the hearer. The banquet table is spread with bread from many a grain field, honey distilled from the nectar of far-off exotic blossoms, sweetmeats from many a bake shop, strong meat from divers markets, and the whole board is garnished by posies from a thousand gardens.

"Often have I been blessed in hearing Dr. Lee preach, have delighted in his southern voice, and have been carried along with joy by his anointed eloquence."

VII.

Are You Thankful?

R. G. LEE

"Be ye thankful." —Col. 3:15.

The great Caruso, knowing that the language of tones belongs equally to all mankind and that melody is the absolute language in which the singer speaks to human hearts, had an artistic temperament. On a tour to Cincinnati, he was exposed to what he considered hardships. A Pittsburgh hotel expected him to sleep on a three-quarter bed, with one mattress and two pillows. Caruso demanded a double bed, three mattresses, and eighteen pillows. "Eighteen pillows, three mattresses, or no concert," he said. So at 1:30 at night closets were ransacked and mattresses and pillows were dragged up as requested. That before the great tenor would sing!

Today some folks must have abundance beyond their needs ere they become thankful—and, even with abundance, they seem to think that God is thanked enough when not thanked at all. "Be ye thankful" is an imperative which nothing must induce you to disregard, and which you must hold in constant reverence.

Let us make here some—

I. INQUIRIES REGARDING THANKFULNESS

Are you thankful?

Does your heart, like David's, go out to God in gratitude as you meditate on God's mercies shown you all your life? Do you thank God for spiritual and temporal blessings abundantly bestowed? Do you receive daily benefits without acknowledging their source—without remembering that all good and perfect gifts come from God "with whom is no variableness nor shadow cast by turning"? (James 1:17). Do you thoughtfully contemplate the marvelous providential care of God and give thanks unto the Lord for having "blessed you with all spiritual blessings in heavenly places in Christ," as well as for the marvelous way in which he "giveth us richly all things to enjoy"? Since "it is a good thing to give thanks unto the Lord" (Ps. 92:1), do you know that it is both ungrateful and unbecoming *not* to give thanks?

Do you know that you can never pass through the day or approach God without cause for gratitude? That thankfulness glorifies God and subdues the lower nature? That thankfulness is a duty or a delight greatly prominent in the Bible? That thankfulness is the declarative mood of gratitude, a bright fire in the world's frigid zone, a well of water in a desert? Do you know that thankfulness is a master force of soul building and the greatest tonic faith has?

The Bible says: "Continue in prayer. . . with thanksgiving" (Col. 4:2). "With thanksgiving let your requests by made known unto God" (Phil. 4:6). "Daniel. . . gave thanks before his God" (6:10). "Offer unto God thanksgiving" (Ps. 50:14).

Jonah said, "I will sacrifice unto thee with the voice of thanksgiving" (2:9). Paul, whose life was one of perils and hardships and sufferings, said, "I thank God."

Cicero calls gratitude the mother of virtues. Seneca said, "He that urges gratitude pleads the cause both of God and men." No metaphysician ever felt the deficiency of language so much as the grateful. 'Tis true God has two dwellings—one in Heaven, the other in a thankful heart.

Think now of the—

II. INIQUITY OF UNTHANKFULNESS

One of the sins charged against the false profession of the last days is that of unthankfulness.

"For men shall be. . . covetous. . . blasphemers. . . *unthankful*. . . unholy. . . fierce, despisers of those that are good, traitors" (II Tim. 3:2-4). Unthankfulness listed with covetousness and blasphemy!

In Luke God puts ingratitude along with evil. "For he is kind unto the unthankful and to the evil" (Luke 6:35).

Ingratitude, sour and peevish, would make you believe that all good folk are dead, youth corrupt, times out of joint like a windmill twisted by a cyclone, and God a merciless tyrant.

Shakespeare wrote:

**I hate ingratitude more in man
Than lying, vainness, babbling, drunkenness,
Or any taint of vice whose strong corruption
Inhabits our frail blood.**

**How sharper than a serpent's tooth it is
To have a thankless child!**

Another has said:

**He that's ungrateful has no guilt but one;
All other crimes may pass for virtues in him.**

The thief may have in him streaks of honesty, the dead beat spots of honor, the liar occasional impulses to tell the truth, the libertine some desires to be pure. But there is nothing redemptive in the ingrate. Trust the ungrateful soul with money, he will steal it; with honor, he will betray it; with virtue, he will violate it; with a blood-bequeathed legacy, he will reduce it in quality and quantity. Trust the ingrate with love—and with hellish alchemy he will transmute it into lust. Trust the ingrate with your good name—and he will besmirch it.

We condemn the nine lepers who came not back to thank Jesus for their healing—and yet put ourselves in their company of cold and unfeeling ingratitude. Ingratitude is a great evil—a most common disease of humanity. Many fail more often in gratitude than in any other Christian graces.

Milton brands ingratitude as besotted and base.

Swift says: "He that calls a man ungrateful sums all the evil of which one can be guilty."

Thomason told the truth when he said that ingratitude is treason to mankind.

Fuller said: "Ingratitude is a fault never found unattended with other viciousness."

Colton claims that brutes leave ingratitude to man.

But we should note the—

III. INCLUSIVENESS OF THANKSGIVING

"In *every thing* give thanks: for this is the will of God in Christ Jesus concerning you."—I Thess. 5:18.

"Giving thanks always for *all things* unto God and the Father in the name of our Lord Jesus Christ."—Eph. 5:20.

You are to give thanks even though a panic of emotions has seized the world and malice torments mankind. Give thanks though the pestilence of hate walketh at noonday and dreadful uncertainties and crises keep life turbulent and hectic. "Be ye thankful"—even though you are fed daily on the aggravating news of horrors.

"Be ye thankful" when barns are filled with plenty and when fields are barren—when the cup of woe is bitter, when money is sufficient and when riches take to themselves wings and the wolf of want howls at the door. "Be ye thankful" when for the affairs of life brain and brawn are at the full and when you, prostrate on the earth, cannot rise and toil—when tides of health are at their full and, also, when all muscles are highways for the running to and fro of pain.

Give thanks in health *and* in sickness—when friends despise *and* forsake you—when the crepe is on the front door *and* the coffin in the house. Give thanks for the gall with the honey, the martyr's fire with its suffering as well as the hearthstone fire with its comfort; for hailstorms that ruin fruitful fields as well as for rains that quench drought; for tribulations severe as well as for triumphs sweet; for good-bys that break hearts as well as for greetings that cheer hearts, for desert places as well as for gardens.

You are to give thanks when bereaved of loved ones, when you find traitors among friends, when sickness brings you prostration, when hopes wither, when you have only summer clothes for wintertime, when only scraps are on your plate—yea, *in everything* you are to give thanks! Think of some who are—

IV. INSPIRATIONS CONCERNING THANKSGIVING

David, giving thanks for the wondrous works of God, speaks the voice of thanksgiving (Ps. 26:7).

The *Levites* were "to stand every morning to thank and praise the Lord, and likewise at even" (I Chron. 23:30).

Daniel, the secret of Nebuchadnezzar's dream revealed from Heaven in a night vision, gave thanks, saying: "I thank thee. . .O thou God of my fathers, who. . .hast made known unto me now what we desired of thee" (Dan. 2:23).

Nehemiah dedicated the wall of Jerusalem "with thanksgiving"— appointing two great companies to "give thanks" (Neh. 12).

Isaiah speaks of how God shall comfort Zion and the voice of *thanksgiving* heard (Isa. 51:3).

Amos, exhorting Israel to repent, says: "Offer a sacrifice of thanksgiving" (Amos 4:5).

Anna, a prophetess of great age, seeing Simeon holding Jesus in his arms and hearing Simeon speak words of wisdom, "gave thanks" (Luke 2:38).

The *apostles*, who suffered persecution, gave thanks that they were "counted worthy to suffer shame for Jesus' name" (Acts 5:41).

The *angels* at God's throne, worshiping God, said, "Thanksgiving...be unto our God" (Rev. 7:12).

Paul, the great apostle of God's Gospel, often lifted his voice and wielded his pen in thanksgiving. Paul was in peril of his life in Damascus, coldly suspected by his fellow believers in Jerusalem, persecuted in Antioch, stoned in Lystra, assaulted in Iconium, beaten with many stripes and put in jail at Philippi, attacked by a lewd and envious crowd in Thessalonica, pursued by jealous enmity in Berea, despised in Athens, blasphemed in Corinth, exposed to the fierce wrath of the Ephesians, bound with chains in Jerusalem, and imprisoned in Rome. Paul was in prison without his freedom, in winter without his coat, in court without friends, in poverty without aid. BUT in none of these was he without his hymn of *thanksgiving*.

Jesus, Son of man without sin, Son of God with power, gave thanks. Jesus gave thanks for FOOD. "And when he had taken the five loaves and the two fishes, he looked up to heaven, and gave thanks" (Mark 6:41). Are *you*, like Jesus, grateful for food?

Jesus was thankful for PERSONAL GIFTS. When Mary, with uncalculating love, broke the costly box of costly nard and anointed His head and feet, He defended her against her critics and immortalized her deed (John 12:7).

Jesus was thankful for FRIENDS. "Henceforth I call you not servants...but friends" (John 15:15).

Jesus was thankful for HELPFUL SERVICE. When seated on the throne under a new relationship, He will recall kindness done to Him by His people. "Then shall the King say unto them on his right hand, Come, ye blessed of my Father...For I was an hungred, and ye gave me meat...thirsty, and ye gave me drink...Naked, and ye clothed me...sick, and ye visited me" (Matt. 25:34-36).

Jesus was grateful for REVEALED TRUTH. "I thank thee, O Father ...because thou hast hid these things from the wise and...hast revealed them unto babes" (Matt. 11:25).

Jesus was thankful for ANSWERED PRAYER. "And Jesus lifted up his eyes, and said, Father, I thank thee that thou hast heard me" (John 11:41).

Jesus was thankful for CALVARY SUFFERINGS. That night, with the shadow of the cross looming darkly and immediately ahead, He "gave thanks." With a song on His lips He went to His agony in Gethsemane—and to the cross.

But we should think, as to ingratitude, of—

V. INSULT

What guilty forgetting is yours—if you forget the Christ! No gratitude, but only abuse, is shown in passing Christ by. Ingrate am I, ingrate are you—if we fail to keep fresh the memory of mighty things Christ has done for us.

To spurn the diamond of His salvation for the paste jewel of a Christ-rejecting life is folly and wickedness. Base ingratitude it is to forget the Emancipator whose power took off your shackles and opened your prison bars—to forget the Redeemer when His redemption has altered your night into confident morning! There never was ingratitude so insultingly base.

Jesus "endured the cross, despising the shame" thereof (Heb. 12:2). Would you, insulting His loving mercy, be listed with those who are "despisers of those that are good"? (II Tim. 3:3; Rom. 2:4-6).

Are you one who, by a will of obstinacy, treats His overtures of love and invitations of mercy with the insult of contempt? Remember: "He that despised Moses' law died without mercy under two or three witnesses: of how much sorer punishment. . . shall he be thought worthy, who hath trodden under foot the Son of God, and hath counted the blood of the covenant. . . an unholy thing, and hath done despite unto the Spirit of grace?" (Heb. 10:28,29).

Oh! Use not despitefully the Christ who offers you costly salvation running in the channel of His precious blood. Be not you among the scorners who delight in their scorning or among the fools who hate knowledge. Wound not again the hand wounded for you—holding forth the Bread of life.

"History knows no disaster," said the *Literary Digest* (Sept. 1923), "which parallels the earthquake and fire that visited Japan this month and laid waste the capital city and the chief seaport."

The *New York Tribune* called this earthquake "undoubtedly the greatest disaster in recorded time." The *New York Times* described the havoc as covering about 45,000 square miles which contained five big cities and a population of 7,000,000. Other dispatches reported that virtually every building in Yokohama was destroyed. Perhaps three-fourths of Tokyo was burned and the entire city with its 5,000,000 inhabitants was shattered by the earthquake.

A joint survey made by Herbert Hoover and the Red Cross estimated the dead at almost 300,000, with 2,500,000 people homeless. Disease and despair rode throughout the island empire.

Then help came! Help from America for helpless Japan! Food, clothing, medical supplies, and volunteer workers came by the shipload. The American Red Cross collected ten million dollars from the people of the United States for the suffering and homeless Nipponese.

Those who lived through the awful earth tremors, the gigantic waves, and the tongues of fire must perish, it seemed, from starvation or disease. But they didn't. Why? Because America remembered—remembered their need, their suffering, their hunger.

The Nipponese were grateful. They even put their appreciation in *writing*. Walter Kiernan, correspondent for the International News Service, recalls their words: "Japan will never forget!"

But Japan did forget! American ships of mercy were forgotten, and the Rising Sun sent planes of destruction in return. On December 7, 1941, Japanese airplanes brought death and destruction to Pearl Harbor—and the Rising Sun proclaimed that America, brought to her knees, would beg for mercy.

But are the Japanese the only ones who overlook past mercies? Long ago the Lord said of Israel, "My people have forgotten me days without number" (Jer. 2:32). God blessed them, but they forgot God!

Are you guilty of forgetting Christ? Just what is your attitude toward the God who "so loved the world, that he gave his only begotten Son, that whosoever believeth in him should not perish, but have everlasting life"? (John 3:16).

The Son of God may be forgotten—the Gift of God rejected—but only at the awful penalty of losing your soul. "For what shall it profit a man, if he shall gain the whole world, and lose his own soul?" (Mark 8:36, 37). God sent His Son to the cross to die for your sins. For you to reject God's mercy can only mean judgment. "For God sent not his Son into the world to condemn the world; but that the world through him might be saved. He that believeth on him is not condemned: but he that believeth not *is* condemned *already*, because he hath not believed in the name of the only begotten Son of God" (John 3:17, 18).

Forget not, I beg you, the Christ who died for you. But with repentance toward God, with faith in Jesus Christ, come out of your loss and defect into His gain and victory—and say to Him:

> Lord, I am Thine, entirely Thine,
> Purchased and saved by blood divine;
> With full consent Thine I would be,
> And own Thy sovereign right in me.
>
> Thine would I live, Thine would I die,
> Be Thine, thro' all eternity;
> The vow is past beyond repeal.
> And now I set the solemn seal.
>
> Here, at the cross where flows the blood
> That bought my guilty soul for God,
> Thee, my new Master, now I call,
> And consecrate to Thee my all.
>
> —Samuel Davies

(From the book, *The Sinner's Saviour,* by R. G. Lee. Published by Broadman Press.)

HENRY (HARRY) ALLEN IRONSIDE
1876-1951

ABOUT THE MAN:

Few preachers had more varied ministries than this man. He was a captain in the Salvation Army, an itinerant preacher with the Plymouth Brethren, pastor of the renowned Moody Memorial Church in Chicago, and conducted Bible conferences throughout the world. Sandwiched between those major ministries, Ironside preached the Gospel on street corners, in missions, in taverns, on Indian reservations, etc.

Never formally ordained and with no experience whatever as a pastor, Ironside took over the 4,000-seat Moody Memorial Church in Chicago and often filled it to capacity for 18½ years. A seminary president once said of him, *"He has the most unique ministry of any man living."* Although he had little formal education, his tremendous mental capacity and photographic memory caused him to be called the "Archbishop of Fundamentalism."

Preaching—warm, soul-saving preaching—was his forte. Special speakers in his great church often meant nothing; the crowds came when he was there. He traveled constantly; at his prime, he averaged 40 weeks in the year on the road—always returning to Moody Memorial for Sunday services.

His pen moved, too; he contributed regularly to various religious periodicals and journals in addition to publishing 80 books and pamphlets. His writings included addresses or commentaries on the entire New Testament, all of the prophetic books of the Old Testament, and a great many volumes on specific Bible themes and subjects.

In 1951, Dr. Ironside died in Cambridge, New Zealand, and was buried there at his own request.

VIII.

The Presentation of First Fruits

H. A. IRONSIDE

"By him therefore let us offer the sacrifice of praise to God continually, that is, the fruit of our lips giving thanks to his name. But to do good and to communicate forget not: for with such sacrifices God is well pleased."—Heb. 13:15, 16.

In chapter 26 of Deuteronomy we have what undoubtedly gave rise to the Puritans' harvest home festival. It was Israel's national Thanksgiving Day and most suggestive of that which should occupy our hearts at this present time.

The chapter is divided into two parts. In verses 1 to 11 the people are seen bringing the first fruits to God and rejoicing before Him as they give thanks for all the mercies of the past year.

In verses 12 to 19 the same people are seen ministering to the Levites, the strangers, the fatherless, the widows and all the poor and needy among them. And by these acts of consideration for their less fortunate fellow men and for the servants of the Lord, who were largely dependent upon their bounty, we see evidences of grace working in their souls, and can understand something of what our own attitude ought to be when, blessed ourselves, we look upon a vast host who are suffering for the lack of what God has so graciously lavished upon us.

These two divisions of this great chapter answer to the two aspects of sacrifice brought before us in our text. In verse 15 we have the sacrifice of praise to God; the fruit of lips that confess the name of Jesus. Whereas in verse 16 we have the sacrifice of ministering to those in need; doing good and sharing with others what God has given to us.

I. THE FIRST FRUITS OF OUR LIPS, THE SACRIFICE OF PRAISE TO GOD

This sacrifice of praise can be presented to God only by those who are in happy relationship with Himself. None but redeemed people can come into His holy presence as worshipers. Worship is not merely the observance of some religious ceremony; neither does it consist in listening to a sermon nor in presenting our petitions in prayer. It is a great mistake to think of worship as the enjoyment of soulful and beautiful music. Carnal and even unconverted people may have their sentimental natures thoroughly aroused by the dulcet strains of the organ or by the sweet singing of a trained choir. But this enjoyment does not necessarily imply that the spirit is worshiping God in reality. Our Lord Himself said to the Samaritan woman, "God is a Spirit: and they that worship him must worship him in Spirit and in truth" (John 4:24).

The highest worship is when the saint of God enters by faith into the holiest, passing through the rent veil and prostrating himself before the throne of the Eternal, there to gaze with adoring love and gratitude upon our blessed Lord Jesus Christ who now sits exalted on the Father's throne. There can be no true worship apart from our occupation with Himself. Outward observances may often hinder rather than help because there is ever the danger of distracting the mind, of fixing the attention upon some religious performance instead of on Christ Himself. It is when the spirit enters into the stillness, the quiet of God's own presence, there to be overwhelmed with a sense of the divine holiness and the divine love as manifested in the Lord Jesus Christ, that we really worship.

And this is pictured for us very beautifully in these first eleven verses of Deuteronomy 26. We read in verses 1 and 2:

> "And it shall be, when thou art come in unto the land which the Lord thy God giveth thee for an inheritance, and possessest it, and dwellest therein; That thou shalt take of all the fruit of the earth, which thou shalt bring of thy land that the Lord thy God giveth thee, and shalt put it in a basket, and shalt go unto the place which the Lord thy God shall choose to place his name there."

Observe, this was something that could never be carried out in the wilderness, and certainly not in Egypt. God says, "When thou shalt come in unto the land." As a redeemed people, redeemed by blood and redeemed by power and dwelling in the inheritance which God had given them, the Israelites were called to observe this festival. No unsaved person, no one who is still in nature's darkness and in bondage to sin and Satan, no one who has not been washed from his sins in the blood of Jesus and raised up together and made to sit together in heavenly places in Christ can be a true worshiper. Men often speak of public worship, but this is a mistake. The public cannot worship. Worship is a very selective thing, and it is the glad privilege of those who are complete in Christ.

Now notice the form their service was to take. They were commanded to bring the first fruits of the land which the Lord had given them, to put it in a basket and go to the place where the Lord had chosen to set His name.

How significant all this is. The first fruits speak of Christ Himself, even as we read in I Corinthians 15:20: "But now is Christ risen from the dead, and become the firstfruits of them that slept." Again in verse 23: "Christ the firstfruits; afterwards they that are Christ's at his coming." The first fruits tell of the great harvest soon to be gathered in, even as a risen Christ has entered into the presence of God as our forerunner, the pledge of the ingathering when millions of the redeemed will be transformed and translated at the moment of His return.

The basket may well speak of our poor hearts, straitened indeed as we often are in ourselves, yet in which Christ is pleased to dwell, "that Christ may dwell in your hearts by faith." We come to God with a heart filled with Christ, thinking of Him, praising Him, occupied alone with Him, rejoicing in Jesus Christ and having no confidence in the flesh. How God delights to see His people thus before Him!

When I was trying to expound this passage some years ago, a dear little golden-haired girl was present. On the way home she said to her father, "Daddy dear, I didn't have anything in my basket for the Lord today."

Thinking she had not understood, the father said, "Well, Flossy, what do you mean?"

"I was so busy," she said, "going to school and playing, that I didn't put anything in my basket."

"You didn't?" the father asked, still not sure that she had understood.

"No," she said. They walked along silently for a few moments, then she said, "Daddy, I am going to have my basket full by next Sunday."

"How are you going to get it full?" her father asked.

"Every day," said the little one, "I am going to stop playing for a little while and think of Jesus, and I think by Sunday I will have it full."

"Out of the mouth of babes and sucklings thou hast perfected praise" (Matt. 21:16). A heart filled with Christ constitutes a worshiper.

Of old there was only one place where the first fruits could be presented, and that was at the place where God had set His name, where the tabernacle had been pitched, or later on, the Temple built, and where He dwelt between the cherubim.

Now it is to no earthly sanctuary we are invited to come, but the word is,

"Having therefore, brethren, boldness to enter into the holiest by the blood of Jesus, By a new and living way, which he hath consecrated for us, through the veil, that is to say, his flesh; And having an high priest over the house of God; Let us draw near with a true heart in full assurance of faith, having our hearts sprinkled from an evil conscience, and our bodies washed with pure water."—Heb. 10:19-22.

Accompanied with the presentation, we have the confession as in verse 3: "And thou shalt go unto the priest that shall be in those days, and say unto him, I profess this day unto the Lord thy God, that I am come unto the country which the Lord sware unto our fathers for to give us." It was a recognition and an acknowledgment of the fact that there had not failed one word of all God's good promise.

And so today as a worshiping company, we gladly confess that we have by faith entered into the inheritance which is ours in Christ.

The priest is another picture of our Lord Jesus Christ. We read, "The priest shall take the basket out of thine hand, and set it down before the altar of the Lord thy God" (vs. 4). It is our great High Priest who presents to God our worship and praises, and it is His perfection which alone can make our feeble adoration acceptable to the Father.

No thought of merit was to be in the mind of the Israelite and surely there can be none with us. We are saved by grace apart from works, and so have nothing of which to boast. Their confession was most abject:

"A Syrian ready to perish was my father, and he went down into Egypt, and sojourned there with a few, and became there a nation, great, mighty, and populous: And the Egyptians evil entreated us, and afflicted us, and laid upon us hard bondage: And when we cried unto the Lord God of our fathers, the Lord heard our voice, and looked on our affliction, and our labour, and our oppression: And the Lord brought us forth out of Egypt with a mighty hand, and with an outstretched arm, and with great terribleness, and with signs, and with wonders: And he hath brought us into this place, and hath given us this land, even a land that floweth with milk and honey. And now,

behold, I have brought the firstfruits of the land, which thou, O Lord, hast given me. And thou shalt set it before thy God, and worship before the Lord thy God."—Deut. 26:5-10.

What an acknowledgment was this that they owed every blessing to divine grace! They merited nothing, they purchased nothing, but all came to them through the wondrous lovingkindness of the Lord. And so in response to that matchless mercy, they brought the first fruits and set them down before Him, rejoicing in His presence because of all the good things He had lavished upon them.

Shall we not emulate them this morning as we think of a nobler inheritance, a greater deliverance, and a more marvelous exhibition of divine grace than they ever dreamed of, all ours in Christ Jesus? Surely we can rejoice in Him today and offer the fruit of lips that confess His name.

II. THE SACRIFICE OF DOING GOOD, OF MINISTERING TO THOSE IN NEED

But what about the needy all around us? The spiritually needy and the temporally needy also? We have been blessed in Christ; and concerning earthly things, we are told, "He hath given us all things richly to enjoy."

But at our very doors are those who know nothing of the grace of God revealed in Christ. All about us are those who are suffering for lack of the everyday mercies that mean so much to us.

God has given us an example in His further commandment to Israel of what His pleasure is in regard to this. We read in verses 12 to 14:

"When thou hast made an end of tithing all the tithes of thine increase the third year, which is the year of tithing, and hast given it unto the Levite, the stranger, the fatherless, and the widow, that they may eat within thy gates, and be filled; Then thou shalt say before the Lord thy God, I have brought away the hallowed things out of mine house, and also have given them unto the Levite, and unto the stranger, to the fatherless, and to the widow, according to all thy commandments which thou hast commanded me: I have not transgressed thy commandments, neither have I forgotten them: I have not eaten thereof in my mourning, neither have I taken away ought thereof for any unclean use, nor given ought thereof for the dead: but I have hearkened to the voice of the Lord my God, and have done according to all that thou hast commanded me."

Here was grace in activity; here was love manifested. Here was the kindness of God seen in His people as they ministered to the need of others. In Hebrews 13:16 we have the same thing where God says, "But to do good and to communicate forget not, for with such sacrifices God is well pleased." He would not have those who have been so richly blessed forget the needs of others, and I am quite sure that no one who truly enjoys Christ can help telling of Him to men and women who are still strangers to His grace.

And as we thank God today for the temporal mercies He has lavished upon us, our enjoyment will be the greater as we share these good things with those whose circumstances are not so agreeable as ours, passing on to them what will brighten their lives and gladden their hearts in the name of Him who said, "It is more blessed to give than to receive."

You have heard of the old gentleman who was so pious that all through the church service he would sit with enraptured face looking up to Heaven, but when they passed the collection plate, he closed his eyes so as not to be disturbed in his meditation.

Dear friends, spirituality is manifested just as truly in sharing with others what God has entrusted to us; whether it is making known the Gospel or giving to others that which would alleviate their distress. But whosoever seeth his brother in need and says, "Depart in peace, be ye warmed and filled; notwithstanding ye give them not those things which are needful to the body; what doth it profit?" (Jas. 2:16).

You see, as priestly believers we are called upon to present our sacrifice of praise to God, and our sacrifice of giving to the world outside. May we truly enter into the responsibilities and the privileges of our priesthood, that the name of our Lord Jesus Christ may be magnified.

(From the book, *The Unchanging Christ and Other Sermons,* Loizeaux Brothers.)

HUGH F. PYLE
1918-

ABOUT THE MAN:

Before his call into the ministry, Hugh Pyle had been in the newspaper field, associated with the *Tampa Tribune*.

Born in Portsmouth, Virginia, Pyle was called to preach in 1940. At age 22 he married a wife (Esther Webber), was ordained a Baptist preacher and began pastoring two country churches near Tampa. After awhile he accepted a call to the First Baptist Church, Graveland, then Pensacola; and later, Panama City, all in Florida.

Between the two latter pastorates, Pyle accepted a position with Dr. John R. Rice and The Sword of the Lord. There he enjoyed a very fruitful ministry; but when his children entered into their teenage years, Hugh returned to the pastorate.

Central Baptist Church, Panama City, was without a doubt Pyle's most productive pastorate. In 15½ years the membership grew to 1,600. He founded a Christian day school which eventually enrolled nearly 1,000 students. There he conducted a daily broadcast for 14 years. In addition to the above Pyle made time to conduct revival campaigns, Bible conferences, speak in summer camps and write booklets and articles.

In 1973 he resigned his fruitful Panama City pastorate to go on the road again as an evangelist.

Pyle campaigns are planned to meet needs. Before each service he dramatizes a Bible story especially designed for the children; his sermons are sin-exposing and repentance-producing which challenge and charge Christians to obey God in baptism, spiritual living, soul winning, strong Christian homes—sold-out lives for Christ! At the conclusion of each service, he conducts a brief session called "Good Ship Courtship," tailored for teenagers.

Hugh Pyle, his wife and their children practice what he preaches in his campaigns! All three children are happily and fruitfully serving the Lord today!

His sermons are regularly read in THE SWORD OF THE LORD. He has published several books and booklets—24 titles at the last count are now in circulation, most published by Sword of the Lord Publishers. Many of his books have to do with the home, marriage and family life.

Dr. Hugh Pyle is desperately desirous of seeing an old-time revival from God sweep our land. It is a worthy desire and prayer of a worthy preacher who has his eyes, ears and heart tuned in on a nation's needs!

IX

Thrill to the Theme of Thanksgiving

HUGH F. PYLE

"They glorified him not as God, neither were thankful."—Rom. 1:21.

The way to be unhappy is to be ungrateful. Romans 1:21 expresses the character of the unregenerate heart: "Neither were thankful"!

That a man can breathe God's fresh air, bask in His sunshine, walk freely on God's ground and enjoy God-given health and not be thankful is a frightening commentary on the depravity of the human heart.

Thanksgiving Day first came about because godly Pilgrims, in spite of privation and hardship, could not overlook the blessing of God in their lives.

Then in 1846, Mrs. Sarah Hale, editor of *Godey's Lady's Book*, began a campaign to have Thanksgiving Day established as a national holiday. Though some states responded to this "mother of magazines for women," the federal government ignored her pleas for seventeen years. In 1863 Abraham Lincoln listened to Mrs. Hale and proclaimed the first Thanksgiving proclamation since George Washington. And I am glad!

"Enter into his gates with thanksgiving," the psalmist cries in Psalm 100. Surely the blood-bought child of God should experience thanksgiving every day, for "blessed be the Lord, who daily loadeth us with benefits, even the God of our salvation" (Ps. 68:19). "Every thing that hath breath" should praise the Lord (Ps. 150:6), and Paul commands, "Let the peace of God rule in your hearts . . . and be ye thankful" (Col. 3:15).

"All things work together for good to them that love God" (Rom. 8:28), and therefore, "From the rising of the sun unto the going down of the same the Lord's name is to be praised" (Ps. 113:3).

I love Thanksgiving Day. The happy reunion with members of the family, the relaxed atmosphere as we take time off from pressing duties, the tantalizing aroma of the turkey in the oven along with all of the trimmings—then the bountiful feast! But I am thankful for other things today, things that matter much for time and eternity and, along with me, all Christians should be grateful for these things.

See if your heart does not thrill to the theme of Thanksgiving as we think about them. How sad that many public schools today do not truly celebrate thanksgiving. Many homes do not. Thus millions of youngsters find it hard to say "thank you." Many husbands do not show appreciation to their wives nor wives to their husbands. This is a selfish, ungrateful generation, for we do not "offer unto God thanksgiving" and pay our vows unto the Most High (Ps. 50:14). If we did, we could call upon Him in this day of trouble and He would deliver us and we would glorify God! (See Ps. 50:15.)

A missionary, studying a large boar lying in four inches of mud, pondered, *What are the ambitions of a pig?* He listened to the animal as he gulped down his meal at the feeding trough and grunted his contentment while splashing in the mud for his siesta. He said he could have written "greed" on one side of the pig's belly and "personal well-being" on the other.

But how many of *us* are like that? Paul encountered Philippian Christians who broke his heart because they were minding earthly things, whose god was their belly and whose glory was in their shame (Phil. 3:19).

What a contrast the testimony of Fanny Crosby who at eight wrote:

O what a happy soul am I,
Although I cannot see.
I am resolved that in this world
Contented I will be.
How many blessings I enjoy
That other people don't—
To weep and sigh because I'm blind,
I cannot, and I won't!

It seems that some have just enough religion to innoculate them against a good case of happy salvation!

R. C. Trench wrote, "When thou hast thanked God for every blessing sent, what time will then remain for murmurs and lament?"

Oh, thrill to the theme of Thanksgiving!
Today

I Am Thankful for Salvation

"The Lord is my light and my salvation," David exclaimed in Psalm 27:1. "Thanks be unto God for his unspeakable gift," wrote Paul to the Corinthians (II Cor. 9:15). Anything this side of Hell for us is pure grace. We do not have this great salvation because we deserve it. Oh, how we should praise the Lord daily for saving us "out of the horrible pit, and from the mirey clay."

On a clockmaker's window was a sign, **Clocks Converted to Chiming**. So, if we truly are converted, we should be chiming our thanks for His wonderful grace.

"By him therefore let us offer the sacrifice of praise to God continually, that is, the fruit of our lips giving thanks to his name" (Heb. 13:15).

If you are among those described in Romans, chapter 1, of whom it is said, "neither were thankful," then you should come to Christ and today experience this so-great salvation. Then you'll have something to sing and shout about. But remember that salvation is found only in one way, in one divine Person: "Neither is there salvation in any other; for there is none other name under heaven given among men, whereby we must be saved" (Acts 4:12). Receive Him and have a real Thanksgiving!

I Am Thankful for Sustenance

He "daily loadeth us with benefits," David assures us. And how those of us who know Him realize this! (Ps. 68:19). "Every good gift and every perfect gift is from above" (Jas. 1:17). Many times He provides and we don't realize it; other times He would provide if we would but trust Him to.

The children of Israel loathed the manna which God sent to them in the wilderness after it became commonplace. Even so, God has been blessing us so long that for many of us it has become merely routine. We take His bountiful provision for granted. What shame! "It is a good thing to give thanks unto the Lord" (Ps. 92:1). God knows what He's talking about. The more your children thank you and show appreciation to you for what you give them, the more you want to do for them. Is it not so? And does our Heavenly Father not do the same?

When a Thanksgiving turkey was taken by Christians to a poor woman, the ungrateful creature exclaimed, "Whar are them thar cranberries?" Thank Him first for the turkey He has sent and perhaps He'll add the cranberries later. Someone has suggested that the number one problem in the world today is hunger. It is hard for us to realize in sleek, well-fed, indulgent America that millions do not really get enough to eat each day.

I Am Thankful for Service

The same sweet singer of Israel who cried, "Enter into his gates with thanksgiving and into his courts with praise," also said, "Serve the Lord with gladness" (Ps. 100:2).

What a privilege to serve Him! Oh, what joy! Jesus took the cup and gave thanks. For what? For suffering! He came to do the Father's will. He was willing to pour out His life's blood in sacrificial giving that we might be saved. Do we serve the Lord with gladness, even when it involves a bit of sacrifice or hardship?

Daniel knew the decree had been signed. He knew that he was the target of a fiendish plot. But "he went into his house; and his windows being open in his chamber toward Jerusalem, he kneeled upon his knees three times a day, and prayed, and gave thanks before his God, as he did aforetime" (Dan. 6:10).

We are saved to serve. We are left in this world to glorify His name. What a pleasure to serve Him!

"In the grave who shall give thee thanks?" David asked. The time is short. Let us thank Him for the privilege and get busy serving the Lord!

I Am Thankful for Strength

"My help cometh from the Lord" (Ps. 121:2). "The Lord is the strength of my life" (Ps. 27:1).

A noted Bible teacher was asked if he had a "Living Bible." He replied, "Well, I certainly don't have a dead one"!

Oh, the strength that comes from this blessed, living Book! Day by day strength and solace come from Him. Do we pause to thank Him for it? "Thanks be unto God which always causeth us to triumph in Christ, and maketh manifest the savour of his knowledge by us in every place" (II Cor. 2:14).

When the thorn in the flesh stings us with pain, then it is that we learn afresh that His grace is sufficient for us and that His strength is made perfect in our weakness (II Cor. 12:9). Be thankful for that! The 147th Psalm that begins, "Praise ye the Lord," continues by citing the gathering together of the outcasts and the healing of the broken in heart, along with the binding up of their wounds (Ps. 147:2,3). Oh, praise Him for strength!

I Am Thankful for Satisfactions

"Who satisfieth thy mouth with good things" (Ps. 103:5). Do you know anyone else who really satisfies? Yes, His grace is sufficient. "In his presence is fulness of joy and at his right hand there are pleasures for evermore" (Ps. 16:11). "Jesus saves, keeps and satisfies" has become a trite testimony. Yet, how true!

The seventy-seven-year-old doorkeeper of a Manhattan apartment building bought a quarter-page advertisement in the *New York Times*. He spent nearly $1,000.00—a portion of his life's savings, to print an essay at Thanksgiving, entitled "Thanks." It was his way to thank God publicly for his good life in this country, for loving parents, his jobs, this free land. He said, "This last year has been such a wonderful year, so I pray to God that I may never forget to thank Him each day."

At this Thanksgiving it will be so easy to forget God in the noisy stadium or stuffed to the brim at the dining table, if we are not careful. Let us remember the source of our satisfactions. See Philippians 4:19. A dangerous bit of road on the way to the Celestial City was called "Forgetful Green" in *Pilgrim's Progress*. Let us not be stricken with spiritual amnesia. Let us remember to thank the Lord. If you enjoy your dinner, try thanking the Lord for taste buds.

At the feeding of the five thousand, Jesus paused to "give thanks" over the loaves and fishes (John 6:11) before He distributed to the disciples. And He, who is our supreme example in all things, thanked the Father for hearing Him (John 11:41) before exercising His power to raise Lazarus from the dead. Thus, Christ is the true author of Thanksgiving.

I Am Thankful for a Song

"He hath put a new song in my heart" (Ps. 40:3). A thankless heart is a cheerless heart. "A merry heart doeth good like a medicine" (Prov. 17:22). Oh, how sweet the song of salvation! "Rejoice in the Lord alway; and again I say rejoice" (Phil. 4:4).

When I survey the misery written in the faces of the Christless generation around me, I thank Him afresh for this joy that He alone can impart. The Psalms are so cheerful and inspiring because they are the expressions of thankful hearts who have experienced the joy of God's salvation. "Many are the afflictions of the righteous; but the Lord delivereth him out of them all" (Ps. 34:19).

A man in a wheelchair was asked what his favorite hymn was. Without any hesitation he exclaimed, "Count Your Blessings"! Yes, think and you'll thank! One who had lost a leg was at least thankful that the rheumatism that had bothered him so much in that leg was gone. This song we must share with others that they, too, may become thankful.

This poem I found somewhere along the way, and frequently when a pastor I would read it to the congregation at our Thanksgiving service, to the delight of all.

> Said old gentleman Gay: "On a Thanksgiving Day:
> If you want a good time, then give something away."
> So he sent a fat turkey to shoemaker Price,
> And the shoemaker said: "What a big bird! How nice!
> With such a good dinner before me I ought
> To give Widow Lee the small chicken I bought."
> "This fine chicken, oh, see!" said the sweet Widow Lee,
> "And the kindness that sent it how precious to me!
> I'll give washwoman Biddy my big pumpkin pie,"
> "And, oh sure," Biddy said, " 'tis the queen o' all pies!
> Just to look at its yellow face gladdens my eyes!
> Now it's my turn, I think, and a sweet ginger cake
> For the motherless Finnigan children I'll bake."
> Cried the Finnigan children, Rose, Denny and Hugh:
> "It smells sweet of spice, and we'll carry a slice
> To little lame Jake, who has nothing that's nice."
> "Oh, I thank you and thank you!" said little lame Jake;
> "What a bootiful, bootiful, bootiful cake
> And the crumbs, I'll give them to each little sparrow that comes."
> Like old gentleman Gay: "On a Thanksgiving Day,
> If you want a good time, then give something away."
>
> —Selected

Yes, give something away if you would be happy. And cast your burdens and cares upon the divine Burden-Bearer if you would have the peace of Thanksgiving at all times. "Casting all your care upon him; for he careth for you" (I Pet. 5:7).

I Am Thankful for the Saints

With all of their faults (which I have plenty of, too) they are still my crowd. "If we walk in the light as he is in the light we have fellowship one with another" (I John 1:7). Mark Twain said, "Heaven for climate, Hell for society," but not for me! I praise Him for the real Christians who mean so much to us along the pilgrim pathway. And I'd hate to think I had to spend eternity in the company of the damned where the smoke of their torment ascendeth forever, and where the only music would be weeping, and wailing, and gnashing of teeth! (Matt. 8:12; 13:42).

Yes, I would say to the saints with Paul, "I thank my God always on your behalf" (I Cor. 1:4).

I Am Thankful for the Second Coming

Now this is really something to be thankful for! "In every thing give thanks" (I Thess. 5:18), Paul said, but no one ought ever to have to urge the saints to thank God for the promised second coming of Jesus! What a day that will be! When we look into the last great book of the Bible, the second-coming book, we see the angels of God about the throne falling on their faces and worshiping God, and saying, "Amen; Blessing, and glory, and wisdom, and thanksgiving, and honour, and power, and might, be unto our God for ever and ever. Amen" (Rev. 7:12). There it is: "Thanksgiving" tucked away there right in the midst of all those other wonderful words used to honor the Lord! And the chapter ends by reminding us that "the Lamb which is in the midst of the throne shall feed them, and shall lead them unto living fountains of waters; and God shall wipe away all tears from their eyes" (Rev. 7:17). Yes, beloved, as we look forward to His coming we have something to truly be thankful for. Let us hasten to tell others about Jesus so they, too, can have a real Thanksgiving.

Let us move from Grumbling Plaza to Thanksgiving Place and truly advertise the grace of God. And, until He comes, let us in all things give thanks!

THOMAS DeWITT TALMAGE
1832-1902

ABOUT THE MAN:

If Charles Spurgeon was the "Prince of Preachers," then T. DeWitt Talmage must be considered as one of the princes of the American pulpit. In fact, Spurgeon stated of Talmage's ministry: "His sermons take hold of my inmost soul. The Lord is with the mighty man. I am astonished when God blesses me but not surprised when He blesses him." He was probably the most spectacular pulpit orator of his time—and one of the most widely read.

Like Spurgeon, Talmage's ministry was multiplied not only from the pulpit to immense congregations, but in the printed pages of newspapers and in the making of many books. His sermons appeared in 3,000 newspapers and magazines a week, and he is said to have had 25 million readers.

And for 25 years, Talmage—a Presbyterian—filled the 4,000 to 5,000-seat auditorium of his Brooklyn church, as well as auditoriums across America and the British Isles. He counted converts to Christ in the thousands annually.

He was the founding editor of *Christian Herald,* and continued as editor of this widely circulated Protestant religious journal from 1877 until his death in 1902.

He had the face of a frontiersman and the voice of a golden bell; sonorous, dramatic, fluent, he was, first of all, an orator for God; few other evangelists had his speech. He poured forth torrents, deluges of words, flinging glory and singing phrases like a spendthrift; there was glow and warmth and color in every syllable. He played upon the heart-strings like an artist. One writer described him as the cultured Billy Sunday of his time. Many of his critics found fault with his methods; but they could not deny his mastery, nor could they successfully cloud his dynamic loyalty to his Saviour and Lord, Jesus Christ.

X.

"The Earth Is Full of the Goodness of the Lord." — Ps. 33:5

T. DeWITT TALMAGE

Good, grand, old-fashioned Thanksgiving Day has come. Nothing could stop it. It pressed on down through the weeks and months, its way lighted by burning cities, or cleft by cavernous graves; now strewn with orange blossoms, and then with funeral weeds; amid instruments that piped "the quickstep" and drummed "the dead march." Through the gates of this morning it came, carrying on one shoulder a sheaf of wheat, and on the other a shock of corn. Children, in holiday dress, hold up their hands to bless it, and old age goes out to bid it welcome, asking that it come in, and by the altars of God rest a while.

Come in, O Day, fragrant with a thousand memories, and borne down under the weight of innumerable mercies, and tell to our thankful hearts how great is the goodness of God.

An aged Christian man in Massachusetts recently died. Instead of the flowers usually put upon the bier there was laid upon his coffin a sheaf of wheat fully ripe. Beautifully significant! Oh, that on the remains of this harvest year we might place today a sheaf of prayer, a sheaf of thanksgiving, a sheaf of joy fully ripe!

By a sublime egotism man has come to appropriate this world to himself, when the fact is that our race is in a small minority. The instances of human life, as compared with the instances of animal life, are not one to a million. We shall enlarge our ideas of God's goodness and come to a better understanding of the text if, before we come to look at the cup of our blessing, we look at

The Goodness of God to the Irrational Creation

Although nature is out of joint, yet even in its disruption I am surprised to find the almost universal happiness of the animal creation. On a summer day, when the air and the grass are most populous with life, you will not hear a sound of distress unless, perchance, a heartless schoolboy has robbed a bird's nest, or a hunter has broken a bird's wing, or a pasture has been robbed of a lamb and there goes up a bleating from the flocks.

The whole earth is filled with animal delight—joy feathered, and scaled, and horned, and hoofed. The bee hums it; the frog croaks it; the squirrel chatters it; the quail whistles it; the lark carols it; the whale spouts it.

The snail, the rhinoceros, the grizzly bear, the toad, the wasp, the spider, the shellfish, have their homely delights—joy as great to them as our joy is to us.

Goat climbing the rocks; anaconda crawling through the jungle; buffalo plunging across the prairie; crocodile basking in tropical sun; seal puffing on the ice; ostrich striding across the desert, are so many bundles of joy; they do not go moping or melancholy; they are not only half supplied; God says *they are filled with good.*

The worm squirming through the sod upturned of plowshare, and the ants racing up and down the hillock, are happy by day and happy by night. Take up a drop of stagnant water under the microscope, and you find that within it there are millions of creatures that swim in a hallelujah of gladness. The sounds in nature that are repulsive to our ears are often only utterances of joy—the growl, the croak, the bark, the howl. The good God made these creatures, thinks of them ever, and will not let a plowshare turn up a mole's nest, or fisherman's hook transfix a worm, until by eternal decree its time has come.

God's hand feeds all these broods, and shepherds all these flocks, and tends all these herds. He sweetens the clover-top for the oxen's taste; and pours out crystalline waters in mossed cups of rock for the hind to drink out of on his way down the crags; and pours nectar into the cup of the honeysuckle to refresh the hummingbird; and spreads a banquet of a hundred fields of buckwheat, and lets the honeybee put his mouth to any cup of all the banquet; and tells the grasshopper to go anywhere he likes; and gives the flocks of Heaven the choice of all the grainfields.

The sea anemone, half animal, half flower, clinging to the rock in mid-ocean, with its tentacles spread to catch its food, has the Owner of the universe to provide for it.

We are repulsed at the hideousness of the elephant, but God, for the comfort and convenience of the monster, puts forty thousand distinct muscles in its proboscis.

I go down on the barren seashore and say no animal can live in this place of desolation; but all through the sands are myriads of little insects that leap with happy life.

I go down by the marsh and say that in this damp place and in these loathsome pools of stagnant water, there will be the quietness of death; but lo! I see the turtles on the rotten log sunning themselves, and hear the bogs quake with multitudinous life.

When the unfledged robins are hungry, God shows the old robin where she can get food to put into their open mouths.

Winter is not allowed to come until the ants have granaried their harvest, and the squirrels have filled their cellar with nuts.

God shows the hungry ichneumon where it may find the crocodile's eggs; and in arctic climes there are animals that God so lavishly clothes that they can afford to walk through snowstorms in the finest sable and ermine, and chinchilla, and no sooner is one set of furs worn out than God gives them a new one.

He helps the spider in its architecture of its gossamer bridge, takes care of the color of the butterfly's wing, tinges the cochineal, and helps the moth out of the chrysalis.

The animal creation also has its army and navy. The most insignificant has its means of defense: the wasp its sting; the reptile its tooth; the bear its paw; the dog its muzzle; the elephant its tusk; the fish its scale; the bird its swift wing; the reindeer its antlers; the roe its fleet foot. We are repelled at the thought of sting and tusk and hoof, but God's goodness provides them for the defense of the animal's rights.

Yea, God in the Bible announces His care for these orders of creation. He says that He has heaved up fortifications for their defense—Psalm 104:18: "The high hills are a refuge for the wild goats, and the rocks for the conies."

He watches the bird's nest—Psalm 104:17: "As for the stork, the fir trees are her house."

He sees that the cattle have enough grass—Psalm 104:14: "He causeth the grass to grow for the cattle."

He sees to it that the cows and sheep and horses have enough to drink—Psalm 104:10, 11: "He sendeth the springs into the valleys, which run among the hills. They give drink to every beast of the field: the wild asses quench their thirst."

Amid the thunders of Sinai God uttered the rights of cattle and said that they should have a Sabbath: "Thou shalt not do any work, thou . . . nor thy cattle."

He declared with infinite emphasis that the ox on the threshingfloor should have the privilege of eating some of the grain as he trod it out, and muzzling was forbidden.

If young birds were taken from the nest for food, the despoiler's life depended on the mother going free. God would not let the mother bird suffer in one day the loss of her young and her own liberty.

And He who regarded in olden time the conduct of man toward the brutes, today looks down from Heaven and is interested in every minnow that swims the stream, every rook that cleaves the air, every herd that bleats, or neighs, or lows in the pasture.

Why did God make all these, and why make them so happy? How account for all this singing and dancing and frisking amid the *irrational creation*? Why this heaven for the animalcule in a dewdrop? Why for the condor a throne on Chimborazo? Why the glitter of the phosphorus in the ship's wake on the sea, which is said to be only the frolic of millions of insects? Why the perpetual chanting of so many voices from the irrational creation in earth, and air, and ocean—beasts, and all cattle, creeping things and flying fowl, permitted to join in the praise that goes up from seraph and archangel?

Only one solution, one explanation, one answer—God is good. "The earth is full of the goodness of the Lord."

I take a step higher and notice

The Adaptation of the World to the Comfort and Happiness of Man

The sixth day of creation had arrived. The palace of the world was made, but there was no king to live in it. Leviathan ruled the deep; the eagle the air; the lion the field; but where was the sceptre which should rule all?

A new style of being was created. Heaven and earth were represented in his nature. His body from the earth beneath; his soul from the Heaven above. The one reminding him of his origin, the other speaking of his destiny—himself, the connecting link between the animal creation and angelic intelligence. In him a strange commingling of the temporal and eternal, the finite and the infinite, *dust* and *glory*. The earth for his floor, and Heaven for his roof; God for his Father; eternity for his lifetime.

The Christian anatomist, gazing upon the conformation of the human body, exclaims, "Fearfully and wonderfully made." No embroidery so elaborate, no gauze so delicate, no color so exquisite, no mechanism so graceful, no handiwork so divine. So quietly and mysteriously does the human body perform its functions, that it was not until five thousand years after the creation of the race that the circulation of the blood was discovered; and though anatomists of all countries and ages have been so long exploring this castle of life, they have only begun to understand it.

Volumes have been written of the hand. Wondrous instrument! With it we give friendly recognition, grasp the sword, climb the rock, write, carve and build. It constructed the Pyramids, and hoisted the Parthenon. It made the harp, then struck out of it all the world's minstrelsy. In it the white marble of Pentelican mines dreamed itself away into immortal sculpture. It reins in the swift engine; it holds the steamer to its path in the sea; it snatches the fire from Heaven; it feels the pulse of the sick child with its delicate touch, and makes the nations quake with its stupendous achievements.

What power brought down the forests, and made the marshes blossom and burdened the earth with all the cities that thunder on with enterprise and power? Four fingers and a thumb. A hundred million dollars would not purchase for you a machine as exquisite and wonderful as your own hand. Mighty hand! In all its bones and muscles and joints, I learn that God is good.

Behold the eye which, in its Daguerrean gallery, in an instant catches the mountain and the sea. This perpetual telegraphing of the nerves; these joints that are the only hinges that do not wear out; these bones and muscles of the body, with fourteen thousand different adaptations; these one hundred thousand glands; these two hundred million pores; this mysterious heart, contracting four thousand times every hour— two hundred and fifty pounds of blood rushing through it every sixty seconds; this chemical process of digestion; this laboratory, beyond the understanding of the most skillful philosophy; this furnace, whose heat is kept up from cradle to grave; this factory of life whose wheels and spindles and bands are God-directed; this human voice, capable, as has been estimated, of producing seventeen trillions, five hundred and ninety-two billions, one hundred and eighty-six millions, forty-four thousand four hundred and fifteen sounds.

If we could realize the wonders of our physical organization, we would be hypochondriacs, fearing every moment that some part of the machine would break down. But there are men here who have lived through seventy years, and not a nerve has ceased to thrill, or a muscle to contract, or a lung to breathe, or a hand to manipulate.

I take a step higher, and look at

Man's Mental Constitution

Behold the lavish benevolence of God in powers of *perception*, or the faculty you have of transporting this outside world into your own mind—gathering into your brain the majesty of the storm, and the splendors of the day-dawn, and lifting into your mind the ocean as easily as you might put a glass of water to your lips.

Watch the *law of association* or the mysterious linking together of all you ever thought, or knew, or felt, and then giving you the power to take hold of the clewline and draw through your mind the long train with indescribable velocity—one thought starting up a hundred, and this again a thousand—as the chirp of one bird sometimes wakes a whole forest of voices, or the thrum of one string will rouse an orchestra.

Watch *your memory*—that sheafbinder that goes forth to gather the harvest of the past and brings it into the present. Your power and velocity of thought—thought of the swift wing and the lightning foot; thought that outspeeds the star and circles through the heavens and weighs worlds and, from poising amid wheeling constellations, comes down to count the blossoms in a tuft of mignonette, then starts again to try the fathoming of the bottomless, and the scaling of the insurmountable, to be swallowed up in the incomprehensible and lost in God!

In reason and understanding, man is alone. The ox surpasses him in strength, the antelope in speed, the hound in keenness of nostril, the eagle in far-reaching sight, the rabbit in quickness of hearing, the honeybee in delicacy of tongue, the spider in fineness of touch. Man's power, therefore, consisteth not in what he can lift, or how fast he can run, or how strong a wrestler he can throw—for in these respects the ox, the ostrich and the hyena are his superior—but by his reason he comes forth to rule all: through his ingenious contrivance to outrun, outlift, outwrestle, outsee, outhear, outdo.

At his all-conquering decree, the forest that had stood for ages steps aside to let him build his cabin and cultivate his farm. The sea which raved and foamed upon the race has become a crystal pathway for commerce to march on. The thundercloud that slept lazily above the mountain is made to come down and carry mailbags.

Man, dissatisfied with his slowness of advancement, shouted to the Water and the Fire, "Come and lift!" "Come and draw!" "Come and help!" And they answered, "Ay, ay, we come." And they joined hands—the Fire and the Water—and the shuttles fly and the rail-train rattles on, and the steamship comes coughing, panting, flaming across the deep.

He elevates the telescope to the heavens and, as easily as through the stethoscope the physician hears the movement of the lung, the astronomer catches the pulsation of distant systems of worlds throbbing with life.

He takes the microscope and discovers that there are hundreds of thousands of animalcula living, moving, working, dying within a circle that could be covered with the point of a pin—animals to which a raindrop would be an ocean, a roseleaf a hemisphere, and the flash of a firefly lasting enough to give them light to several generations.

I take a step higher, and look at

Man's Moral Nature

Made in the image of God. Vast capacity for enjoyment; capable at first of eternal joy and, though now disordered, still, through the recuperative force of heavenly grace, able to mount up to more than its original felicity: faculties that may blossom and bear fruit inexhaustibly. Immortality written upon every capacity: a soul destined to range in unlimited spheres of activity long after the world has put on ashes and the solar system shall have snapped its axle and the stars that, in their courses, fought against Sisera, shall have been slain and buried amid the tolling thunders of the last day.

You see that God has adapted every thing to our comfort and advantage. Pleasant things for the palate; music for the ear; beauty for the eye; aroma for the nostril; kindred for our affections; poetry for our taste; religion for our soul. We are put in a garden and told that from all the trees we may eat except here and there one. He gives the sun to shine on us, the waters to refresh us, food to strengthen us; the herbs yield medicine when we are sick, and the forests lumber when we would build a house, or cross the water in a ship.

The rocks are transported for our foundation; metals upturned for our currency; wild beasts must give us covering; the mountains must be tunneled to let us pass; the fish of the sea come up in our net; the birds of the air drop at the flash of our guns; and the cattle on a thousand hills come down to give us meat.

For us the peach orchards bend down their fruit and the vineyards their purple clusters. To feed and refresh our intellect, ten thousand wonders in nature and providence—wonders of mind and body, wonders of earth and air and deep, analogies and antitheses; all colors and sounds; lyrics in the air; idyls in the field; conflagrations in the sunset; robes of mist on the mountains; and the "Grand March" of God in the storm.

But for the *soul* still higher adaptation: a fountain in which it may wash; a ladder by which it may climb; a song of endless triumph that it may sing; a crown of unfading light that it may wear. Christ came to save it—came with a cross on His back; came with spikes in His feet; came when no one else would come, to do a work which no one else would do.

See how suited to man's condition is what God has done for him! Man is a sinner; here his pardon. He has lost God's image; Christ retraces it. He is helpless; almighty grace is proffered. He is a lost wanderer; Jesus brings him home. He is blind; and at one touch of Him who cured Bartimaeus, eternal glories stream into his soul.

Jesus, I sing Thy grace! Cure of worst disease! Hammer to smite off heaviest chain! Light for thickest darkness! Grace divine! Devils scoff at it and men reject it, but Heaven celebrates it!

Thanks for Mercies of the Year Just Past

But I must stop this range of thought, for our Chief Executive asks that today we chiefly celebrate the mercies of the past year. Now, my soul, to the altar of incense. Come, all ye people! Great High Priest, kindle the coals! Let the cloud fill the Temple!

I wish you good cheer for the *national health*. Pestilence that in other years has come to drive out its thousand hearses to Greenwood and Laurel Hill, has not visited our nation, or has touched only one or two of the Southern ports.

It is a glorious thing to be well! How strange that we should keep our health when one breath from a marsh, or the sting of an insect, or the slipping of a foot, or the falling of a tree branch might fatally assault our life! Regularly the lungs work, and their motion seems to be a spirit within us panting after its immortality. Our sight fails not, though the air is so full of objects which by one touch could break out the soul's window. What ship, after a year's tossing on the sea, could come in with so little damage as ourselves, though we arrive after a year's voyage today?

I wish you good cheer for the *national harvest*. Reaping machines never swathed thicker rye; cornhusker's peg never ripped out fuller ear; mow-poles never bent down under sweeter hay; and windmill's hopper never shook out larger wheat.

Long trains of white covered wagons have brought the wealth down to the great thoroughfares. The garners are full, the storehouses are overcrowded, the canals are blocked with freights pressing down to the markets. The cars rumble all through the darkness and whistle up the flagmen at dead of night to let the Western harvests come down to feed the mouths of the great cities.

A race of kings has taken possession of this land—King Cotton, King Corn, King Wheat, King Grass, King Coal. Our nets bring up supplies from the cod, salmon and mackerel fisheries; the whaler's harpoon was never more skillfully flung.

I wish you good cheer for *civil and religious liberty*. No official spy watches our entrance here, nor does an armed soldier interfere with the honest utterance of truth. We stand here today with our arms free to work and our tongues free to speak.

This Bible—it is all unclasped. This pulpit—there is no chain round about it. There is no snapping of musketry in the street. Blessed be God that today we are free men, with the prospect and determination of always being free.

No established religion: Jew and Gentile—Arminian and Calvinist—Trinitarian and Unitarian—Protestant and Roman Catholic—on the same footing. If persecution should come against the most unpopular of all the sects, I believe that all other denominations would band together and arm themselves. Hearts would be stout and blood would be free, and the right of men to worship God according to the dictates of their consciences would be contested at the point of the bayonet and with blood flowing up to the bits of the horses' bridles.

I wish you good cheer for our *condition as a church*. We stand today at a point of prosperity that we never expected to reach. Our experiment of a free church has been successful. Considering the fact that a little more than two years ago this church was as near extinction as a church ever goes without absolutely dying, and considering the fact that we have been in this Tabernacle only a little more than one year, we ought to offer a thanksgiving to God, long and loud and deep, for His wonderful works in our behalf. The American church has rejoiced with us in the success of our experiment, and our enemies have been confounded.

Let us render thanksgiving to God that He has given this church a mission to perform and that the thousands who worship with us on the Sunday are but a handful compared with that great multitude of perhaps hundreds of thousands of souls whom, through the printing press, we are now reaching every week in this country and in England and Scotland.

I confess that I am appalled on Sundays when I think of the work that, as a church, we are called to do. Great is the responsibility, O men and women of God, and great the condemnation if, with such wonderful opportunity for usefulness, we prove recreant.

Let us thank God that during the year we have been permitted to inaugurate *"the Tabernacle Free College for training Christian men and women for practical work,"* an institution that has kindled the sympathies of tens of thousands of people all over this land and which, if successful, will be of more value than the building of many churches. A very large number of men and women have enrolled themselves already as students. May the Lord bless and encourage all who are connected with it!

Praise ye the Lord! Let every thing that hath breath praise the Lord! Today let the people come out from their storehouses and offices, from Lowell factories, and from Western prairies, and up from Pennsylvania coal mines, and out from Oregon forests, and in from the whale ships of New London and Cape Ann, and wherever God's light shines and God's rain descends and God's mercy broods, let the thanksgiving arise!

DWIGHT LYMAN MOODY
1837-1899

ABOUT THE MAN:

D. L. Moody may well have been the greatest evangelist of all time.

In a 40-year period, he won a million souls, founded three Christian schools, launched a great Christian publishing business, established a world-renowned Christian conference center, and inspired literally thousands of preachers to win souls and conduct revivals.

A shoe clerk at 17, his ambition was to make $100,000. Converted at 18, he uncovered hidden gospel gold in the hearts of millions for the next half century. He preached to 20,000 a day in Brooklyn and admitted only non-church members by ticket!

He met a young songleader in Indianapolis, said bluntly, "You're the man I've been looking for for eight years. Throw up your job and come with me." Ira D. Sankey did just that; thereafter it was "Moody will preach; Sankey will sing."

He traveled across the American continent and through Great Britain in some of the greatest and most successful evangelistic meetings communities have ever known. His tour of the world with Sankey was considered the greatest evangelistic enterprise of the century.

It was Henry Varley who said, "It remains to be seen what God will do with a man who gives himself up wholly to Him." And Moody endeavored to be, under God, that man; and the world did marvel to see how wonderfully God used him.

Two great monuments stand to the indefatigable work and ministry of this gospel warrior—Moody Bible Institute and the famous Moody Church in Chicago.

Moody went to be with the Lord in 1899.

XI.

"Let Us Offer the Sacrifice of Praise Continually"

D. L. MOODY

We ought to be more thankful for what we get from God. Perhaps some of you mothers have a child in your family who is constantly complaining—never thankful. You know that there is not much pleasure in doing anything for a child like that. If you meet with a beggar who is always grumbling and never seems to be thankful for what you give, you very soon shut the door in his face altogether. Ingratitude is about the hardest thing we have to meet with.

The great English poet says:

> Blow, blow, thou winter wind—
> Thou art not so unkind
>   As man's ingratitude;
> Thy tooth is not so keen,
> Because thou art not seen,
>   Although thy breath be rude.

We cannot speak too plainly of this evil which so demeans those who are guilty of it. Even in Christians there is but too much of it to be seen. Here we are, getting blessings from God day after day; yet how little praise and thanksgiving there is in the church of God!

Referring to the words, "In every thing give thanks," Gurnall, in his *Christian Armor*, says:

"Praise is comely for the upright." "An unthankful saint" carries a contradiction with it. Evil and Unthankful are twins that live and die together; as anyone ceaseth to be evil, he begins to be thankful. It is that which God expects at your hands; He made you for this end. When the vote passed in Heaven for your being—yea, happy being in Christ!—it was upon this account, that you should be a name and a praise to Him on earth in time, and in Heaven to eternity. Should God miss this, He would fail of one main part of His design.

What prompts Him to bestow every mercy, but to afford you matter to compose a song for His praise? "They are my people, children that will not lie; so he was their Saviour."

He looks for fair dealing at your hands. Whom may a father trust with his reputation, if not his child? Where can a prince expect honor, if not among his favorites? Your state is such that the least mercy you have is more than all the world besides. Thou, Christian, and thy few brethren, divide Heaven and earth among you! What hath God that He withholds from you? Sun, moon and stars are set up to give you light; sea and land have their treasures for your use. Others are encroachers upon them; you are the rightful heirs to them; they groan that any others should be served by them.

The angels, bad and good, minister unto you; the evil, against their will, are forced like scullions when they tempt you, to scour and brighten your graces and make way for your greater comforts; the good angels are servants to your Heavenly Father and disdain not to carry you in their arms.

Your God withholds not Himself from you; He is your portion— Father, Husband, Friend. God is His own happiness, and admits you to enjoy Him. Oh, what honor is this, for the subject to drink in his prince's cup! "Thou shalt make them drink of the river of thy pleasures."

And all this is not the purchase of your sweat and blood; the feast is paid for by Another, only He expects your thanks to the Founder. No sin-offering is imposed under the Gospel; thank-offerings are all He looks for.

Charnock, in discoursing on spiritual worship, says:

> The praise of God is the choicest sacrifice and worship under a dispensation of redeeming grace. This is the prime and eternal part of worship under the Gospel. The psalmist, speaking of the gospel times, spurs on to this kind of worship: "Sing unto the Lord a new song; let the children of Zion be joyful in their king; let the saints be joyful in glory; let them sing aloud upon their beds; let the high praises of God be in their mouth."
>
> He begins and ends both Psalms with *Praise ye the Lord!* That cannot be a spiritual and evangelical worship that hath nothing of the praise of God in the heart. The consideration of God's adorable perfections discovered in the Gospel will make us come to Him with more seriousness, beg blessings of Him with more confidence, fly to Him with a winged faith and love, and more spiritually glorify Him in our attendances upon Him.

Praise Is United to Prayer

There is a great deal more said in the Bible about praise than prayer, yet how few praise-meetings there are! In his Psalms, David always mixes praise with prayer. Solomon prevailed much with God in prayer at the dedication of the Temple, but it was the voice of *praise* which brought down the glory that filled the house, for we read:

"And it came to pass, when the priests were come out of the holy place: (for all the priests that were present were sanctified, and did not then wait by course: Also the Levites which were the singers, all of them of Asaph, of Heman, of Jeduthun, with their sons and their brethren, being arrayed in white linen, having cymbals and psalteries and harps, stood at the east end of the altar, and with them an hundred and twenty priests sounding with trumpets:) It came even to pass, as the trumpeters and singers were as one, to make one sound to be heard in praising and thanking the Lord; and when they lifted up their voice with the trumpets and cymbals and instruments of musick, and praised the Lord, saying, For he is good; for his mercy endureth for ever: that then the house was filled with a cloud, even the house of the Lord; So that the priests could not stand to minister by reason of the cloud; for the glory of the Lord had filled the house of God."—II Chron. 5:11-14.

We read, too, of Jehoshaphat, that he gained the victory over the hosts of Ammon and Moab through praise, which was excited by faith and thankfulness to God.

"And they rose early in the morning, and went forth into the wilderness of Tekoa: and as they went forth, Jehoshaphat stood and said, Hear me, O Judah, and ye inhabitants of Jerusalem; Believe in the Lord your God, so shall ye be established; believe his prophets, so shall ye prosper. And when he had consulted with the people, he appointed singers unto the Lord, and that should praise the beauty of holiness, as they went out before the army, and to say, Praise the Lord; for his mercy endureth for ever. And when they began to sing and to praise, the Lord set ambushments against the children of Ammon, Moab, and Mount Seir, which were come against Judah; and they were smitten."—II Chron. 20:20-22.

In Hardest Times Be Thankful

It is said that in a time of great despondency among the first settlers in New England, it was proposed in one of their public assemblies to proclaim a fast. An old farmer arose, spoke of their provoking Heaven with their complaints, reviewed their measures, showed that they had much to be thankful for, and moved that instead of appointing a day of fasting, they should appoint a day of thanksgiving. This was done, and the custom has been continued ever since.

However great our difficulties, or deep even our sorrows, there is room for thankfulness.

Thomas Adams has said:

> Lay up in the ark of thy memory not only the pot of manna, the bread of life; but even Aaron's rod, the very scourge of correction, wherewith thou hast been bettered. Blessed be the Lord, not only giving, but taking away, saith Job. God who sees there is no walking upon roses to Heaven, puts His children into the way of discipline, and by the fire of correction eats out the rust of corruption. God sends trouble, then bids us call upon Him; promiseth our deliverance; and lastly, the all He requires of us is to glorify Him. "Call upon me in the day of trouble; I will deliver thee, and thou shalt glorify me."

Like the nightingale, we can sing in the night and say with John Newton—

> **Since all that I meet shall work for my good,**
> **The bitter is sweet, the medicine food;**
> **Though painful at present, 'twill cease before long,**
> **And then—oh, how pleasant!—the conqueror's song.**

Among all the apostles, none suffered so much as Paul, but none of them do we find so often giving thanks as he. Take his letter to the Philippians. Remember what he suffered at Philippi; how they laid many stripes upon him and cast him into prison. Yet every chapter in that epistle speaks of rejoicing and giving thanks. There is that well-known passage, "Be careful for nothing, but in every thing, by prayer and supplication, with thanksgiving, let your requests be made known unto God."

As someone has said, there are here three precious ideas: "Careful for nothing; prayerful for everything; and thankful for anything." We always get more by being thankful for what God has done for us.

Paul says again, "We give thanks to God, the Father of our Lord Jesus Christ, praying always for you." So he was constantly giving thanks. Take up any one of his epistles and you will find them full of praise to God.

Even if nothing else called for thankfulness, it would always be an ample cause for it that Jesus Christ loved us and gave Himself for us.

A farmer was once found kneeling at a soldier's grave near Nashville. Someone came to him and asked, "Why do you pay so much attention to this grave? Was your son buried here?"

"No," he said. "During the war my family were all sick; I knew not how to leave them. I was drafted. One of my neighbors came over and said, 'I will go for you; I have no family.'

"He went off. He was wounded at Chickamauga. He was carried to the hospital and there died. And, sir, I have come a great many miles that I might write over his grave these words, HE DIED FOR ME!"

This the believer can always say of his blessed Saviour and in the fact may well rejoice. "By him therefore, let us offer the sacrifice of praise continually, that is, the fruit of our lips, giving thanks to his name."

NOEL SMITH
1900-1974

ABOUT THE MAN:

How we thank God for Noel Smith and what he contributed to the world, what he contributed to the Baptist Bible Fellowship, what he contributed to the Baptist Bible College, and what he contributed to High Street Baptist Church, Springfield, Missouri, where he and his family held membership.

Dr. Smith was a scholar in many fields. And being founding editor of the *Baptist Bible Tribune* (1950), he was truly one of the great religious editors of America for 24 years.

When we think of great men, we always are impressed by, first of all, one particular quality of character. And Noel Smith's quality was quality. He despised that which was cheap in the religious life of America, whether it was in music, or in preaching, or in writing. He had no patience with liberalism and modernism. And Noel Smith never denied his Lord, never betrayed a friend, never compromised a principle.

And when one thinks of Noel Smith, he thinks also of fortitude and faithfulness. He was a man of unquestioned integrity and he was a man who had unmovable convictions. What he believed, he believed. What he believed, he said. If he didn't say it with his mouth, he wrote it with his pen. And he didn't apologize for it—ever! When Heaven gets the check list out for Noel Smith and the Lord says, "Check on him," Dr. Smith is going to get an A$^+$ in the fight department. Surely the Lord will have up there some special comfort for those who fought down here the good fight of faith.

Another thing about this good man: he lived by the principle that there is no substitute for hard work. So he died in 1974 at work.

Now, praise God, he's enjoying the respite from the battle! Heaven grows sweeter as our friends go over to the other side!

XII.

The Heartbreaking Sin of Ingratitude

NOEL SMITH

Gratitude is not a spiritual or moral dessert which we may take or push away according to the whims of the moment, and in either case without material consequences. Gratitude is the very bread and meat of spiritual and moral health, individually and collectively.

Gratitude is not a general virtue floating around on the periphery of the personality; gratitude is central, basic, decisive. The success, continuity and climax of individuals and nations are determined by the sovereignty of God; gratitude is the determining factor with that sovereignty.

What was the seed of disintegration that corrupted the heart of the ancient world beyond the point of divine remedy, where God gave it up to wallow in its filth, where men and women became foul with unnatural lusts and perversions, where not a fresh breath of purity blew through the heavy atmosphere of its stench?

What was it but ingratitude? ". . . when they knew God, they glorified him not as God, neither were thankful. . . ." (Rom. 1:21).

What was it that blinded with pride the eyes of that young man of that far-distant time, dethroned him from his seat of authority and dignity and led him a bound slave from the wealth and comforts of his father's house, to the hogpen?

What was it that led him from the music of the voices of father and mother and sister and brother to the hard, cold, barren ground of the far-away country where only swine grunted and fugitive winds wailed their distress?

What was it that tore from his back his woven robe, jerked from his feet his shoes of freedom, pulled from his finger the signet of love, and left his shivering form to the mercy of such tattered rags as he could find?

What was it but ingratitude? When he knew his father, he praised him not as his father, neither was he thankful.

The first step of civilization toward disaster and the first step of an individual toward disaster are one and the same—ingratitude!

The unexcelled genius of William Shakespeare never was more impressively and brilliantly revealed than when he summed up this oldest sin in three words.

Julius Caesar, on the Ides of March, is being stabbed to death there in the senate, near the statue of his great enemy, Pompey. Among the assassins Caesar sees Brutus, whom he had often befriended, and when none but Caesar would have befriended him. Looking at him, Caesar says in his characteristically calm way: "Thou, too, Brutus?"

Ingratitude is the basic sin of the world. It is the basic sin of youth. It is the basic sin of middle age; such gratitude as most middle-aged people have drains into the belly. A girdle will improve the figure but it won't change the heart. Old age, with those rare and beautiful exceptions, finds little for which to be thankful.

How unlike mankind are the heavenly hosts in this matter of being thankful!

"And all the angels stood round about the throne, and about the elders and the four beasts [living creatures], *and fell before the throne on their faces, and worshipped God, Saying, Amen: Blessing, and glory, and wisdom, and thanksgiving, and honour, and power, and might, be unto our God for ever and ever. Amen."*—Rev. 7:11, 12.

Heaven is a place of praise and thanksgiving; Hell is a place of recrimination and ingratitude.

About the Same as Pigs

A deep and genuine sense of gratitude is as foreign to our daily routine as to pigs leisurely rooting around in the orchard. We have about the same sense of appreciation for bread on the table as they have for apples on the ground. Like the ox in the stall and the ass at its master's crib, we take everything without a sense of wonder, appreciation, and thanksgiving; without wonder at the Cause behind everything; without appreciation that God not only flings constellations and systems into infinite space and knows each star by name, but that the same God gives the raven its meat in due season and looks with pity on the sparrow's fall; without thanksgiving that we, unlike the winged creatures of the heavens and four-footed beasts of the field, were conceived and fashioned in His infinite intelligence and born of His infinite love and have engraven upon us His very image.

The gratitude that most men have for their wives is, like a clawhammer coat, for special occasions. There was a time when she to him was dear and sweet, gentle, kind and good. There was a wonderful mystery in her personality, like the glow hovering above the mountain range as the day fades. Her love for him troubled all that was good and kind and pure in him and brought it to the surface. Every lovely thing his eyes saw and every tender note his ears heard reminded him of her. Every breath he drew was a breath of thanksgiving to God that He had fashioned her and breathed into her being all her excellencies and that He had given her to him. He was a thankful creature in those young and fresh and happy days.

But now that he has her, she takes her place among the electric stove, the refrigerator, the radio, television and other utilities.

And to a lot of wives, a hard-working, honest, loyal, sober husband coming home at night is just about as much to be thankful for as the coal the truckman is shoveling into the bin. You need coal and you need a husband. You have both. Both are routine; neither is anything for special thanksgiving.

You should visit some of your sisters and see the hot tears flow down their faces as they tell you how the drunken husband has beaten the children. You will find plenty of them. You will find plenty of women in great and tragic distress because their son-in-law comes home at least once a week and beats up their daughter.

Filial Ingratitude

And, of course, children are lacking in gratitude for their parents. Filial ingratitude! It is one of the great themes of the drama.

Many years ago, very late one night, I was sitting upstairs in a reverie. After a little while I casually reached for the table and took from it a worn, yellowed envelope of old pictures. I fingered through them.

I came across one which was so appealing that it was a long time before I could lay it aside. It haunts me to this day. It was a picture of my father. As I sat there gazing at it, my memory trailed back over the years to the "public square" at Murfreesboro, Tennessee, where it was made. I remembered the time and the occasion.

The eyes, tinged with sadness, had a faraway look. The face was plain and kind. The jaws were not set in defiance; they were relaxed and resigned to whatever winds that blew. He was a plain and simple man. He believed in the "Good Master," and he believed in the "Good Book." He never heard of a "dispensation," but he treaded softly in the house of God and he spoke in subdued tones in the yard of his sick neighbor.

One night, when he had gone beyond his threescore and ten years, he lay his tall form down upon the bed of his sister, placed two large old-fashioned pillows under his tired head; as the night deepened, his breathing became increasingly difficult. He had nothing more to say—no complaints and no requests. Next day, as the sun was high above the Tennessee hills, he looked straight at me; his jaws tightened, he took one last breath and laid down his load.

Back to the picture. That picture made a silent appeal to me for a filial gratitude that I had not given. I had not been positively ungrateful, and I never caused him any trouble. I had simply taken him as a matter of routine. He was my father; I was his son. What was so exciting about that? Why make ado about that? It was natural, wasn't it? It was the ordinary, regular thing, wasn't it?

The strange, silent appeal of that face gazing at me there in that upstairs room deep in that winter night!

But many children—especially nowadays—have just cause to complain of the ingratitude of their parents. Their parents provide them with food and clothing, the radio and television, and there the matter ends.

It will pay you well to have intelligent sympathy and warm love for your children. As they grow up they will become your friends as well as your children. They will confide in you rather than in the neighbors.

The Chief Reason

The chief reason why all of us are so lacking in genuine daily gratitude is that we are so sheep-headed and dumb. We are lacking in intelligence and understanding. We know the Scriptures, but we don't understand them. We know everything in general and understand nothing in particular.

Just now the mountains and hills and valleys are aflame with imperial glory. We talk about "nature." But we don't talk about nature as David did. When David spoke of nature, a river of praise flowed from his soul to God. "Bless the Lord, O my soul." When David was thinking of nature in the 104th Psalm, those were the first words he uttered.

David was intelligent. He knew that nature was the handiwork of a personal God. He knew that nature was as personal as a priceless work of art from a master's hand. He knew that there was thought and design and purpose behind every hue of color, behind every flaming world, every bud and every violet. The clouds were the chariot of the Almighty, and the winds were the wings upon which He walked. Nothing happened "according to the laws of nature." Everything was designed by God.

The springs were in the valleys and among the hills because God had placed them there. God had placed them there to quench the thirst of the beasts of the field and the wild asses. The hills were not watered "according to the laws of nature"; they were watered from the chambers of God. The grass and herbs were not the fruit of "nature"; God had placed the grass here for the cattle and the herbs for man.

God had placed the sap in the trees, and He had thought of the needs of the wild goats when He established the hills.

The sun and moon were for service of both man and beast; when the sun shone, man would have his day and do his work; when the sun went down and the darkness came, the beasts of the forests would come forth and have their night. The whale was no accident of "nature." The whale was made to play around in the great deep (Ps. 104:26). It's tough on the scribes and Pharisees and the straight-laced theologians to have to face the fact that God Almighty made the whale just to play and have a good time in the great waters. And He made another one for the sole purpose of swallowing a backslidden preacher. And that whale was glad when he had completed his mission.

What is nature? It is the handiwork of God, every stroke of it. What is the life of nature? It is the breath of God.

How can a man live in a world like this without praising God and giving thanks unto Him with every breath he draws?

David was intelligent as well as devout; he was devout because he was intelligent. When David considered nature, he said, "I will sing unto the Lord as long as I live: I will sing praise to my God while I have my being."

Nature, when you really understand it, is something to really praise God for and to sing about. It really is.

Personality of Our Lord

Our Lord was the most magnetic personality this world has ever seen.

I am thinking primarily of His humanity. I am thinking primarily of Him as the Son of Man.

When but thirty years old He attracted and drew to Himself twelve of as matured and independent-minded men as could be found in all of Palestine. With the exception of the traitor, He bound them to Himself with hoops stronger than steel. All of those men, but one, sealed their loyalty to Him with their martyr's blood; John, so tradition tells us, died a natural death—died speaking of the Face he had seen, of the Voice he had heard—

"That which was from the beginning, which we have heard, which we have seen with our eyes, which we have looked upon, and our hands have handled. . . ."—I John 1:1.

When He expounded the Scriptures, the hearts of His hearers "burned within" them. When He gave thanks and broke bread, His words and mien and manner were so engraven upon the minds of those present that they never forgot them.

And there never was anything artificial, strained, forced, or unnatural about Him. He was so warm and friendly and human and natural that mothers brought their children to Him.

What was it, from the human standpoint, that made Him the glowing, magnetic, inspiring personality He was? What was it but His innate attitude toward His Father and His Father's world, an attitude that sweetened every breath He drew with thanksgiving and praise. The lily's clothing had not been fashioned by "nature"; the lily's clothing had been fashioned by the hands of His Father. The ravens were not being fed by "nature"; they were being fed by His Father. The pitying eye of His Father was upon every sparrow that fell from its nest. Every hair of every head was "numbered," with all the divine brooding and concern involved.

With our Lord, everything from the throne of God and clouds of glory to the sparrow's fall, the five loaves and two fishes, and every hair of every head was definitely related to His Father; none existed apart from the Father's love and care.

What a degrading sin it is to live in a world like this without the heart constantly reaching up to God in thanksgiving and praise!

"O give thanks unto the Lord; call upon his name: make known his deeds among the people. Sing unto him, sing psalms unto him: talk ye of all his wondrous works. Glory ye in his holy name: let the heart of them rejoice that seek the Lord."—Ps. 105:1-3.

ABOUT THE AUTHOR:

Classics in religious books are few and far between. Many are written which have the appearance of the classic, but few live long enough to make a lasting mark upon the lives of men.

Not so with Hannah Whitall Smith's classic and enduring *The Christian's Secret of a Happy Life,* by which she is best known.

Born in a Quaker home in Philadelphia, she learned early of God's love and was inspired to tell others all she had discovered. In a day when the shadows of human error and apostasy hung heavy on the world, she wrote this book, and held it forth as a key to the happy life. Her generation bought it, read it, kept and treasured it next to the Book of books itself, for her generation saw in it and in her that for which they longed: **a more abundant life.**

Printed first in 1870 (one of the first books published by Revell), over 2 million copies have been sold.

Then she pinned another popular book entitled *God of All Comfort,* from which we lifted this chapter you are about to read. It is published by Moody Press.

XIII.

Thanksgiving Versus Complaining

HANNAH WHITALL SMITH

(Mrs. Smith was an English writer of many years ago, famous for her book, *The Christian's Secret of a Happy Life*. She was not a preacher, and the following article is not a sermon. However, this article did appear in the pages of THE SWORD OF THE LORD, and the content was so worthy on the subject of the Christian's obligation to give thanks that we felt it should be included in this book.)

"In every thing give thanks, for this is the will of God in Christ Jesus concerning you."—I Thess. 5:18.

Thanksgiving or complaining—these words express two contrasting attitudes of the souls of God's children in regard to His dealings with them; and they are more powerful than we are inclined to believe in furthering or frustrating His purposes of comfort and peace toward us. The soul that gives thanks can find comfort in everything; the soul that complains can find comfort in nothing.

God's command is, "In every thing give thanks"; and the command is emphasized by the declaration, "for this is the will of God in Christ Jesus concerning you." It is an actual and positive command; and if we want to obey God, we must simply give thanks in everything. There is no getting around it.

But a great many Christians have never realized this; and, although they may be familiar with the command, they have always looked upon it as a sort of counsel of perfection to which mere flesh and blood could never be expected to attain. And they, unconsciously to themselves perhaps, change the wording of the passage to make it say "be resigned" instead of "give thanks," and "in a few things" instead of "in every thing," leaving out altogether the words, "for this is the will of God in Christ Jesus concerning you."

God Is in Everything for Good: So Be Thankful

If brought face to face with the actual wording of the command, such

Christians will say, "Oh, but it is an impossible command. If everything came direct from God, one might do it perhaps; but most things come through human sources and are often the result of sin; it would not be possible to give thanks for these."

It is true we cannot always give thanks for the things themselves, but we can always give thanks for God's love and care in the things. He may not have ordered them, but He is in them somewhere, to compel even the most grievous to work together for our good.

The "second causes" of the wrong may be full of malice and wickedness, but faith never sees second causes, only the hand of God behind the second causes. They are all under His control, and not one of them can touch us except with His knowledge and permission. The thing itself that happens cannot perhaps be said to be the will of God, but by the time its effects reach us, they have become God's will for us, so must be accepted as from His hands.

The story of Joseph is an illustration of this. Nothing could have seemed more entirely an act of sin or more utterly contrary to the will of God than his being sold to the Ishmaelites by his wicked brethren; and it would not have seemed possible for Joseph, when he was being carried off into slavery in Egypt, to give thanks. Yet, if he had known the end from the beginning, he would have been filled with thanksgiving.

The fact of his having been sold into slavery was the direct doorway to the greatest triumphs and blessings of his life. And, at the end, Joseph himself could say to his wicked brethren: "As for you, ye thought evil against me, but God meant it unto good."

To the eye of sense it was Joseph's wicked brethren who had sent him into Egypt, but Joseph, looking at it with the eye of faith, said, "God did send me."

We can all remember similar instances in our own lives when God has made the wrath of man to praise Him, and has caused even the hardest trials to work together for our greatest good.

I recollect once in my own life when a trial was brought upon me by another person, at which I was filled with bitter rebellion and could not see in it from beginning to end anything to be thankful for. But, as it was in the case of Joseph, that very trial worked out for me the richest blessings and the greatest triumphs of my whole life; and in the end I was filled with thanksgiving for the very things that had caused me such bitter rebellion before. If only I had faith enough to give thanks at first, much sorrow would have been spared me.

Discourtesy and Faultfinding Against God

But I am afraid that the greatest heights to which most Christians in their shortsightedness seem able to rise is to strive after resignation to things they cannot alter, and to seek for patience to endure them. The result is that thanksgiving is almost an unknown exercise among the children of God; and, instead of giving thanks in everything, many of them hardly give thanks in anything.

If the truth were told, Christians as a body must be acknowledged to be but a thankless set. It is considered in the world a very discourteous thing for one man to receive benefits from another man and fail to thank him. Then I cannot see why it is not just as discourteous a thing not to thank God. Yet we find those who would not for the world omit an immediate note of thanks upon the reception of any gift, however trifling, from a human friend, but who have never given God real thanks for any one of the innumerable benefits He has been showering upon them all their long lives.

Moreover, I am afraid a great many not only fail to give thanks, but they do exactly the opposite, allowing themselves instead to complain and murmur about God's dealings with them. Instead of looking out for His goodness, they seem to delight in picking out His shortcomings, and think they show a spirit of discernment in criticizing His laws and His ways.

We are told that "when the people complained, it displeased the Lord"; but we are tempted to think that our special complaining, because it is spiritual complaining, cannot displease Him since it is a pious sort of complaining and a sign of greater zeal on our part, and of deeper spiritual insight than is possessed by the ordinary Christian.

Thanksgiving Is Praise Due God About Everything

But complaining is always alike, whether it is on the temporal or spiritual plane. It always has in it the element of faultfinding.

Webster says to complain means to make a charge or an accusation. It is not merely disliking the thing we have to bear, but it contains the element of finding fault with the agency that lies behind it.

And if we will carefully examine the true inwardness of our complainings, we shall generally find they are founded on a subtle faultfinding with God. We secretly feel as if He were to blame somehow; and, almost unconsciously to ourselves, we make mental charges against Him.

On the other hand, thanksgiving always involves praise of the giver.

Have you ever noticed how much we are urged in the Bible to "praise the Lord"? It seemed to be almost the principal part of the worship of the Israelites. "Praise ye the Lord, for the Lord is good: sing praises to his name, for it is pleasant" is the continual refrain of everything all through the Bible. If we should count up, we would find that there are more commands given and more examples set for the giving of thanks "always for all things" than for the doing or the leaving undone of anything else.

It is very evident from the whole teaching of Scripture that the Lord loves to be thanked and praised just as much as we ourselves like it. I am sure that it gives Him real downright pleasure, just as it does us; and that our failure to thank Him for His "good and perfect gifts" wounds His loving heart, just as our hearts are wounded when our loved ones fail to appreciate the benefits we have so enjoyed bestowing upon them.

What a joy it is to us to receive from our friends an acknowledgment of their thanksgiving for our gifts; is it not likely that it is a joy to the Lord also?

When the apostle is exhorting the Ephesian Christians to be "followers of God as dear children," one of the exhortations he gives in connection with being filled with the Spirit is this: "Giving thanks always for all things unto God and the Father, in the name of our Lord Jesus Christ."

"Always for all things" is a very sweeping expression, and it is impossible to suppose it can be whittled down to mean only the few and scanty thanks, which seem all that many Christians manage to give. It must mean that there can be nothing in our lives which has not in it somewhere a cause for thanksgiving, and that, no matter who or what may be the channel to convey it, everything contains for us a hidden blessing from God.

The apostle tells us that "every creature of God is good, and nothing to be refused, if it be received with thanksgiving." But it is very hard for us to believe things are good when they do not look so. Often the things God sends into our lives look like curses instead of blessings; and those who have no eyes that can see below surfaces judge by the outward seemings only and never see the blessed realities beneath.

How many "good and perfect gifts" we must have had during our lives, which we have looked upon only as curses and for which we have never returned one thought of thanks! And for how many gifts also, which we have even acknowledged to be good, have we thanked ourselves, or our friends, or our circumstances, without once looking behind the earthly givers to thank the heavenly Giver from whom in reality they all come! It is as if we should thank the messengers who bring us our friends' gifts, but should never send any word of thanks to our friends themselves.

All Complaining Is Against God

But, even when we realize that things come directly from God, we find it very hard to give thanks for what hurts us. Do we not, however, all know what it is to thank a skillful physician for his treatment of our diseases, even though that treatment may have been very severe? And surely we should no less give thanks to our divine Physician, when He is obliged to give us bitter medicine to cure our spiritual diseases, or to perform a painful operation to rid us of something that harms.

But instead of thanking Him, we complain against Him; although we generally direct our complaints, not against the divine Physician Himself who has ordered our medicine, but against the "bottle" in which He has sent it. This "bottle" is usually some human being, whose unkindness or carelessness, or neglect, or cruelty has caused our suffering, but who has been after all only the instrumentality or "second cause" that God has used for our healing.

Good common sense tells us that it would be folly to rail against the bottles in which the medicines, prescribed by our earthly physicians, come to us; and it is equal folly to rail against the "second causes" that are meant to teach us the lessons our souls need to learn.

When the children of Israel found themselves wandering in the wilderness, they "murmured against Moses and Aaron" and complained that they had brought them forth into the wilderness to kill them with hunger. But in reality their complaining was against God, for it was really He who had brought them there, not Moses and Aaron, who were only the "second causes." And the psalmist in recounting the story afterward called this murmuring against Moses and Aaron a "speaking against God." Divine history takes no account of second causes, but goes directly to the real cause behind them.

We may settle it, therefore, that all complaining is at the bottom "speaking against God," whether we are conscious of it or not. We may think, as the Israelites did, that our discomforts and deprivations have come from human hands only, and may therefore feel at liberty to "murmur against" the second causes which have, we may think, brought about our trials. But God is the great Cause behind all second causes. The second causes are only the instrumentalities that He uses; and when we murmur against these, we are really murmuring, not against the instrumentalities, but against God Himself. Second causes are powerless to act except by God's permission; and what He permits becomes really His arranging.

The psalmist tells us that when the Lord heard the complainings of His people "he was wroth," and His anger came up against them "because they believed not in God, and trusted not in his salvation."

At the bottom, all complainings mean just this: that we do not believe in God, and do not trust in His salvation.

"The Sacrifice of Thanksgiving"

The psalmist says: "I will praise the name of God with a song, and magnify him with thanksgiving. This also shall please the Lord better than an ox or bullock that hath horns and hoofs."

A great many people seem quite ready and willing to offer up an "ox or a bullock," or some great sacrifice to the Lord, but never seem to have realized that a little genuine praise and thanksgiving offered to Him now and then would 'please Him better' than all their great sacrifices made in His cause.

As I said before, the Bible is full of this thought from beginning to end. Over and over it is called a "sacrifice of thanksgiving," showing that it is as really an act of religious worship as is any other religious act. In fact, the "sacrifice of thanksgiving" was one of the regular sacrifices ordained by God in the Book of Leviticus. "Oh that men would praise the Lord for his goodness, and for his wonderful works to the children of men! And let them sacrifice the sacrifices of thanksgiving and declare his works with rejoicing." "By him therefore let us offer the sacrifice of praise to God continually, that is, the fruit of our lips giving thanks to his name."

It is such an easy thing to offer the "sacrifice of thanksgiving," that one would suppose everybody would be keen to do it. But somehow the contrary seems to be the case; and if the prayers of Christians were all to be noted down for any one single day, I fear it would be found that with them, as it was with the ten lepers who had been cleansed, nine out of every ten had offered no genuine thanks at all. Our Lord Himself was grieved at these ungrateful lepers, and said: "Were there not ten cleansed? But where are the nine? There are not found that returned to give glory to God, save this stranger."

Will He have to ask the same question regarding any of us? We have often, it may be, wondered at the ingratitude of those nine cleansed lepers; but what about our own ingratitude? Do we not continually pass by blessings innumerable without notice, and instead fix our eyes on what we feel to be our trials and our losses, and think and talk about these, until our whole horizon is filled with them, and we almost begin to think we have no blessings at all?

God Is Grieved at Our Complaining

We can judge of how this must grieve the Lord by our own feelings. A child who complains about the provision the parent has made wounds that parent's heart often beyond words. Some people are always complaining. Nothing ever pleases them. No kindness seems ever to be appreciated. We know how uncomfortable the society of such people makes us; and we know, on the contrary, how life is brightened by the presence of one who never complains, but who finds something to be pleased with in all that comes.

I believe far more misery than we imagine is caused in human hearts by the grumblings of those they love; and I believe also that woundings we never dream of are given to the heart of our Father in Heaven by the continual murmuring of His children.

How often is it despairingly said of fretful, complaining spirits upon whom every care and attention has been lavished, "Will nothing ever satisfy them?" And how often must God turn away, grieved by our complainings, when His love has been lavished upon us in untold blessings.

I have sometimes thought that if we could but realize this, we would check our inordinate grief over even the trials that come from the death of those we love and would try, for His dear sake, to be cheerful and content even in our lonely and bereft condition.

I remember hearing of a dear girl who was obliged to undergo a serious and very painful treatment for some disease and how the doctors had dreaded the thought of her groans and outcries. But to their amazement not even a moan escaped her lips, but all the time she smiled at her father who was present, and uttered only words of love and tenderness. The doctors could not understand.

And when the worst was over, one asked her how it could have been. "Ah," she said, "I knew how much my father loved me, and I knew how he would suffer if he saw that I suffered, so I tried to hide my suffering and to smile to make him think I did not mind."

Can any of us do this for our Heavenly Father?

Job was a great complainer; and we may perhaps think, as we read his story, that if ever anyone had good cause for complaining, he had. His circumstances seemed to be full of hopeless misery.

"My soul is weary of my life; I will leave my complaint upon myself; I will speak in the bitterness of my soul. I will say unto God, Do not condemn me; show me wherefore thou contendest with me. Is it good unto thee that thou shouldest oppress, that thou shouldest despise the work of thine hands?"

We can hardly wonder at Job's complaint. Yet could he but have seen the divine side of all his troubles, he would have known that they were permitted in the tenderest love and were to bring him a revelation of God such as he could have had by no other means. Could he have seen that this was to be the outcome, he would not have uttered a single complaint, but would have given triumphant thanks for the trials which were to bring him such a glorious fruition.

And could we but see in our heaviest trials the end from the beginning, I am sure that thanksgiving would take the place of complaining in every case.

The Rebellious Israelites Complained

The children of Israel were always complaining about something. They complained because they had no water; and when water was supplied, they complained that it was bitter to their taste. And we likewise complain because the spiritual water we have to drink seems bitter to our taste.

Our souls are athirst, and we do not like the supply that seems to be provided. Our experiences do not quench our thirst; our religious exercises seem dull and unsatisfying; we feel ourselves to be in a dry and thirsty land where no water is. We have turned from the "fountain of living waters," then we complain because the cisterns we have hewed out for ourselves hold no water.

The Israelites complained about their food. They had so little confidence in God that they were afraid they would die of starvation. Then when the heavenly manna was provided, they complained again because they "loathed such light food."

We also complain about our spiritual food. Like the Israelites, we have so little confidence in God that we are always afraid we shall die of spiritual starvation. We complain because our preacher does not feed us, or because our religious privileges are very scanty, or because we are not supplied with the same spiritual fare as others are, who seem to us more highly favored; and we covet their circumstances or their experiences. We have asked God to feed us, then our souls "loathe" the food He gives. We think it is too "light" to sustain or strengthen us. We have asked for bread, and we complain that He has given a stone.

Even Our Trials and Sorrows Are What Is Best for Us

But, if we only knew it, the provision our divine Master has made of spiritual drink and spiritual food is just that which is best for us, and is that for which we would be the most thankful if we knew. The amazing thing is that we cannot believe now, without waiting for the end, that the Shepherd knows what pasture is best for His sheep. Surely if we did, our hearts would be filled with thanksgiving and our mouths with praise even in the wilderness.

Jonah was a wonderful illustration of this. His prayer of thanksgiving out of the "belly of hell" is a tremendous lesson.

"I have cried by reason of mine affliction unto the Lord, and he heard me; out of the belly of hell cried I, and thou heardest my voice. For thou hadst cast me into the deep, in the midst of the sea: and the floods compassed me about; all thy billows and thy waves passed over me. . . . But I will sacrifice unto thee with a voice of thanksgiving; I will pay that I have vowed. Salvation is of the Lord."

No depth of misery, not even the "belly of hell," is too great for the sacrifice of thanksgiving. We cannot, it is true, give thanks for the misery, but we can give thanks to the Lord in the misery, just as Jonah did. No matter what our trouble, the Lord is in it somewhere; and, of course, being there, He is there to help and bless us. Therefore, when our "souls faint within us" because of our trouble, we have only to remember this, and to thank Him for His presence and love.

It is not because things are good that we are to thank the Lord, but because He is good. We are not wise enough to judge as to things, whether they are really, in their essence, joys or sorrows. But we always know that the Lord is good and that His goodness makes it absolutely certain that everything He provides or permits must be good and must therefore be something for which we would be heartily thankful, if only we could see it with His eyes.

Uncounted Blessings for a Widow

In a little tract called, *Mrs. Pickett's Missionary Box*, a poor woman, who had never done anything but complain all her life long and who, consequently, had got to thinking that she had no benefits for which to give thanks, received a missionary box with the words written on it: "What shall I render unto the Lord for all his benefits toward me?" And she was asked by her niece, who believed in being thankful, to put a penny into the box for every benefit she could discover in her life. I will let her tell her own story.

"Great benefits I have!" says I, standing with my arms akimbo, an' lookin' that box all over. "Guess the heathen won't get much out of me at that rate." An' I jest made up my mind I would keep count, jest to show myself how little I did have. *Them few pennies won't break me,* I thought, and I really seemed to kinder enjoy thinkin' over the hard times I had.

Well, the box sot there all that week, an' I used to say it must be kinder lonesome with nothin' in it; for not a penny went into it until next missionary meetin' day. I was sittin' on the back steps gettin' a breath of fresh air when Mary came home, an' sat down alongside o' me an' began to tell me about the meetin', an' it was all about Injy an' the widders there, poor creturs, an' they bein' abused, an' starved, an' not let to think for themselves—you know all about it better'n I do!—an' before I thought I up an' said—

"Well, if I be a widder, I'm thankful I'm where I kin earn my own livin', an' no thanks to nobody, an' no one to interfere!"

Then Mary, she laughed an' said there was my fust benefit. Well, that tickled me, for I thought a woman must be pretty hard up for benefits when she had to go clear off to Injy to find them, an' I dropped in one penny, an' it rattled round a few days without any company. I used to shake it every time I passed the shelf, an' the thought of them poor things in Injy kep' a comin' up before me, an' I really was glad I got a new boarder for me best room, an' felt as if I'd oughter put in another.

An' next meetin', Mary she told me about China, an' I thought about that till I put in another because I warn't a Chinese. An' all the while I felt kinder proud of how little there was in that box. Then one day, when I got a chance to turn a little penny sellin' eggs, which I warn't in the habit of, Mary brought the box in, where I was countin' of my money, an' says—

"A penny for your benefit, Aunt Mirandy."

An' I says, "This ain't the Lord's benefit."

An' she answered, "If 'tain't His whose is it?" An' she begun to hum over somethin' out of one of the poetry books that she was always a readin' of—

> **"God's grace is the only grace,**
> **And all grace is the grace of God."**

Well, I dropped in my penny, an' them words kep' ringin' in my ears, till I couldn't help puttin' more to it, on account of some other things I never thought of callin' the Lord's benefits before. An' by that time, what with Mary's tellin' me about them meetin's, an' me most always findin' somethin' to put in a penny for, to be thankful that I warn't it, an' what with gettin' interested about it all, and sorter searchin' round a little now and then to think of somethin' or other to put a penny in for, there really come to be quite a few pennies in the box, an' it didn't rattle near so much when I shook it.

Remember "All His Benefits"

One Psalm I call our Benefit Psalm, Psalm 103. It recounts some of the benefits the Lord has bestowed upon us, and urges us not to forget them. "Bless the Lord, O my soul, and forget not all his benefits." Our dear sister's Benefit Box had taught her something of the meaning of this Psalm. All her life she had been forgetting the benefits the Lord had bestowed upon her; now she was beginning to remember them.

Have we begun to remember ours?

If during the past year we had kept count of those benefits for which we had actually given thanks, how many pennies, I wonder, would our boxes have contained?

We sometimes sing at mission meetings a hymn of thanksgiving,

> **"Count your many blessings, name them one by one,**
> **And it will surprise you what the Lord has done."**

And sometimes I have wondered whether any of us who were singing it so heartily had ever kept the slightest record of our blessings, or even, in fact, knew that we had any.

For the trouble is that very often God's gifts come to us wrapped up in such rough coverings that we are tempted to reject them as worthless; or the messengers who bring them come in the guise of enemies, and we want to shut the door against them, and not give them entrance. But we lose far more than we know when we reject even the most unlikely.

Evil is only the slave of good,
And sorrow the servant of joy:
And the soul is mad that refuses food
From the meanest in God's employ.

We are commanded to enter into His gates with thanksgiving and into His courts with praise. And I am convinced that the giving of thanks is the key that opens these gates more quickly than anything else.

Try it, dear reader. The next time you feel dead, cold and low-spirited, begin to praise and thank the Lord. Enumerate to yourself the benefits He has bestowed upon you, thank Him heartily for each one, then see if your spirits do not begin to rise and your heart get warmed up.

Sometimes it may be that you feel too disheartened to pray; then try giving thanks instead. Before you know it, you will find yourself "glad" in the multitude of His lovingkindnesses and His tender mercies.

One of my friends told me that her little boy one night flatly refused to say his prayers. He said there was not a single thing in all the world he wanted, and he did not see what was the good of asking for things that he did not want.

A happy thought came to his mother as she said, "Well, Charlie, suppose then we give thanks for all the things you have got."

The idea pleased the child, and he very willingly knelt down and began to give thanks. He thanked God for his marbles, for a new top that had just been given him, for his strong legs that could run so fast, that he was not blind like a little boy he knew, for his kind father and mother, for his nice bed, for one after another of his blessings, until the list grew so long that at last he said he believed he would never get done.

When finally they rose from their knees, he said to his mother, with his face shining with happiness, "O Mother, I never knew before how perfectly splendid God is!"

If we would sometimes follow the example of this little boy, we too would find out, as never before, the goodness of our God.

It is very striking to notice how much thanksgiving had to do with the building of the Temple. When they had collected the treasures for the Temple, David gave thanks to the Lord for enabling them to do it. When the Temple was finished, they gave thanks again. Then a wonderful thing happened. It came to pass as the trumpeters and singers were as one to make one sound to be heard in praising and thanking the Lord...then the house was filled with a cloud, even the house of the Lord, so that the priests could not stand to minister by reason of the cloud; for the glory of the Lord had filled the house of God. When the people praised and gave thanks, then the house was filled with the glory of the Lord.

And we may be sure that the reason our hearts are not oftener filled with the "glory of the Lord" is because we do not often enough make our voices to be heard in praising and thanking Him.

If the giving of thanks is the way to open the gates of the Lord, complaining on the other hand closes these gates. Jude quotes a prophecy of Enoch's concerning murmurers:

"The Lord cometh to execute judgment upon all, and to convince all that are ungodly among them. . . of all their hard speeches which ungodly sinners have spoken against him. These are murmurers, complainers, walking after their own lusts."

People who are "murmurers" and "complainers" make in their complainings more "hard speeches" against the Lord than they would like to own, or than they will care at the last day to face. And it is not to be wondered that the judgment of God, instead of the "glory of God," is the result.

Read the Thanksgiving Psalms

I wish I had room to quote all the passages in the Bible about giving thanks and praises to the Lord. It is safe to say that there are hundreds and hundreds of them; and it is an amazing thing how they can have been so persistently ignored.

I beg of you to read the last seven Psalms and see what you think. They are simply full to overflowing with a list of the things for which the psalmist calls upon us to give thanks. All of them are things relating to the character and the ways of God, which we dare not dispute. They are not for the most part private blessings of our own but the common blessings that belong to all humanity and that contain within themselves every blessing we can possibly need. But they are blessings which we continually forget, because we take them for granted, hardly noticing their existence, and never give thanks for them.

But the psalmist knew how to count his many blessings and name them one by one, and he would have us do likewise. Try it, dear reader, and you will indeed be surprised to see what the Lord has done. Go over these Psalms verse by verse, and blessing by blessing, and see if, like the little boy of our story, you are not made to confess that you never knew before "how perfectly splendid God is."

The last verse of the Book of Psalms, taken in connection with the vision of John in the Book of Revelation, is very significant. The psalmist says, "Let every thing that hath breath praise the Lord." And in the Book of Revelation, John, who declares himself to be our brother and our companion in tribulation, tells us that he heard this being done.

"And every creature which is in heaven, and on the earth, and under the earth, and such as are in the sea, and all that are in them, heard I saying, Blessing, and honour, and glory, and power, be unto him that sitteth upon the throne, and unto the Lamb, for ever and ever."

The time for universal praise is sure to come some day. Let us begin to do our part now.

I heard once of a discontented, complaining man who, to the great surprise of his friends, became bright, happy and full of thanksgiving. After watching him for a little while and being convinced that the change was permanent, they asked what had happened.

"Oh," he replied, "I have changed my residence. I used to live in Grumbling Lane, but now I have moved into Thanksgiving Square, and I find that I am so rich in blessings that I am always happy."

Shall we each one make this move now?

(From the book, *The God of All Comfort,* by Hannah Whitall Smith. Published by Moody Press.)

XIV.

Rejoice Always

JOHN R. RICE

"Rejoice in the Lord alway: and again I say, Rejoice."—Phil. 4:4.

"Rejoice evermore."—I Thess. 5:16.

An old song my mother used to sing says:

> **Once I thought I walked with Jesus,**
> **Yet such strangeful feelings had,**
> **Sometimes trusting, sometimes doubting,**
> **Sometimes joyful, sometimes sad.**

Alas, that is the sad state of most Christians. Most are "sometimes joyful, sometimes sad." But the command of Scripture is, "Rejoice in the Lord alway: and again I say, Rejoice." A plain order from Heaven is—"Rejoice evermore."

Philippians is one of the "rejoicingest" little books in the Bible! In chapter 3, Paul is inspired to write:

"Finally, my brethren, rejoice in the Lord. To write the same things to you, to me indeed is not grievous, but for you it is safe."

That word *finally* is not a last word, for it comes slightly before the middle of the epistle, but Paul wants them to "remember this is as the final summing up of what I am inspired to write you." Being happy is to be the final truth of a Christian!

Paul reminded them that to rejoice "indeed is not grievous." He was in jail at Rome, where he would die later as a martyr, beheaded for Christ's sake. But he could rejoice in the Lord. He told these same Philippian brethren, "For I have learned, in whatsoever state I am, therewith to be content" (4:11). He urged them, "Be careful for nothing" (4:6). He called them, "my brethren dearly beloved and longed for, my joy and crown . . ." (4:1).

Rejoicing Paul, Paul with chains on his hands and feet, Paul in prison awaiting the executioner's sword—if he could rejoice in all this, then surely it was not grievous for these saints at Philippi to rejoice!

But he had written the same way to the Thessalonians, commanding them, "Rejoice evermore." Three words later he was telling them, "In every thing give thanks: for this is the will of God in Christ Jesus concerning you" (I Thess. 5:18). Thankful about everything, rejoicing evermore is God's plan for the Christian!

Obviously then, the joy of the Lord can abound in the midst of trouble and sorrow. All of us know that even in this life there is pain, sorrow, sickness, misunderstanding, death of loved ones. The best Christian may be the most persecuted. And the better Christians enter into the sorrow of the Lord over a poor, dying and sinful race about us. Paul could write:

"I say the truth in Christ, I lie not, my conscience also bearing me witness in the Holy Ghost, That I have great heaviness and continual sorrow in my heart. For I could wish that myself were accursed from Christ for my brethren, my kinsmen according to the flesh."—Rom. 9:1-3.

Paul knew what sorrow was, but it did not affect his rejoicing. In II Corinthians 6 he tells of the afflictions, necessities, distresses, stripes, imprisonments, tumults, labors, watchings, fastings, which are the proper evidence of a good minister of Christ; then he gives the triumphant truth that we can have honor in dishonor; have good report at the same time we have evil report; can be branded as deceivers, yet walk in the truth of God; can be "unknown and yet well known, as dying, and, behold, we live; as chastened, and not killed." Then he adds, "As sorrowful, yet always rejoicing." So all the sorrows that God's apostle went through never dimmed his constant joy. Indeed, we find that his sorrows were a part of his joy. He rejoiced that his persecution had "fallen out rather unto the furtherance of the gospel" (Phil. 1:12). He could give thanks for everything, knowing that "all things work together for good to them that love God, to them who are the called according to his purpose" (Rom. 8:28).

All things are from God. As Dr. Bob Jones, Sr., well said, "For a Christian, life is not divided into the secular and sacred. To him all ground is holy ground, every bush a burning bush, every place a temple of worship."

Since God has things under perfect control and His infinite love constantly remembers His dear ones, we can rejoice in whatever He sends, whether we understand it or not. That which tastes bitter will turn out to be sweet to the Christian; that which seems great loss will turn out to be rich gain.

Our rejoicing is not to be affected by circumstances. The Christian can be as happy on a cloudy day as when the sun shines; as happy when lonely as when in the presence of loved ones; as happy when sick as when well. The rejoicing of a Christian is a divine rejoicing which comes from eternal springs of blessing that God Himself puts within and about. So the Christian should rejoice evermore and "rejoice alway: and again I say, Rejoice."

Surely this constant rejoicing is to flow out of that inward peace which Jesus promised to His disciples: "Let not your heart be troubled . . ." and "I will pray the Father, and he shall give you another Comforter, that he may abide with you for ever; Even the Spirit of truth . . ." (John 14:1, 16, 17), and when He said, "Peace I leave with you, my peace I give unto you: not as the world giveth, give I unto you. Let not your heart be troubled, neither let it be afraid," in verse 27.

Peace is just lack of trouble. Joy is a more positive emotion. And we Christians are commanded to "rejoice evermore," to "rejoice in the Lord alway: and again I say, Rejoice."

Do you think it impossible? No, dear child of God! Let us go through the Blessed Word and see some things about which we are commanded and invited to rejoice. We will learn that any time a Christian does not rejoice, it is because he does not pay attention to the riches and blessings which are present to rejoice his heart every time he lets them. We will find that rejoicing evermore is the great privilege and basic duty of every child of God.

I. REJOICE IN YOUR SALVATION

The psalmist David reminded himself:

"Bless the Lord, O my soul: and all that is within me, bless his holy name. Bless the Lord, O my soul, and forget not all his benefits."

Then he began to name the principal blessings for which we ought to bless God. First of all he named:

"Who forgiveth all thine iniquities." —Ps. 103:1-3.

Oh, how blessed to have sins forgiven!

Once Jesus sent seventy unnamed converts out "two and two before his face into every city and place, whither he himself would come." What a blessed time they had!

"And the seventy returned again with joy, saying, Lord, even the devils are subject unto us through thy name. And he said unto them, I beheld Satan as lightning fall from heaven. Behold, I give unto you power to tread on serpents and scorpions, and over all the power of the enemy: and nothing shall by any means hurt you. Notwithstanding in this rejoice not, that the spirits are subject unto you; but rather rejoice, because your names are written in heaven."—Luke 10:17-20.

Imagine the joy of these new converts with the mighty power of God upon them. They cast out devils and doubtless raised the sick and saw many turn to God. It was wonderful to minister under the power of the Holy Spirit, and they rejoiced. But the One who gave them that power said, "Notwithstanding in this rejoice not, that the spirits are subject unto you; but rather rejoice, because your names are written in heaven."

Sins forgiven! A name written down in Heaven! A possessor of eternal life! Partaker of the divine nature! Born of God, and passed out of condemnation into everlasting life! Oh, how blessed it is to be saved!

I am afraid we preachers, Sunday school teachers and old-time Christians get far away from the sweet joy of being saved. It would do us good to go again down to the rescue missions and see how the converted Skid Row bums rejoice when God forgives them and makes them sober.

I have often marveled that when I have a Christian congregation quote verses of Scripture which are to them a great blessing, hardly anyone quotes John 3:16! And if a child quotes that sweet verse, we smile and say we are glad he has learned that familiar verse. But for us it has become commonplace.

I fear that in our familiarity there is a certain contempt. I fear that we have gotten used to the love of God which is so great that He gave His only begotten Son to keep us out of Hell! I fear we Christians have forgotten the pit from which we were dug and mire out of which the dear Lord pulled us! Some of us have forgotten the pigpen of sin in the far-off country now that we are back eating at the Father's table!

Let each stop and thank God for "so great salvation."

What superlatives there are in this matter of salvation: "Everlasting life," "No condemnation," "They shall never perish," "Heirs of God and joint heirs with Christ," "All things are yours." The psalmist says, "That I may shew forth all thy praise in the gates of the daughter of Zion: I will rejoice in thy salvation" (9:14).

Oh, resolve to praise God publicly at your first opportunity because your name is written down in Heaven.

This proper joy of salvation is indicated in Isaiah 61:10:

"I will greatly rejoice in the Lord, my soul shall be joyful in my God; for he hath clothed me with the garments of salvation, he hath covered me with the robe of righteousness, as a bridegroom decketh himself with ornaments, and as a bride adorneth herself with her jewels."

Let all who have on the garments of salvation, who have been covered with the white robe of righteousness of Christ, rejoice! Be glad! Rejoice as a bridegroom decked with ornaments or as a bride adorned with her jewels! We who have trusted Christ already have on the white robe for the wedding feast and the robe in which we will see the bridegroom. So let us rejoice.

Isaiah 12:2 and 3 speaks of this joy of salvation:

"Behold, God is my salvation; I will trust, and not be afraid: for the Lord Jehovah is my strength and my song; he also is become my salvation. Therefore with joy shall ye draw water out of the wells of salvation."

"The wells of salvation!" I have a well of salvation. One day I heard this great call, "Ho, every one that thirsteth, come ye to the waters . . ." (Isa. 55:1), and I came.

To that poor, frustrated, shabby woman of Samaria, Jesus said:

"Whosoever drinketh of this water shall thirst again: But whosoever drinketh of the water that I shall give him shall never thirst; but the water that I shall give him shall be in him a well of water springing up into everlasting life." —John 4:13, 14.

She drank, and the Lord Jesus put within her a living well of water that will never run dry. Every Christian has within a well of salvation. Sometimes the well is an artesian well which flows and flows. Sometimes the well seems deep and the water low, but the water is there, and the promises are ours. "Therefore with joy shall ye draw water out of the wells of salvation." A Christian is to enjoy his salvation every day, but if he doesn't, still it is there. David lost the joy of his salvation because of his sin. But when he begged God to restore it, He did.

If there were no other reason, our hearts ought to overflow day and night because our sins are forgiven, our names are written in Heaven, we are God's own dear children and headed for Glory!

May I urge you to cultivate again a happy, glad heart over your salvation, the forgiveness of sins and the grace of God to such a poor, unworthy sinner!

II. REJOICE DAILY IN THE WORD OF GOD

Every Christian should make the happy decision of the inspired psalmist:

"Thy testimonies have I taken as an heritage for ever: for they are the rejoicing of my heart." —Ps. 119:111.

A millionaire lumberman built a marvelous mansion for his wife and daughter. It was on half a city block, in a great city. I saw the tapestried walls, the parquet floors, the solid silver doorknobs and hinges on the solid Honduran mahogany doors. The building was of the most expensive face brick and ceramic tile. Even the servants' quarters were a mansion. This man delighted in the little private elevator to save steps for his beloved wife. That was a dream home built with infinite care, and he expected to delight in it all his life.

But when his wife died of a heart attack and his daughter ran away and married a drunkard, he moved out and insisted that his agent sell it at any price. So it sold for only a fraction of its worth.

But what a rich heritage in the Word which gets sweeter by the moment! Blessed is the man who can say, "Thy testimonies have I taken as an heritage for ever: for they are the rejoicing of my heart" (Ps. 119:111).

The young girl rejoices in the love letters from the man she hopes to marry, saving each one and tying them with a pink ribbon to keep forever. But years afterward they seem a little silly. She smiles at them. And the ardent swain who wrote them is ashamed of all that mush!

Not so with the precious Word of God, our love letter from Heaven. It gets sweeter all the time.

Jeremiah knew this sweetness, this joy of the Word:

"Thy words were found, and I did eat them; and thy word was unto me the joy and rejoicing of mine heart: for I am called by thy name, O Lord God of hosts." —Jer. 15:16.

One very lonely and dreaded Christmas turned out to be one of my sweetest. I was about sixteen when during the Christmas holiday all the family went to visit relatives, leaving me on the stock farm to milk the cows, feed the horses and take care of the place. I anticipated a lonely, sad week while others were away celebrating.

But I started reading the Bible. How wonderfully sweet it was! I reveled in it for days. Now I regard that as one of the happiest of Christmases. I found that no Christian need ever be lonely when he has the Word of God. "Thy words were found, and I did eat them; and thy word was unto me the joy and rejoicing of mine heart." Rejoice in the Bible every day and discover its treasures.

"Blessed is the man that walketh not in the counsel of the ungodly, nor standeth in the way of sinners, nor sitteth in the seat of the scornful. But his delight is in the law of the Lord; and in his law doth he meditate day and night."—Ps. 1:1, 2.

His delight is in the law of the Lord, and in his law he meditates day and night. Ever-available happiness is found in the Word.

III. THE JOY OF ANSWERED PRAYER

No doubt the disciples were fearful, though trying to be glad, as Jesus said they should, since the Saviour insisted He was going to the cross the next day. Jesus talked to them the night of the Last Supper in the Upper Room and on the trip to Gethsemane, saying, "But because I have said these things unto you, sorrow hath filled your heart" (John 16:6), yet He insisted that it was expedient that He go away. It was then that He gave this wonderful key to joy: "Hitherto have ye asked nothing in my name: ask, and ye shall receive, that your joy may be full" (vs. 24).

The life of answered prayer is the life full of joy! Many times were the children of Israel reminded to thank God that He brought them out of Egypt through the Red Sea, while smiting Pharaoh and his army. Many times they were reminded about the forty years' supply of manna from Heaven; of the water for the whole multitude gushing out of the cliff side smitten by Moses' rod; of their deliverance, and how God brought them into the land of Canaan. Often were they delivered in answer to prayer, so God taught them to rejoice in these deliverances.

When the prayers of Esther and her maidens were answered and the Jews delivered from the intended suffering by wicked Haman, they set a feast of rejoicing to celebrate. The Jews to this day have the Feast of Purim.

I am sure that the three Hebrew children were joyful in the Lord when they were brought out of the fiery furnace.

I suspect that the darkest hour the Apostle Paul ever saw, with more soul trouble than his stoning at Lystra, or his trial when none stood by him at Rome, or when death approached, is revealed in II Corinthians 1:8, 9:

"For we would not, brethren, have you ignorant of our trouble which came to us in Asia, that we were pressed out of measure, above strength, insomuch that we despaired even of life: But we had the sentence of death in ourselves, that we should not trust in ourselves, but in God which raiseth the dead."

He had heard of the strife among his beloved Corinthians, of divisions into sects, of drunkenness at the Lord's table, of a man living in sin with his stepmother, unrebuked but rather defended. The strain of the work itself pressed him so much that he seemed broken down and "despaired . . . of life." Besides this, he writes, "I had no rest in my spirit, because I found not Titus my brother . . ." (II Cor. 2:13).

Paul tells us that, living under the constant sentence of death, he learned "that we should not trust in ourselves, but in God which raiseth the dead." Then he entered into praise for answered prayer:

"Who delivered us from so great a death, and doth deliver: in whom we trust that he will yet deliver us; Ye also helping together by prayer for us. . . ."—II Cor. 1:10, 11.

So we go back to the exuberant rejoicing in the first verses of the epistle:

"Blessed be God, even the Father of our Lord Jesus Christ, the Father of mercies, and the God of all comfort; Who comforteth us in all our tribulation. . . ."—II Cor. 1:3, 4.

Now, after hearing the good news from the church at Corinth of penitence, revival and restitution, he writes, "Now thanks be unto God, which always causeth us to triumph in Christ . . ." (II Cor. 2:14).

Oh, yes, and he rejoiced much over the coming of Titus for whom he had prayed so long. "Nevertheless God, that comforteth those that are cast down, comforted us by the coming of Titus" (II Cor. 7:6).

In the midst of troubles and sorrow, Paul was thanking God for answered prayer. And so in the midst of his inspired report of his troubles and God's loving deliverance and answer, Paul wrote, "As sorrowful, yet always rejoicing" (II Cor. 6:10).

I, too, can join in the comfort and rejoicing over the coming of my Titus. Years ago I had set out by God's grace to bring back great city-wide revival campaigns to America. With heartbroken pleading I asked God daily for almost two years for a songleader of the stature to help carry on such campaigns.

I remember the day the word came that a great singer was leaving one of the largest and most prominent churches in America, Moody Church, Chicago, and was joining with me to hold revival campaigns and lead the singing. When the word came that he had accepted my invitation, with what joy I walked the floor and praised God! Strat Shufelt and I had two great and happy years together with citywide campaigns in Minneapolis, Buffalo, Cleveland, Chicago, and in other cities.

"Ask, and ye shall receive, that your joy may be full," Jesus admonished in John 16:24. Oh, the triumphs, the blessings, the deliverances, the victories in answer to prayer which have rejoiced my heart through vigorous, happy, yet trying years!

And the joy that overflowed my heart came just as great over a matter that seemed small.

While conducting a conference on soul winning and revival at the great Church of the Open Door, Los Angeles, along with two or three other nationally known evangelists, I became so dizzy that I consulted a doctor. He discovered I was anemic and insisted I lighten my schedule, leave off some revival campaigns, and rest. He also urged that I eat lots of beef, which was needed to build up my blood.

But we were in the midst of World War II, and steaks and prime rib roasts went to the men in service and to the big hotels and expensive eating places which I did not patronize.

One day at Checotah, Oklahoma, I walked down to the little cafe where I ate my noon meal daily during a revival. In those war days, with rationing, the plate lunch would usually be pig knuckles and sauerkraut or Polish sausage or macaroni and cheese. But as I walked toward the cafe I prayed, "Lord, if I were home and my wife asked me today what I wanted and she could get it for me, I would suggest short ribs of beef. Lord, it is such a little matter, and I will love You just as much if You do not want to bother with my request; but it would make me very happy if I could have the beef my body needs."

Immediately when I sat down in the little cafe, the waitress suggested a choice of two plate lunches; and the first one included short ribs of beef! She brought me a great serving, and I had all I could eat.

For days I was as thrilled as a girl who has just gotten a letter from her sweetheart! I mean I had a holy joy remembering I had a God who loved me and cared for my needs and would provide even such a little detail as the kind of meat I had requested.

I remember well in 1938 when in the early days of THE SWORD OF THE LORD and getting out free literature everywhere, there were bills amounting to $920.00. I laid them out before the Lord. I cannot relate the full story now. I had gone to a small church in Nebraska for a meeting. Because of the small love offering, the pastor wanted to extend the meeting. I refused to break my plans and go on with services in the hope that I could get more money.

The revival campaign closed. I got $25.00 for my two weeks. I had committed the matter to God so completely the night before that I was not surprised when the next morning as the Rock Island Rocket left Wichita, Kansas, the porter came through the car holding a telegram and calling my name.

I took the telegram, opened it and read from my secretary: YOU HAVE JUST RECEIVED CHECK FOR ONE THOUSAND DOLLARS FOR YOUR WORK!

I walked up and down the aisles clutching that telegram and laughing and praising God in my soul! I could hardly refrain from telling the porter, the hostess, the passengers, how God hears prayer!

That money came from a man I had never seen. I had never corresponded with him. Nor have I had a letter or gift from him since, though I have since met the noble good man.

Oh, the Christian need not be downcast who learns to take his burdens to the Lord day by day, to ask and receive and be so in the will of God that he can ask for what the Lord would delight to give him.

No Christian need ever be unhappy. If only he will take his burdens to the Lord, he can "rejoice evermore" in answered prayer.

IV. THE JOY OF SOULS WON BY MINISTRY
OR TESTIMONY AND PLEADING!

Doubtless every reader knows the familiar story of the shepherd with one lost sheep which he sought in the wilderness until he found it.

"And when he hath found it, he layeth it on his shoulders, rejoicing. And when he cometh home, he calleth together his friends and neighbours, saying unto them, Rejoice with me; for I have found my sheep which was lost. I say unto you, that likewise joy shall be in heaven over one sinner that repenteth, more than over ninety and nine just persons, which need no repentance." —Luke 15:5-7.

Oh, the dear Lord calls together all the saints in Heaven to rejoice over every soul saved.

Then Jesus told about the woman who lost a piece of her dowry money and how she lighted a candle and searched the house diligently till she found it.

". . . when she hath found it, she calleth her friends and her neighbours together, saying, Rejoice with me; for I have found the piece which I had lost. Likewise, I say unto you, there is joy in the presence of the angels of God over one sinner that repenteth." —Luke 15:9, 10.

Even the heart of God and the hearts of all the redeemed are made glad in Heaven when a soul is saved. The inference is that Christians should find their highest joy in the salvation of sinners.

The prodigal son came home in penitence from the far country to the father's arms and table, and to his good gifts, forgiveness and provision. The story tells how they killed the fatted calf and made merry.

The father explained to the older brother:

"It was meet that we should make merry, and be glad: for this thy brother was dead, and is alive again; and was lost, and is found." — Luke 15:32.

A time of soul-winning revival, when the power of God convicts and saves the lost, is one of great joy. It was so in Bible times, too. Philip went down to Samaria and preached Christ. Devils were cast out; the sick were healed, and a multitude turned to Christ. Then "there was great joy in that city" (Acts 8:8).

The Apostle Paul delighted in those converted under his ministry. To those at Corinth he wrote, "Ye are our epistle written in our hearts, known and read of all men" (II Cor. 3:2). He addressed the Philippians as "my brethren dearly beloved and longed for, my joy and crown" (Phil. 4:1). The Thessalonian Christians were called his "crown of rejoicing" and he said, "For ye are our glory and joy" (I Thess. 2:20).

In that wonderful Old Testament Scripture on soul winning, Psalm

126:5, 6, we have this word about the soul winner's joy:

"They that sow in tears shall reap in joy. He that goeth forth and weepeth, bearing precious seed, shall doubtless come again with rejoicing, bringing his sheaves with him."

We sow in tears, but when we win souls, we reap with joy!

We go to labor sowing everywhere. Some seeds fall by the wayside, and Satan takes the Word out of the hearts of people. Some fall on stony ground, and in unregenerate hearts they do not take root. But some seeds fall on good ground and bring forth an abundant harvest.

How sweet is the soul winner's joy!

I can assure every Christian who makes soul winning the main thing in his life that he will have constant joy and will find himself able to largely approximate this constant joy.

V. THE CHRISTIAN CAN HAVE COMPLETE JOY IN TRIBULATION

Before now it was mentioned that Paul said a good minister of Jesus Christ would prove himself "as sorrowful, yet always rejoicing." So this godly, blessed rejoicing can coexist with sorrow. At one and the same time we may have the sorrows and burdens of this world, and the joys and glory of the next.

Paul said that he proved himself a minister of God:

". . .by honour and dishonour, by evil report and good report: as deceivers, and yet true; As unknown, and yet well known; as dying, and behold, we live; as chastened, and not killed; As sorrowful, yet alway rejoicing; as poor, yet making many rich; as having nothing, and yet possessing all things."—II Cor. 6:8-10.

There is a paradox in the Christian life. To be unknown, chastened, sorrowful, poor and destitute, does not hinder being well known, alive, protected, rejoicing, making many rich and possessing all things! The world's sorrows and troubles need not hinder a Christian's constant joy. He can "rejoice alway," can "rejoice evermore."

But the sweet truth is greater than that! It is not only that a Christian can rejoice *in spite of* suffering, sorrow and trouble; he can delight *in* the suffering, sorrow and trouble!

Paul was inspired to write:

"And not only so, but we glory in tribulations also: knowing that tribula-

tion worketh patience; And patience, experience; and experience, hope; And hope maketh not ashamed; because the love of God is shed abroad in our hearts by the Holy Ghost which is given unto us." — Rom. 5:3-5.

It is not that we glory in something else in a time of tribulation, but we glory in tribulation. As Paul did, so can a Christian do, for tribulation is part of the "all things" which "work together for good" for us. A Christian can know that "no chastening for the present seemeth to be joyous, but grievous: nevertheless afterward it yieldeth the peaceable fruit of righteousness unto them which are exercised thereby" (Heb. 12:11). A Christian can glory in the midst of his chastening, his tribulation.

Paul had a thorn in the flesh. The Greek word used does not mean a small thorn, but a "stake," such as a big peg driven into a helpless prisoner to torture him. And this thorn was "a messenger of Satan" sent to buffet Paul (II Cor. 12:7). How earnestly Paul besought the Lord, in three different periods, that this punishment, this handicap, this buffeting, this temptation, this torment, be taken away! But the Lord answered back: "My grace is sufficient for thee: for my strength is made perfect in weakness" (II Cor. 12:9).

We now see Paul changing his prayer. Now he is rejoicing in his trouble. Now Paul could say, "Most gladly therefore will I rather glory in my infirmities, that the power of Christ may rest upon me." He could even say, "Therefore I take pleasure in infirmities, in reproaches, in necessities, in persecutions, in distresses, for Christ's sake." He knew that in his weakness he would be strong.

Someone has said that the Lord is too wise to make a mistake and too good to do wrong. What He planned, Paul would, by faith, glory and delight in!

I do not know what his thorn in the flesh was. Was it half-blinded eyes that made it so he must have others do his writing unless he scrawled with great letters? Was it some temptation perhaps to drink? Or the temptation which might naturally come to a lonely, wifeless, strong man? Or was it pride in his great intellect and the mighty revelations? We do not know. We know it was in the flesh, and from Satan. Satan meant it for evil, but God meant it for good! And since Paul knew that God had included it in His plan, he could glory in that infirmity.

It is far better to have trouble and have Christ prove Himself the ever-present Friend, the answer to every need, the satisfaction of every hunger and thirst, than not to have the trouble!

In Fort Worth, Texas, I went to a home with some dread to preach the funeral service for a lovely girl of fifteen. I knew the little family well. During the Depression, the husband had deserted his family; so the mother of two children set out to make a living for them. She toiled day and night. Indeed she toiled so much that her strength was soon gone, and in her fatigue, the white plague of tuberculosis brought her down. Then, to the concern of a proud and independent heart, she must go on relief. And to top her calamities, the teenager took sick and died.

We were to take this frail, thin body of the mother in our arms to the next room to look in the face of her dead child for the last good-by. What would I say to this sick woman, deserted by husband, health gone, and in poverty, and her beloved daughter now dead?

But coming into her presence was like coming into a sunlit place of flowers and beauty! She smiled so sweetly as she took my hand into hers. Although the tears ran down her face, she smiled. "Brother Rice, Jesus said He would not leave us comfortless. He said He would come to us. He came! He came!" So it was she who comforted me!

This world has no sorrows that Heaven cannot heal. And they can be healed now. We can rejoice evermore. We can even glory in tribulation that Christ's will may be done and that God's good plan may be worked out!

VI. IN PERSECUTION, REJOICE FOR CHRIST'S SAKE

It is sad that Christians are so well received in the midst of a wicked race that crucified Jesus Christ and scorns sin still! It is sad that our kind of Christianity, our churches, our sermons, our Christian work, should be so popular in a condemned world, a world which does not know and will not have Jesus Christ! When will we Christians learn, "Be not conformed to this world: but be ye transformed. . . ."? Don't we know that while we are in this world, we are not at home in this world? This day ought not be a day for crowns but for crosses. Christ is still despised and rejected; and if we were enough like Him, we, too, would be despised and rejected!

Some boast that more than half of the population of the United States belongs to some church. Alas, for our boasting, that includes the modernists, Catholics, false cults, Christian Scientists, Unitarians, and all Christ-rejecting Jews. These days our church membership has very little relationship to real Bible Christianity.

O God, give us again some of the reproach and persecution of New Testament Christianity! The servant is no better than his Lord. If the Lord Jesus was hated and crucified, surely God's people ought to suffer some. There is a curse of God on our popular Christianity, for Jesus said, "Woe unto you, when all men shall speak well of you! for so did their fathers to the false prophets" (Luke 6:26).

Oh, it is blessed to be persecuted, to suffer for Jesus' sake.

In Matthew 5:1-12 we have the Beatitudes, then we come down to a grand climax. Let us read them again and put the emphasis where the Lord Jesus put it. Jesus said:

"Blessed are the poor in spirit: for their's is the kingdom of heaven" —13 words.

"Blessed are they that mourn: for they shall be comforted" —10 words.

"Blessed are the meek: for they shall inherit the earth" —10 words.

"Blessed are they which do hunger and thirst after righteousness: for they shall be filled" —15 words.

"Blessed are the merciful: for they shall obtain mercy" —9 words.

"Blessed are the pure in heart: for they shall see God" —11 words.

"Blessed are the peacemakers: for they shall be called the children of God" —13 words.

Then comes the climaxing beatitude on persecution:

"Blessed are they which are persecuted for righteousness' sake: for their's is the kingdom of heaven. Blessed are ye, when men shall revile you, and persecute you, and shall say all manner of evil against you falsely, for my sake. Rejoice, and be exceeding glad: for great is your reward in heaven: for so persecuted they the prophets which were before you" —62 words!

I believe that the order of the Beatitudes was planned by the Saviour and that His strong elaboration of this Beatitude is an emphasis which ought not be overlooked.

The shortest of the Beatitudes with its promised blessing is— "Blessed are the merciful: for they shall obtain mercy" —9 words—while the blessing on the persecuted is almost seven times as great!

We can understand why the Lord did not say that all these others are to rejoice. They are blessed. But the one persecuted for Jesus' sake is so blessed that he should "rejoice, and be exceeding glad." Or in the language of Jesus in Luke 6:23, "Rejoice ye in that day, and leap for joy."

Then we are commanded to rejoice in persecution for righteousness' sake and for Jesus' sake! All the prophets of the past did. And these have great reward in Heaven!

> **Faith of our fathers! living still**
> **In spite of dungeon, fire and sword:**
> **O how our hearts beat high with joy**
> **Whene'er we hear that glorious word!**
> **Faith of our fathers! holy faith!**
> **We will be true to thee till death!**
>
> **Our fathers, chained in prisons dark,**
> **Were still in heart and conscience free:**
> **How sweet would be their children's fate,**
> **If they, like them, could die for Thee!**
> **Faith of our fathers! holy faith!**
> **We will be true to thee till death!**

I have lost many friends for Jesus' sake, lost them because I preach plain the Scripture truths, because I expose sin, because I oppose modernism, and because I stress soul winning. And God knows that I did not always rejoice over the suffering and sorrow! But I say also that there have been great joys and a happy expectancy of reward because I have been counted worthy to suffer some loss, some shame for Him.

Once in a time of trial I prayed that the Lord would help me to be resigned to abuse and misunderstanding and that I would not be rebellious about losing friends. But He seemed to rebuke me sharply and say, "I do not ask you to be resigned; I ask you to delight, to rejoice in persecution and tribulation."

Resignation is not enough! A Christian should take real joy in being counted worthy to suffer shame for Jesus! For great is the reward in Heaven! If we suffer with Him, we shall also reign with Him.

VII. A CHRISTIAN MAY HAVE THE JOY OF DAILY FORGIVE-NESS, CLEANSING, FELLOWSHIP WITH GOD

God is not far away. God the Spirit dwells in our bodies, which are His temple. Every Christian has "Christ in you, the hope of glory." So happy fellowship is not only possible, but normal and proper. This is part of the joy of salvation, part of the reason why the Christian can and ought to "rejoice alway" and "rejoice evermore."

But we are still in the flesh. Like Paul, all of us can say, "When I would do good, evil is present with me" (Rom. 7:21). We can say with inspired language, "In me (that is, in my flesh,) dwelleth no good thing." Every Christian struggles with the old man, but provision is made so that we can have the joy of daily cleansing, forgiveness and continued fellowship.

In I John 1:3 and 4, this matter of fullness of joy, in fellowship with the Father and the Son, is mentioned.

"That which we have seen and heard declare we unto you, that ye also may have fellowship with us: and truly our fellowship is with the Father, and with his Son Jesus Christ. And these things write we unto you, that your joy may be full."

Now let us read on and see what the plan of God is for a Christian, written by the inspired pen of John, "that your joy may be full."

"This then is the message which we have heard of him, and declare unto you, that God is light, and in him is no darkness at all. If we say that we have fellowship with him, and walk in darkness, we lie, and do not the truth: But if we walk in the light, as he is in the light, we have fellowship one with another, and the blood of Jesus Christ his Son cleanseth us from all sin. If we say that we have no sin, we deceive ourselves, and the truth is not in us. If we confess our sins, he is faithful and just to forgive us our sins, and to cleanse us from all unrighteousness."—I John 1:5-9.

God is light. Real fellowship with God means that we walk in the light, and so in joy. And as we walk in the light, "we have fellowship one with another, and the blood of Jesus Christ his Son cleanseth us from all sin."

We are solemnly warned that we need not depend on sinlessness, for "if we say that we have no sin, we deceive ourselves, and the truth is not in us." But here is the blessed promise: "If we confess our sins, he is faithful and just to forgive us our sins, and to cleanse us from all unrighteousness."

We notice with great joy that in verse 7 above, "The blood of Jesus Christ his Son *cleanseth* us from all sin." Note the tense: not *cleansed* one time, but *cleanseth*, continually. It is a continuing action, daily experienced by the Christian, if we walk in the light, and if every known sin is confessed and forsaken. Christians do sin; but as long as we never harbor sin nor excuse it, nor long for it, but openly confess it and take sides with God against sin when it comes to our attention, then the fellowship will be unbroken and we will walk in the light and have the fellowship of God. And thus, the Scripture says our joy may be full!

It is a great tragedy when Christians sin. Sin is always a tragedy and hateful to God, even though it be in the dearest of His children. And so in the following chapter, I John 2:1, 2, we read:

"My little children, these things write I unto you, that ye sin not. And if any man sin, we have an advocate with the Father, Jesus Christ the righteous: And he is the propitiation for our sins: and not for our's only, but also for the sins of the whole world."

We ought not sin. Oh, with holy concern we should buffet our bodies, mortify the deeds of the flesh, and flee youthful lusts. But "if any man sin, we have an advocate with the Father, Jesus Christ the righteous."

Oh, the blood of Jesus still avails! Not only was the blood of Christ sufficient to redeem my soul and save me, but the blood is still available for daily cleansing. That is part of the bargain. Christ is faithful to forgive and cleanse out of the way of fellowship every sin that is confessed to Him. And He ever lives—our blessed High Priest—to intercede for us.

Thus a Christian may live a life of daily cleansing and daily walk in sweet fellowship and know "that your joy may be full"!

Sin is a sad thing; but I thank God for the mercy beyond all measure, the lovingkindness that cannot be explained or understood but can be accepted with a grateful heart!

The dear Lord knows our frame. He remembers that we are dust. "Like as a father pitieth his children, so the Lord pitieth them that fear him" (Ps. 103:13). So as we seek to please the Lord and walk in the light, when we sin and confess and turn from it, we need never lack the fellowship, the joy of salvation, the fullness of joy.

VIII. WE LIVE IN JOYFUL ANTICIPATION OF HEAVEN, THE HOPE OF GLORY

The child of God is certain for Heaven. He has been made "a partaker of the divine nature" (II Pet. 1:4). He can properly say, "We have now received the atonement." He can say, "Beloved, now are we the sons of God..." (I John 3:2). "There is therefore now no condemnation to them that are in Christ Jesus..." (Rom. 8:1). And "He that believeth on the Son hath everlasting life..." (John 3:36). Oh, the glad certainty, the eternal blessedness for everyone who has trusted Christ for salvation.

That is the plain statement of God in Romans 5:1 and 2:

"Therefore being justified by faith, we have peace with God through our Lord Jesus Christ: By whom also we have access by faith into this grace wherein we stand, and rejoice in hope of the glory of God."

We are justified. We have peace with God. God has counted us as if we had never sinned. Jesus was counted guilty and died in our place. We are counted innocent and righteous, because His righteousness is now imputed to us. The Scripture says we stand in grace, "and rejoice in the hope of the glory of God."

A glad hope, an expectancy of eternal glory, the same glory of the Father is to be ours. It is a blessed anticipation!

Of course we understand that if our salvation depended on our own righteousness, on holding out faithful, we would have no assurance of the future. Many do not have the joy of their salvation because they largely depend on getting to Heaven on their own faithfulness. No one can have perfect assurance of salvation until he casts the entire burden on the Lord Jesus and depends on the price already paid, on the blood poured out. By His death on the cross Christ has satisfied the proper divine judgment on sin; and when we put our trust in the atoning sacrifice Christ offered on Calvary, we are held guiltless as far as the duty of our souls is concerned.

It is proper to rejoice in the prospect of Heaven. Jesus told His disciples before He went away:

"Let not your heart be troubled: ye believe in God, believe also in me. In my Father's house are many mansions: if it were not so, I would have told you. I go to prepare a place for you. And if I go and prepare a place for you, I will come again, and receive you unto myself; that where I am, there ye may be also."—John 14:1-3.

Here He gives the prospect of Heaven, the prospect of the Father's House where there is plenty of room. And He has promised to come again to receive us unto Himself.

The Lord set us a good example in looking forward with joy to that time when all saints come from the east and west to sit down with Abraham, Isaac and Jacob in the kingdom of God.

Oh, happy wedding feast, when Christ Himself is the Bridegroom and when His bride is adorned in the perfect righteousness which He has furnished.

We are told that we should look to Jesus and be like Him, "who for the joy that was set before him endured the cross, despising the shame, and is set down at the right hand of the throne of God" (Heb. 12:2). The Lord, buoyed up by the anticipation of joyfully greeting all the multitude of the saved in Heaven, was glad to face the cross.

And that joy of the Saviour is anticipated in Isaiah: "He shall see of the travail of his soul, and shall be satisfied..." (53:11).

It is not surprising that the last two chapters of the Bible tell such marvelous truths about the Heavenly City, the New Jerusalem, the river of life and the tree of life, with leaves for the healing of the nations, and all manner of fruit! Oh, that fair city with streets of gold, with gates of pearl and foundation of precious stones and jasper! Oh, that city forever lighted by the presence of God and the Lamb! Oh, that city where God Himself shall wipe away all tears and there will be no more death nor sorrow nor crying, for the former things are passed away!

So the Christian can properly delight in the prospect of Heaven. We can remember that there is a payday coming for the faithful. Those who suffer now for Christ will rule with Him then. Those who turn many to righteousness now shall shine as the stars forever and ever. Those who mourn shall be comforted. And many who are last now will be first then!

Wonderful joy of Heaven! We ought to think often of Heaven, sing happy songs about Heaven, and look forward with glad anticipation to our reunion with Christ and loved ones.

Surely, surely, the Christian who meditates on all these grounds of holy joy and happiness will ask for grace to obey the Scriptures and "rejoice alway, and again I say, Rejoice," and again, "Rejoice evermore."

How the Christian Should React in a Life
of Constant Rejoicing

What is the normal expression of Christian joy? "What shall I render to the Lord for all his benefits?"

Let me suggest that these manifestations are part of the secret of joy. One should rejoice not only as he becomes the passive receiver of joy that may flood his heart from on high, but he ought actively to rejoice, to comfort and encourage himself in the Lord and to live in the fullness of joy.

How, then, should a Christian express and cultivate this joy?
First, be thankful.

First Thessalonians 5:16 commands, "Rejoice evermore." And verse
18 commands, "In every thing give thanks: for this is the will of God
in Christ Jesus concerning you."

These are twin commands for twin blessings, or perhaps they are parts
of the same thing. How could one be properly joyful without being properly thankful?

In Philippians, too, rejoicing and thanksgiving are connected.

*"Rejoice in the Lord alway: and again I say, Rejoice. Let your modera-
tion be known unto all men. The Lord is at hand. Be careful for nothing;
but in every thing by prayer and supplication with thanksgiving let your
requests be made known unto God. And the peace of God, which
passeth all understanding, shall keep your hearts and minds through
Christ Jesus."* —Phil. 4:4-7.

Rejoice in the Lord always. Part of this rejoicing is being free of care
and anxiety. And the way is "in every thing by prayer and supplication
with thanksgiving let your requests be made known unto God." In this
way that inexpressible peace of God will surround, master, protect and
keep our hearts.

To rejoice always one must in everything pray with thanksgiving!
Ingratitude is one of the basest of sins. When his wicked older daughters
took his property and cast him out, Shakespeare's King Lear cried out,
"How sharper than a serpent's tooth it is to have a thankless child!"
Then how must God feel about His thankless children!

The psalmist was inspired to write, "Bless the Lord, O my soul: and
all that is within me, bless his holy name. Bless the Lord, O my soul,
and forget not all his benefits" (103:1, 2). Then he counted all the
major benefits. We Christians should count our blessings, name them,
be joyful about them, and thank God for them!

Psalm 34:1 says, "I will bless the Lord at all times: his praise shall
continually be in my mouth." Praise is the normal and proper expression of joy. Since all our joy is from God, then He should have the glory.

> **Oh, how can I love Thee enough, dear Redeemer,**
>   **How e'er repay my Friend?**
> **I'll spread the glad sound of my praise and my heart love**
>   **On every joyful wind.**

Thanks and praise to God before others should be the normal

outcome of the Christian's joyful heart.

The Lord delights in our praises. "Let every thing that hath breath praise the Lord" (Ps. 150:6). Surely, better than angels who never sinned and never knew forgiveness, better than lost people would ever do, better than animals or plants and planets and worlds, the born-again child of God should praise the Lord.

And the joyful heart ought to sing. The holy exultation should put lilt in our voices and melody in our hearts. We are commanded to be:

"Speaking to yourselves in psalms and hymns and spiritual songs, singing and making melody in your heart to the Lord; Giving thanks always for all things unto God and the Father in the name of our Lord Jesus Christ."—Eph. 5:19, 20.

Too often our singing is left only for the trained voice or for those with musical gifts. Rather, songs should be an outburst of praise, petition and joy, normal for every Christian.

And, of course, the joyful Christian must be the obedient one. With glad witness, we should urge people to trust the Saviour. And an overflowing joy in the power of the Spirit will have more to do with results from our testimony than nearly anything else.

Too often our testimony is weak because the happy glow in the heart is weak. But a happy heart proves sincerity. And this poor, sad, frustrated world, with all its tranquilizers, psychiatric couches, mental hospitals, frustrations, divorces and suicides, surely needs to learn the secret of happiness!

So let us "rejoice in the Lord alway." Let God's people "rejoice evermore."

CHARLES HADDON SPURGEON
1835-1892

ABOUT THE MAN:

Many times it has been said that this was the greatest preacher this side of the Apostle Paul. He began preaching at the age of 16. At 25 he built London's famous Metropolitan Tabernacle, seating around 5,000. It was never large enough. Even when traveling he preached to 10,000 eager listeners a week. Crowds thronged to hear him as they came to hear John the Baptist by the River Jordan. The fire of God was on him as on the Prophet Elijah facing assembled Israel at Mount Carmel.

Royalty sat in his Tabernacle, as did washerwomen. Mr. Gladstone had him to dinner; and cabbies refused his fare, considering it an honor to drive for this "Prince of Preachers." To a housewife kneading bread, he would say, "Have you ever tried the Bread of life?" Many a carpenter was asked, "Have you ever tried to build a house on sand?"

He preached in all the principal cities of England, Scotland and Ireland. And although invited to the United States on several occasions, he was never able to visit this country.

HOW GREAT WAS HIS HEART: for preachers, so the Pastors' College was founded; for orphans, so the orphans' houses came to be; for people around the world, so his literature poured forth in an almost unmeasurable volume. He was a national voice; so every national issue affecting morals, religion or the poor had his interpretation, his counsel.

Oh, but his passion for souls! You can see it in every sermon.

Spurgeon published thousands of poems, tracts, sermons and songs.

HIS MESSAGE TO LOST SINNERS WILL LIVE AS LONG AS THE GOSPEL IS PREACHED.

XV.

A Thanksgiving Psalm
Exposition of Psalm 136

CHARLES H. SPURGEON

When the chorus was taken up by the whole of the people, accompanied by a blast of trumpets, this must have been a magnificent hymn of praise.

Verse 1: *"O give thanks unto the Lord; for he is good: for his mercy endureth for ever."*

The Psalm begins with the august name, the incommunicable title of the one living and true God, Jah, Jehovah. For this name the Jews had a high respect, which degenerated into superstition, for they would not write it in their Bibles, but put another word instead, in which our translators have imitated the version.

Sure, if it is "Jehovah" in the original, we should have it "Jehovah" here. The name is a very wonderful one—"Je-ho-vah." No man knows exactly how it should be pronounced; it is said to consist of a succession of breathings, therefore is it written, "Let every thing that hath breath praise the Lord," whose name is a breathing, and in whom dwells the life of all who breathe.

Let us take care that we never trifle with the name of God. I think that the common use of the word "Hallelujah" or "Praise ye the Lord" is simply profane. Sure, this is not a word to be dragged in the mire; it should be pronounced with solemn awe and sacred joy.

Verse 2: *"O give thanks unto the God of gods: for his mercy endureth for ever."*

If there be any other god, if there can be imagined to be any, our God is infinitely above them all. The gods of the heathen are idols, but our God made the heavens. If there be any reverence due to magistrates, of whom we read in Psalm 82: "I have said, Ye are gods," yet are they nothing at all compared with Jehovah, "the God of gods."

Verse 3: *"O give thanks to the Lord of lords: for his mercy endureth for ever."*

Whatever there be of authority or lordship or kingship of any kind in the world, it is all in subjection to Him who is "the Lord of lords."

I think I hear the trumpets sounding it out, and all the people joining in chorus, "O give thanks to the Lord of lords: for his mercy endureth for ever." It is ever the same strain, the enduring mercy of God, that bore the strain of Israel's sin and Israel's need and Israel's wandering.

Verse 4: *"To him who alone doeth great wonders: for his mercy endureth for ever."*

Nobody does wonders that can be compared with Jehovah's wonders. Nobody helps Him in the doing of His wonders; He asks no aid from any of His creatures.

Verse 5: *"To him that by wisdom made the heavens: for his mercy endureth for ever."*

Every time you lift up your eyes to that one great arch which spans all mankind, praise the name of the great Builder who made that one enormous span, unbuttressed and unpropped. What a work it was! And it was made by mercy as well as by wisdom. If we go into the scientific account of the atmosphere, of the firmament, and of the stellar heavens, we see that the hand of mercy was at the back of wisdom in the making of it all: "for his mercy endureth for ever."

Verse 6: *"To him that stretched out the earth above the waters: for his mercy endureth for ever."*

We ought to praise Him for the making of every country, especially, I think, we who dwell on these favored islands, because He has placed our lot in an island.

"He bade the waters round thee flow;
Not bars of brass could guard thee so."

We might have been beneath the tyrant's foot, had it not been for "the silver streak" that gives us liberty. The whole earth, wherever men dwell, will afford some peculiar reason for their praise to Jehovah.

Verses 7 to 9: *"To him that made great lights: for his mercy endureth for ever: The sun to rule by day: for his mercy endureth for ever: The moon and stars to rule by night: for his mercy endureth for ever."*

Why three verses about one thing? Because we are not wont to dwell upon God's goodness as we should. We are therefore bidden, first, to remember light in general, then the sun, the moon, the stars, each one in particular; and each time we do so, we may say, "His mercy endureth for ever."

We are not left in the daytime without the sun; and, when the day is over, the darkness of the night is cheered either by the moon or by the stars, which show us that not only day unto day, but night unto night He thinks upon us, "for his mercy endureth for ever."

Praise Him, praise Him, whether it be high noon or midnight, when the day is renewed or when the curtains of your rest are drawn, still praise Him, "for his mercy endureth for ever."

Verse 10: *"To him that smote Egypt in their firstborn: for his mercy endureth for ever."*

It is not a common mercy of which we have to sing, but a peculiar theme for thanksgiving. He "smote Egypt in their firstborn."

Verse 11: *"And brought out Israel from among them: for his mercy endureth for ever."*

Sing of His goodness to His chosen, even though it involved a terrible stroke upon His proud adversary. There are some who cannot praise God's left hand, but we can; not only the right hand that helps His people out, but the left hand that smites the Egyptians. We praise Him still with unabated joy in Him. What He doeth must be right; and in His vengeance there is justice, and justice is mercy to mankind.

Verse 12: *"With a strong hand, and with a stretched out arm: for his mercy endureth for ever."*

In all God's acts there is some peculiarity which commands especial attention. He "brought out Israel" —praise Him for that. He did it "with a strong hand, and with a stretched out arm," therefore again praise Him. The ring is precious, but the brilliance in the ring is that to which in this verse you are bidden to look, namely, Jehovah's strong hand and stretched out arm.

Verses 13, 14: *"To him which divided the Red sea into parts: for his mercy endureth for ever: And made Israel to pass through the midst of it: for his mercy endureth for ever."*

And when you, too, come to the Red Sea on your way to the heavenly Canaan, when your path is blocked, God will divide it for you; and as He gently leads you through the very deeps, He will have you sing, "His mercy endureth for ever." No floods can drown His love, nor divide you from it. "Who shall separate us from the love of Christ?" Jehovah will split seas in two to make a passage for His people, "for his mercy endureth for ever."

Verse 15: *"But overthrew Pharaoh and his host in the Red sea: for his mercy endureth for ever."*

This is the deep bass of the hymn. He "overthrew Pharaoh." "The horse and his rider hath he thrown into the sea." We cannot give up that verse; we cannot refuse to sing the song of Moses; we must praise and bless God for all that He did at the Red Sea, even though terrible were His deeds of righteousness, when the chivalry of Egypt sank to the bottom of the sea like a stone.

Verse 16: *"To him which led his people through the wilderness: for his mercy endureth for ever."*

Here is another point where you can join with Israel. This world is a wilderness to you; but the Lord leads you through it. By His fiery cloudy pillar, He conducts you all your journey through. By His manna, gently dropping from Heaven, He feeds you still; and He will guide you till He brings you over "Jordan's stormy banks" "To Canaan's fair and happy land."

Verses 17 to 20: *"To him which smote great kings: for his mercy endureth for ever: And slew famous kings: for his mercy endureth for ever: Sihon king of the Amorites: for his mercy endureth for ever: And Og the king of Bashan: for his mercy endureth for ever."*

Here you have the repetitions of God. I have sometimes said that I like the tunes which allow us to repeat the line of a hymn; and certainly one likes a Psalm which turns over some great mercy of God and makes us see the various facets of the wonderful jewel.

The psalmist does not merely say that Jehovah smote great kings; but these kings were famous in battle, which rendered their greatness or power the more formidable. But whether men be great, or whether they be valorous, or both, they cannot prevent God's mercy to His people. He will push a way for them against the horns of their adversaries, and they shall be victorious.

As if to show the depth of His gratitude, the psalmist gives the names of these kings and of the countries over which they ruled; and He dwells with emphasis upon these points of the mercy of God to His people, in that He slew famous kings, Sihon, king of the Amorites, and Og, the king of Bashan.

Verses 21, 22: *"And gave their land for an heritage: for his mercy endureth for ever: Even an heritage unto Israel his servant: for his mercy endureth for ever."*

He gave those countries which were beyond the land of promise, because these foes tried to stop their way. He did not limit Palestine; but, on the contrary, He stretched the ordained bounds of it and enclosed the land of the Amorites and Bashan within the territory He gave to His people.

Now comes a soft, sweet verse; I think I hear the harps leading the singing:

Verse 23: *"Who remembered us in our low estate: for his mercy endureth for ever."*

Can you not sing this tonight? Some of you who were very poor, very sad, despairing, abhorred of men, slandered, persecuted, very low, perhaps some here who once were in the slums of this city, now can sing, "Who remembered us in our low estate."

Spiritually, our estate was low enough; it had ebbed out, till we had no comfort nor hope left; but the Lord remembered us. That is a blessed prayer, "Lord, remember me." That prayer has been answered for many here; ay, even before we prayed it. He remembered us in our low estate, "for his mercy endureth for ever."

Dear heart, are you in a very low estate tonight? Do you feel as if you were at death's dark door and at Hell's dread brink, by reason of the greatness and blackness of your sin? "His mercy endureth for ever." Catch at that rope. Drowning men clutch at straws; but this is no straw. Do you cling to it; it will bear your weight. It has been a means of salvation to myriads before you. Trust God's mercy in Christ and you are saved, "for his mercy endureth for ever." "Who remembered us" — what next?

Verse 24: *"And hath redeemed us...."*

This song is climbing up; it begins to ascend the heavenly ladder; it has already reached redemption.

Verses 24, 25: *"...from our enemies: for his mercy endureth for ever. Who giveth food to all flesh: for his mercy endureth for ever."*

God is the great Feeder of the world. What a commissariat is that of the universe! One cannot think of the wants of the five millions in London without shuddering lest, some day, there should not be food enough for them; but there always is. I will not trace it to the mere fact that trade and commerce supply us. No, there is an overruling power at the back of it all, depends upon it. All the world seems eager to supply our markets, and to make the loaf for the laborer; but it is God who has planned it all. Let us praise Him "who giveth food to all flesh." As for spiritual meat, He will give us that; I trust we shall all have a portion of meat in due season tonight.

If any shall be hungry at the end of the service, it shall be surely from want of willingness to be fed rather than lack of suitability in the Word of God to sustain the spirit, and bless the soul.

Verse 26: *"O give thanks unto the God of heaven: for his mercy endureth for ever."*

ROBERT MURRAY McCHEYNE
1813 — 1843

ABOUT THE MAN:

Born in Edinburgh, Scotland in 1813, Robert Murray McCheyne was one of God's blessings given to Scotland in the early part of the 19th century.

Robert displayed outstanding intellectual skills as a child: at the age of four, he taught himself to name and to write the Greek alphabet, while recovering from an illness. He later used a remarkable memory to memorize long passages of Scripture.

Attending the University of Edinburgh, he was greatly influenced by Thomas Chalmers; he graduated in 1830. Having been licensed to preach when he was 22, McCheyne was ordained a year later and began pastoring in Dundee, Scotland.

For six years he was pastor of St. Peter's Church (of the Church of Scotland), which grew to over one thousand members.

In 1839 he visited Palestine concerning future evangelization of the Jewish people. While there, he prayed fervently for his congregation back home. Upon his return he found that a spiritual awakening was in progress. His preaching consequently made a significant contribution to the revival and helped it spread across Scotland to northern England.

He used his intellectual ability to design sermons that had a tremendous persuasion upon the unconverted. He was only 30 when he died in 1843, reportedly of typhoid fever.

Few men have had the impact in a long lifetime that Robert Murray McCheyne had in his 30 years. Though his ministry lasted only seven years, he is recognized as one of the great spiritual leaders of his day. His was a daily walk with God, and it was perhaps his Christlike dependence upon God's Spirit that left such a deep impression on men's lives.

After hearing him preach, one Scottish evangelist reportedly said, "He preached with eternity stamped upon his brow. I trembled, and never felt God so near."

McCheyne's life undoubtedly exemplified the words he so often repeated: "Live so as to be missed."

XVI.

Thanksgiving Obtains the Spirit

ROBERT MURRAY McCHEYNE

(Preached 1839 after returning from Palestine)

"It came even to pass, as the trumpeters and singers were as one, to make one sound to be heard in praising and thanking the Lord; and when they lifted up their voice with the trumpets and cymbals and instruments of musick, and praised the Lord, saying, For he is good; for his mercy endureth for ever: that then the house was filled with a cloud, even the house of the Lord; So that the priests could not stand to minister by reason of the cloud; for the glory of the Lord had filled the house of God."—II Chron. 5:13, 14.

The day here spoken of appears to have been a day of days. It seems to have been the day of Pentecost in Old Testament times—a type of all the glorious days of an outpoured Spirit that ever have been in the world—a foretaste of that glorious day when God will fulfill that amazing, soul-satisfying promise: "I will pour out my Spirit upon all flesh."

My dearly beloved flock, it is my heart's desire and prayer that this very day might be such a day among us—that God would indeed open the windows of Heaven, as He has done in times past, and pour down a blessing, till there be no room to receive it.

Let us observe, then, how thanksgiving brings down the Spirit of God.

I. THE REASON FOR THEIR PRAISE

". . . in praising and thanking the Lord." Yea, you have their very words: *"For he is good; for his mercy endureth for ever."*

It was thus the people were engaged when the cloud came down and filled the house. They had been engaged in many other most affecting duties. The Levites had been carrying the ark from Mount Zion and placing it under the wings of the cherubim; Solomon and all his people had been offering sacrifices, sheep and oxen, which could not be told for multitude—still no answer came from Heaven.

But when the trumpeters and singers were as one in praising and thanking the Lord, when they lifted up their voices, saying, "For he is good; for his mercy endureth for ever"—then the windows of Heaven were opened—then the cloud came down and filled the whole Temple.

My dear flock, I am deeply persuaded that there will be no full, soul-filling, heart-ravishing, heart-satisfying outpouring of the Spirit of God till there be more praise and thanking the Lord. Let me stir up your hearts to praise.

1. **"He is good."** Believers should praise God for what He is in Himself. Those who have never seen the Lord cannot praise Him. Those who have not come to Christ have never seen the King in His beauty.

An unconverted man sees no loveliness in God. He sees a beauty in the blue sky—in the glorious sun—in the green earth—in the spangling stars—in the lily of the field; but he sees no beauty in God. He hath not seen Him, neither known Him; therefore there is no melody of praise in that heart.

When a sinner is brought to Christ, he is brought to the Father. Jesus gave Himself for us, "that he might bring us to God." Oh, what a sight breaks in upon the soul—the infinite, eternal, unchangeable God!

I know that some of you have been brought to see this sight. Oh, praise Him, then, for what He is!

Praise Him for His *pure, lovely holiness* that cannot bear any sin in His sight. Cry, like the angels, "Holy, holy, holy, Lord God Almighty."

Praise Him for His *infinite wisdom*—that He knows the end from the beginning. In Him are hid all the treasures of wisdom and knowledge.

Praise Him for His *power*—that all matter is in His hand. The heart of the king, the heart of saint and sinner, are all in His hand. Hallelujah! for the Lord God Omnipotent reigneth.

Praise Him for His *love*; for God is love. Some of you have been at sea. When far out of sight of land, you have stood high on the vessel's prow and looked round and round—one vast circle of ocean without any bound. So it is to stand in Christ justified and to behold the love of God—a vast ocean all around you, without a bottom and without a shore!

Oh, praise Him for what He is! Heaven will be all praise. If you cannot praise God now, how can you praise Him there?

2. **"For his mercy" — for what He has done for us.** The Lord has done much for me since we parted. We were once in perils of waters, but the Lord saved the ship. Again and again we were in danger of plague—we nightly heard the cry of the mourner, yet no plague came near our dwelling. Again and again we were in perils of robbers—the gun of the murderer has been leveled at us, but the Lord stayed his hand.

I have been at the gates of death since we parted. No man who saw me would have believed that I could be here this day, yet He hath healed our diseases and brought me back to open once more to you the unsearchable riches of Christ. I, then, have reason to praise Him; for His mercy endureth forever.

The Lord has done much for you since we parted. My eyes filled with tears when I left you, for I thought He had done it in anger. I thought it was anger to me, and I thought it was anger to you, but now I see it was all love—it was all mercy to unworthy you and to unworthy me. The Lord gave you my dear brother [the one ministering in M'Cheyne's absence] to care for your souls, and far better than that—for to give you a man only would have been a poor gift—but He has given you His Holy Spirit.

"Bless the Lord, O my soul!" Praise Him, O my people, for He is good; for His mercy endureth forever.

Are there not some of you brands plucked out of the burning? You were in the burning; the pains of Hell were actually getting hold on you. You had a hell in your own hearts—you had a Hell yawning to receive you, but the Lord snatched you from the burning. Will you not praise Him?

Are there not some of you whom I left blind and deaf and dumb and dead? You saw no beauty in Him who is fairer than the children of men; you saw no glory in Immanuel—God manifest in flesh. But the Lord has said: "Go, wash in the pool of Siloam"; and whereas you were blind, now you see. Oh, praise Him that hath done it!

In Heaven, they praise God most of all for this: "Worthy is the Lamb that was slain." Oh, have you no praise for Jesus for all His love—for the Father—for the Spirit? Some of you cannot sing, "No man could learn that song but those who were redeemed from the earth."

Some of you are worse than when I left you. You have resisted me— you have resisted my brother; and, worse than all—you have resisted the Holy Ghost. You are prayerless yet—Christless yet.

Unhappy souls, unredeemed, unrenewed, remember it will be too late to learn to praise when you die. You must begin now.

I will tell you what a dear friend of my own once said before dying. She desired all the servants to be brought in; and she said very solemnly: "There's nothing but Christ between me and weeping and wailing and gnashing of teeth." Oh, if you have not Christ, then there is nothing between you and weeping and wailing and gnashing of teeth. You who will not praise Christ now, shall wail because of Him soon.

II. THE MANNER OF THEIR PRAISE

They were "as one." Their hearts were all as one heart in this exercise. There were a thousand tongues, but only one heart. Not only were their harps and cymbals and dulcimers in tune, giving out a harmonious melody, but their hearts were all in tune. God had given them one heart, and then the blessing came down.

The same was the case on the day of Pentecost; they were all with *one accord* in one place; they were looking to the same Lamb of God. The same thing will be the case in that day prophesied of in Psalm 133, "Behold, how good and how pleasant it is for brethren to dwell together in unity!" 'There God commands the blessing, even life for evermore.'

This is the very thing which Jesus prayed for in that prayer which none but God could have asked, and none but God could answer:

"Neither pray I for these alone, but for them also which shall believe on me through their word; That they all may be one; as thou, Father, art in me, and I in thee, that they also may be one in us: that the world may believe that thou hast sent me."

And then follows the blessing:

"And the glory which thou gavest me I have given them; that they may be one, even as we are one: I in them, and thou in me, that they may be made perfect in one; and that the world may know that thou hast sent me, and hast loved them, as thou hast loved me."

Dear children of God, unite your praises. Let your hearts no more be divided. You are divided from the world by a great gulf. Soon it will be an infinite gulf; but you are united to one another by the same Spirit—you have been chosen by the same free, sovereign love—you have been washed in the same precious blood—you have been filled by the same blessed Spirit.

Little children, love one another. He that loveth is born of God. Be one in your praises. Join in one cry: 'Worthy is the Lamb that was slain: thou art worthy to open the book—thou art worthy to reign in our hearts.' Be fervent in praise! Lift up your voices in it—lift up your hearts in it.

In Heaven they wax louder and louder. John heard the sound of a great multitude, then it was like many waters, then it was like mighty thunderings, crying, "Hallelujah! hallelujah!"

I remember Edwards' remark, that it was in the singing of praises that his people felt themselves most enlarged, and that then God was worshiped somewhat in the beauty of holiness.

Let it be so among yourselves. Learn, dearly beloved, to praise God heartily—to sing with all your heart and soul in the family and in the congregation. But remember that even your praises must be sprinkled with blood, and can be acceptable to God only by Jesus Christ.

III. THE EFFECTS OF THEIR PRAISE

1. **"The house was filled with a cloud."** This cloud is the very same which led them through the Red Sea and went before them forty years in the wilderness. It was a pillar of cloud by day—to shade them from the heat; it was a pillar of fire by night—to guide Israel on her way to the promised rest; now it came and filled the holiest of all and the holy place. Such was the wonderful effect which followed their united fervent praises.

God Himself came down and filled every chamber of the house with His presence. "This is my rest for ever: here will I dwell; for I have desired it."

My dear friends, we are not now to expect that God will answer our prayers or follow our praises with a pillar of cloud or a pillar of fire. These were but the shadows; now we receive the reality—the substance. If ye will but unite in unanimous and heartfelt praises, then am I persuaded that God will give His Holy Spirit to fill this house—to fill every heart in the spiritual temple. How glorious this will be:

(1) *For the children of God.*

Are there not some of you who have come to Christ, and nothing more? Guilty, weary, heavy laden, you have found rest—redemption through His blood—even the forgiveness of sins. Do not stop there! Do not rest in mere forgiveness. Cry for the fullness of the Holy Ghost, the Comforter.

Are there not some of you groaning under a body of sin and death and crying with the apostle, "Oh! wretched man, who shall deliver me from the body of this death?" Do you not feel the plague of your own heart? Do you not feel the power of your old nature? How many in this state lean upon themselves—trust in their resolutions—attempt, as it were, by force, to put down their sins! But here is the remedy. Oh, cry for the flood tide of God's Spirit, that He may fill every chamber of your heart—that He may renew you in the spirit of your mind.

Are there not many who are cold, worldly Christians—those who were long ago converted, but have fallen sadly back under the power of the world—either its gaiety or its business, its mirth or its money—and they have gotten into worldly habits, deep ruts of sin? Ah, see what you need! It is He only who can melt your icy heart and make it flow out in love to God—who can fill you with all the fullness of God.

Are there not some who read the Bible, but get little from it? You feel that it does not sink into your heart—it does not remain with you through the week. It is like the seed cast in the wayside, easily plucked away.

Oh, it is just such an outpoured Spirit you require, to hide the Word in your heart. When you write with a dry pen, no impression is made upon the paper.

Now, ministers are the pens and the Spirit of God is the ink. Pray that the pen may be filled with that living ink—that the Word may remain in your heart, known and read of all men—that you may be sanctified through the truth.

(2) *For the unconverted.*

So it was in the day of Pentecost—the Spirit came first upon the small company of disciples, then on the three thousand.

You have seen the hills attracting the clouds, and so drawing down the shower into the valleys—so do God's children, having their heads within the veil, obtain the Spirit of God in fullness, and dispense it to all around. You have seen some tall tree or spire catching the lightning and conveying it down into the ground—so does the fire of God's Spirit come first upon the trees of righteousness, and from them descends to the dead souls around them.

A Word to Dead Souls

Keep near to God's children at such a time as this. Do not separate from them—do not mock at them; you may yet receive the grace of God through them. Dear believers, for the sake of the dead souls around you—for the sake of this great town, full of wickedness—for the sake of our land, filled with formality and hypocrisy—unite in prayer and unite in praise and prove the Lord, if He will not pour out a blessing. Not for your own sakes only, but for the sake of those perishing around you, let us wrestle and pray for a fuller time of the Spirit's working than has ever been seen in Scotland yet.

2. **"The priests could not stand to minister."** Before the cloud came down, no doubt the priests were all busily engaged burning incense and offering sacrifices; but when the cloud came down, they could only wonder and adore.

So it ever will be when the Lord gives much of His Spirit; He will make it evident that it is not the work of man. If He were to give only a little, then ministers would begin to think they had some hand in it; but when He fills the house, then He makes it plain that man had nothing to do with it.

David Brainerd said that when God awakened his whole congregation of Indians, he stood by amazed and felt that he was as nothing— that God alone was working.

It is this, dear friends, that we desire and pray for—that the Lord the Spirit would Himself descend and, with His almighty power, tear away the veil from your hearts, convince you of sin, of righteousness, and of judgment—that Jesus Himself would take His sceptre and break your hard hearts and take all the glory—that we may cry out, "Not unto us, Lord, not unto us, but unto thy name give glory."

AMZI CLARENCE DIXON
1854-1925

ABOUT THE MAN:

Born on a plantation near Shelby, North Carolina, on July 6, 1854, Amzi Clarence Dixon was a microcosm of an era of Fundamentalism. His father, a Baptist preacher, was a godly man, so young Clarence consistently received the highest caliber of Christian example and training.

Destined to become a great Bible expositor and elegant pulpiteer, A. C. Dixon knew early in life that he must preach the Gospel.

After graduating from Wake Forest College, Dixon served two country churches in North Carolina. Leaving both congregations in a state of revival, he then went to study under John A. Broadus at Southern Baptist Theological Seminary.

Dixon is most often remembered for his big-city churches in the North, though he always considered himself a Southerner. He enjoyed powerful and fruitful pastorates at many places, but particularly at the well-known Chicago's Moody Church and London's Metropolitan Tabernacle.

During his 10-year ministry at Hanson Place Baptist Church in Brooklyn (1890-1900) Dixon often rented the Brooklyn Opera House for Sunday afternoon evangelistic services.

In 1901, he became pastor of Ruggles Street Baptist Church, Roxbury, Massachusetts, a Boston suburb. Here Dixon taught at the Gordon Bible and Missionary Training School and wrote his famous *Evangelism Old and New,* an attack on the Social Gospel movement.

In 1906 he accepted the pulpit of the Chicago Avenue Church (Moody Memorial Church), and he spent the war years ministering at Spurgeon's Tabernacle in London.

During these years he was conspicuous at Fundamentalist gatherings; he spoke at great Bible conferences.

A. C. Dixon suffered a heart attack and died on June 14, 1925, just one month before the Scopes Trial. Dixon, like many other Fundamentalists, fought the good fight almost to the midnight hour of his life.

XVII.

Hallelujah!

A. C. DIXON

"Praise Ye the Lord" — Psalm 146:1

The word *hallelujah*, translated "Praise ye the Lord," occurs, as I have counted, twenty-four times in the Book of Psalms and four times in chapter 19 of Revelation, making twenty-eight times altogether. In the Psalms it is the hallelujah of earth, and in Revelation it is the hallelujah of Heaven.

This word *hallelujah* cannot be translated by one word into any other language, and is, therefore, transferred. It is about the same in Greek, Latin, German, French, Italian, Dutch and English. It looks as if all nations were practicing for the Hallelujah Chorus of Heaven!

There are six hallelujahs; let us pass them in review.

I. THE HALLELUJAHS OF EARTH

1. The Hallelujah of Nature

The first use of the word is at the close of Psalm 104.

This Psalm is a fine poem on nature. It begins by calling on the soul to bless God, then ascribes to God the greatness, honor and majesty which a study of nature suggests to a religious mind. The light is God's garment. The heaven is the canopy which He has spread. The foundations of the ocean were laid by Him. He makes the clouds His chariot and rides upon the wings of the wind. The thunder is His voice. He makes the springs which water bird and beast. The grass for the cattle, the trees for the nesting birds, the hills for the wild goats and the rocks for the conies are the expressions of His love and wisdom.

He made the laws which govern the sun and moon. Even the darkness serves a benevolent purpose. In the midst of this beautiful scene, man "goeth forth to his labour until the evening."

Then the psalmist-poet turns to the ocean, "this great and wide sea, wherein are things creeping innumerable," with the ships on its surface and the monsters playing in its depths. God gives life and sustenance to all these.

The study of nature fills the psalmist with praise to God. He says, "My meditation of him shall be sweet. I will be glad in the Lord." There is no conflict between the two books God has written for us, the Book of Nature and the Book of Revelation. God reveals Himself in both.

The naturalist who does not see God in His works simply shuts his eyes and refuses to see. An agnostic is one who chooses blindness rather than sight. Everything on earth and sea and sky proclaims a God.

Over the door of the great museum of McGill University in Montreal, Sir William Dawson wrote the 24th verse of this Psalm, "O Lord, how manifold are thy works: in wisdom hast thou made them all." Sir William was a scientist, but he did not allow scientific prejudice to blind the eyes of his soul.

2. The Hallelujah of Providence

Psalm 105, which also closes with *hallelujah*, deals with the history of Israel, and the psalmist sees the footprints of God in history as well as in nature.

It was God who covenanted with Abraham, "made oath unto Isaac," and "confirmed the same to Jacob."

It was God who protected His people when they "were but few in number."

It was God who "called for a famine upon the land" when prosperity had caused them to forget His laws.

It was God who sent Joseph into Egypt, and then Moses as the deliverer of His people.

It was God who sent the darkness and turned their water into blood.

It was God who spread a cloud over them for a covering and gave them "fire to give light in the night."

It was God who "opened the rock" and quenched thirst.

The psalmist closes this review of God's providential dealings with a *hallelujah*.

With some it is easier to see God in nature than in providence. Jacob could praise God for grass and trees and stars, but when Joseph was taken, he said, "All these things are against me." On another occasion the psalmist did not feel like praising and he refused to shout *hallelujah* with his lips when his heart did not prompt it. "Why art thou cast down, O my soul," he exclaims, "and why art thou disquieted within me? Hope thou in God; for I will yet praise him." I do not feel like praising now; but I will hope for the time to come when I will praise Him. Indeed I will praise God that I will yet praise Him.

There is no kind of experience in which a Christian has a right to refuse to praise God, for "all things work together for good to them that love God."

Praise God in the dark, for He maketh the light to shine out of darkness.

Praise God for sorrow, for Jesus said, "Your sorrow shall be turned into joy."

Praise God for clouds, for it is upon the clouds that God shows His rainbow of love.

Praise God for the furnace, for it is in the fire that the Son of Man delights to walk with you, and when you come out, you will find that only your bonds have been burned. He who obeys the command, "Rejoice in the Lord," has a hallelujah in his soul every minute of the day and night.

3. The Hallelujah of Grace

Psalm 106 begins and closes with *hallelujah*, and the keynote of its contents is in the first verse, "Give thanks unto the Lord, for his mercy endureth for ever."

He prays, "O visit me with thy salvation," and he makes confession of sin: "We have sinned with our fathers; we have committed iniquity, we have done wickedly." Then follows a recountal of God's merciful dealings with His people in spite of their sins. "He remembered for them his covenant and repented according to the multitude of his mercies."

The saved sinner can sing this *hallelujah* of mercy more loudly and sweetly than any other. And God's mercy fills him with song because His justice has been satisfied in Jesus Christ. Mercy can now rejoice against judgment because judgment has been met and mercy made possible through the atoning sacrifice of Christ.

"Hallelujah for the cross" is the song of the redeemed; it comes to us from Heaven and will return with us to Heaven.

4. The Hallelujah of Praise

The hallelujahs of nature, providence and grace continue to the end, but the works of God receded while God Himself is more clearly seen.

After *hallelujah* in Psalm 111 come the words, "I will praise the Lord with my whole heart."

After *hallelujah* in Psalm 112: "Blessed is the man that feareth the Lord."

After *hallelujah* in Psalm 113: "Praise, O ye servants of the Lord, praise the name of the Lord."

And as the hallelujahs increase toward the end of the book, God alone is the object of praise.

In Psalm 146: "Hallelujah. Praise the Lord, O my soul."

In Psalm 147: "Hallelujah, for it is good to sing praises unto our God."

In Psalm 148: "Hallelujah. Praise ye the Lord from the heavens."

And the psalmist calls the roll of the Hallelujah choir consisting of angels, sun, moon, and stars, the heavens, "the dragons and all deeps," fire and hail, snow and vapors, strong wind, mountain and hills, trees, beasts and cattle, creeping things and flying fowl, men and maidens, old men and children. "Let them praise the name of the Lord, for his name alone is excellent."

In Psalm 149: "Hallelujah. Sing unto the Lord a new song," as if thought and words were failing the psalmist to express his praise to God. And the climax comes in the last verse of the last Psalm, "Let every thing that hath breath praise the Lord. Hallelujah." God is greater and more worthy of praise than are His works in nature, providence and grace.

II. THE HALLELUJAHS OF HEAVEN

5. The Hallelujah of Judgment

This appears in Revelation 19:1-3:

"Hallelujah. Salvation, and glory, and honour, and power, unto the Lord our God: For true and righteous are his judgments: for he hath judged the great whore, which did corrupt the earth with her fornica- tion. . . And again they said, Hallelujah. And her smoke rose up for ever and ever."

The Hallelujah of Judgment seems to shock sentimental natures who cannot endure the thought that God could allow anyone to go to Hell. Yet anyone with a spark of nobility of character must rejoice over the apprehension and punishment of certain criminals.

When the papers published the fact that a young man entered a large room in Buffalo, New York, and stood in line with those who were receiving the greetings of President McKinley that he might murder the man who was ready to greet him with kindness, some theologians in New England who had been preaching that there was no Hell, were frank enough to confess that there ought to be a Hell for at least one man, for McKinley and his murderer ought not to be together in the same place.

For such men to escape Hell unless they repent would be cause for everlasting regret. The smoke of their torment satisfies the sense of justice which every righteous soul has. For them to escape punishment would make a discordant note in God's universe.

The Hallelujah of Judgment is the response of noble natures to the justice of the retribution which comes upon those who wreck the character and destroy the happiness of others.

6. The Hallelujah of Sovereignty

"Hallelujah: for the Lord God omnipotent reigneth."—Rev. 19:6.

> **Truth forever on the scaffold,**
> **Wrong forever on the throne,**
> **Yet the scaffold sways the future,**
> **And behind the dim unknown**
> **Standeth God within the shadow,**
> **Keeping watch above His own.**

God seems to be dethroned, but He is not. The fact that He does not strike dead monsters of iniquity in human shape is proof that He is merciful. When, therefore, I read in the press of the orgies of those who lie in wait for the innocent and seek their destruction, I say, "Hallelujah! God is merciful." And when I read that some monster has been overtaken by retribution, I say with equal emphasis, "Hallelujah! God is just." When I hear a blasphemer revile God and the Bible, I say, "Hallelujah! God is merciful or he would be smitten dumb." And when I hear the same man, yet not the same, because he has been transformed by grace, praising God for redemption through the blood of Christ, I say, "Hallelujah! Hallelujah, for the Lord God Omnipotent reigneth!"

XVIII.

Gratitude for Great Deliverances

C. H. SPURGEON

(Delivered at the Metropolitan Tabernacle, Newington, on Thursday evening, October 29, 1874.)

"For he hath looked down from the height of his sanctuary; from heaven did the Lord behold the earth; to hear the groaning of the prisoner; to loose those that are appointed to death; to declare the name of the Lord in Zion, and his praise in Jerusalem; when the people are gathered together, and the kingdoms, to serve the Lord." —Ps. 102:19-22.

I suppose the first sense of this passage would be just this. Israel had been carried away captive, and only the poorest of the people had been left in the land. Jerusalem was a heap, Zion had been ploughed with the plough of desolation—the whole country was, compared with its former state, like a desert.

But in due time God, who had peculiar favor towards His people, though He had sorely smitten them, would look down upon them. From the height of His sanctuary in Heaven, He would look down upon the ruins of His sanctuary on earth; from His heavenly city above, He would look down upon His earthly city below. And as He looked and listened, He would be attracted by the moans of His people, especially of some who were appointed to death, or, as the margin renders it, "the children of death." Upon these He would look with tender pity and, in due time, He would so come to the deliverance of His scattered people, Israel, and bring them back to their own land, and work for them such wonderful mercy that, ever afterwards, that deliverance would be spoken of with praise and thanksgiving.

Even in the last days, when all nations shall serve the Lord, the memory of this deliverance shall not be forgotten. Still shall it be the theme of joyous song and the subject of holy contemplation, just as when Israel was in Egypt, the Lord heard their groaning, and with a high hand and a stretched-out arm brought them up out of the land of bondage; and ever afterwards, among the sweetest patriotic songs of the nation was the one which Moses and Miriam sang on the further shore of the Red Sea, "Sing ye to the Lord, for he hath triumphed gloriously; the horse and his rider hath he thrown into the sea."

And all along Jewish history, whatever other songs there may have been, that one has never gone into oblivion. And even in Heaven itself "they sing the song of Moses the servant of God, and the song of the Lamb." So the deliverance promised here to Israel was to be as noteworthy as that which was given at the Red Sea, and it was to be forever kept in memory by the Lord's chosen people.

Now I am going to leave the more immediate sense of our text, yet still to give you its meaning.

It has been said that if a great crystal be broken into the smallest fragments, each piece will still be crystallized in the same form; and, in like manner, the dealings of God with His church, as a whole, will be found to be of the same kind as His dealings with the various parts of His church, and also with individuals. And in dealing with individuals, each separate act of God will have about it the same attributes and be of the same character as His dealings on a large scale with the whole of His people.

So if we break down the great truth of the text, which is like a mass of bread, into small crumbs, so that each one of the Lord's children may have a portion, it will still be bread. The truth will be the same as we try to bring it home to individual experience, and that we shall now try to do. May the eternal Spirit, the Comforter, help us in the doing of it!

First, our text speaks of

Misery at Its Extreme

You observe that it speaks of prisoners who are groaning and of those who are appointed unto death, who are evidently in chains, because they are spoken of as being loosed.

It has been well said that one half of the people in the world do not know how the other half live. And it is certainly true that there are sorrows in this world of which some of us have no conception or imagination.

Complaint was made some time ago by a hearer in a certain place of worship, that most of the sermons he heard there were composed upon the principle that everybody was happy; and it did not appear to him that the preacher had much, if any, sympathy with those who were of a sorrowful spirit, like Hannah, or those who were in an afflicted and depressed condition, who could not rejoice as he could.

I do not think that charge could be truthfully brought against me. If it could, I should be sorry; for where the Spirit of God rests upon any man at all after the manner in which it rested upon Christ, that man will repeat, in his measure, what his Lord could say in the fullest possible sense, "He hath sent me to heal the brokenhearted, to preach deliverance to the captives, and recovering of sight to the blind, to set at liberty them that are bruised, to preach the acceptable year of the Lord."

The ministry that God sends, though it will be a ministry of warning and threatening to the ungodly, will be a ministry of consolation to those who are sorrowing over their sins and seeking divine deliverance from them.

So you who are the sons and daughters of joy will pardon me if there should seem to be less than usual for you in my present discourse.

When someone is sick, nobody blames the physician for giving his main attention to the invalid of the house, nor finds fault with the nurse for her assiduous attentions to the poor suffering one.

There are many sorrows, brethren and sisters, in this world, and there are many sorrows even in the church of God; yet, for my part, I see much for which I can thank God, especially when I look upon the people of God. Then I say, with Moses, "Happy art thou, O Israel: who is like unto thee, O people saved by the Lord?"

Yet there are still many sons and daughters of affliction, and there are many trials and tribulations for each of us to pass through ere we reach that land where sorrow is unknown.

There are some sad souls who are comparable to prisoners, prisoners that groan most mournfully; some who are convinced of sin, but who have not yet found the Saviour; and some who, having found that Saviour, have fallen into doubts and fears, or who have backslidden from Him, and so lost their comforting assurance, and are now crying, "Oh that I knew where I might find Him!"

There are also some who have experienced heavy losses and are bearing heavy crosses, some who have seen the desire of their eyes taken away with a stroke, some to whom the shafts of death have flown once, twice, thrice, each time smiting down a beloved one.

There are some very dear children of God who do not always see the light of His countenance—precious sons of God who are like fruit brought forth by the moon—those who are like the bruised spices of the sanctuary all the sweeter for being bruised; and just now is the time of their sorrow, when they are prisoners who cry and sigh and groan by reason of their hard bondage.

A prisoner is often a solitary man. Very much of the sorrow of imprisonment lies in separation from friends and in utter loneliness.

Perhaps I am addressing some whose condition is that of extreme solitude. You are alone in the streets of this great wilderness of a city, and there is no such loneliness as that. Or you live in a house where you wish that you could be alone in one sense, for you are sadly alone in another sense, for nobody seems to understand your case or to enter into your experience. You wear a fetter which never fretted human wrists before; at least, so you think. You are in solitary confinement, and in that confinement you are in the dark. The light in which you once rejoiced has gone from you. The joyous flow of spirits and the cheery countenance which you used to possess have departed from you. Your heart is toubled. You are vexed with inward doubts and fears.

It is a sorrowful case when a man is in that condition, and is alone in it.

It may be, also, that you feel as if you were chained. The power to act, which you once had, has gone from you. Your former energy has departed; you are like a man spellbound. Just as sometimes, in troubled dreams, a man tries to run, but cannot even lift a foot or seeks to grasp something, but his hand seems turned to stone, so is it with you; or so, at any rate, has it been with some of us. We were chained and in the dark and solitary. We have tried hard to convince ourselves of the truth of what people said to us—that it was only a matter of nerves and that we must be energetic and make up our minds to get out of that state—which is what only fools say, for wise men know that such talk as this is like pouring vinegar into open wounds, making them smart still more and never producing any healing effects.

You have, perhaps, been like a prisoner who has well-nigh escaped, but who has been detected by the ever-watchful guards, and so had to go back again to his cell and to wear double chains through trying to escape. And, possibly, your imprisonment has lasted long.

Some of you young people may feel frightened while you hear me talk like this. Do not be alarmed, yet lay up in your memories what

I am saying, because, if these dark days never come to you, you will be all the more thankful that they do not; and if they do, you will remember that I told you about them. You will then say, "This is no strange thing that has happened to us, for the preacher said it might be so. The preacher was a man of a cheery spirit, yet he said it might be so with us."

As it now is so, we need not be surprised, and we may know that we may be the children of God, and that God may be looking down from Heaven in pity upon us and resolving to set us free, yet for the present we are fettered, and unable to escape from our prison house.

Now observe that, according to the text, *there are some who are in a worse plight than prisoners,* for they are "appointed to death"—some who feel in their bodies that they will soon die, but who have not yet learned to exult in that fact. They have not looked at the Heavenward side of it and said, "Ah! we shall soon be where we shall shake off every infirmity and sickness, and see our Saviour face to face, and praise Him without sinning forever," but they have said, "We are appointed to death; we have sharp pains to undergo and the dying strife to endure, when the clammy sweat will thicken upon our brow." As yet, that is all they have thought of, or, at least, they think most of that.

If there are any such people here, I pray God now to give you the comfort which you so sorely need, that you may even rejoice in the prospect of departing to be with that dear Lord whom you have so long loved and served.

And, alas! there are some who are "appointed to death" in a far worse sense than that; for "to die is gain" to us who are believers in Christ, but the ungodly feel that they are "appointed to death" in a much more terrible meaning of the word "death." Their sins are standing out before them and crying out against them. They feel like a murderer who is standing under the gallows. They are afraid that the floor will fall from beneath their feet, and that they will sink down to destruction. They have not yet learned the power of the precious blood of Jesus, and they have not yet heard the voice of God saying to them, "Your sins, which are many, are all forgiven you for Christ's sake."

They are under conviction of sin and, under that conviction, they feel that they are "appointed to death" eternal. Their own conscience affirms that the divine sentence is a just one, and they dare not cavil at it. Such is their own sense of their condition in the sight of God that, if they had to judge themselves, they would have to condemn themselves.

And, perhaps, meanwhile, Satan is reminding them of the wrath to come and making them feel how certain it is that it will be their portion.

They also believe themselves to be "appointed to death" because even their fellows seem to shun them. Christian people appear to have given them up as hopeless, their old companions look upon them as though they were too far gone for the mercy of God to reach them.

If there should be one such sinner in this building, I am right glad of it, for it is to you, and to those like you, that this text is especially sent. The Lord is at this moment looking down from Heaven with those piercing eyes of His which can discern the exact condition of all hearts here, and those eyes of His are gazing with infinite pity upon the groaning prisoners who are "appointed to death."

Now, brothers and sisters in Christ, there are some of us who are neither prisoners nor "appointed to death." Let us bless the Lord who has set us free and given us eternal life in His Son, Jesus Christ; but let us not forget what we used to be, nor forget those who are still in bonds and under sentence of death. Let us pray the Lord to bless them and to bring them out into liberty and joy this very hour.

Whenever I meet with a poor bondaged, sin-sick soul, I say, "Ah, my friend! I can pity you. I still have the scars upon my soul where the iron fetters used to hold me fast; and the bitterness of heart that I then experienced makes me ever feel a tender, loving sympathy with the weak ones among God's people, and the tried ones among His saints."

Those who are pushed about by many as though they were not fit to live are the very ones for whom I would fain make a way, and bring them to the softest place and say, "Be of good comfort, for it is for you and such as you that God has sent His Son and His Spirit into the world."

Now, secondly, in our text we notice

Misery Observed

I want you carefully to note these words, "For the Lord hath looked down from the height of his sanctuary; from heaven did the Lord behold the earth; to hear the groaning of the prisoner."

This expression is, of course, not strictly applicable to God, for He seeth all things; but, speaking after the manner of men, it describes Him as going up to the highest part of Heaven, as a watchman goes up to the top of the tower, where the widest range of vision can be obtained, and looks over sea and land with keen and searching eye. The original appears to mean, "The Lord leans from the height of his sanctuary," as if He bent down over the battlements of Heaven in order to get nearer to the object of His search, and to gaze the more intently at it.

He looks and listens, His eye and ear are riveted upon a prison, through whose dreary, grated window He sees what others cannot—a pining prisoner, and He hears a moan which others cannot bear to hear. And far off yonder, in the place of shame and death, He sees poor wretches taken out to die; and all His heart goes out in pity towards them.

We naturally look for some pleasing sight. We like to let our eye rest upon that beautiful lake in the distance, or that forest browning with the tints of autumn, or that green hill, or that skyscape checkered with a thousand hues as the sun is setting. But here is the great God looking out for miserable objects, keenly observing those who are the most miserable of men and women.

We like to have our ears charmed by the sweet sounds of melody and harmony; but God opens His ear to catch the sound of a moan or a groan, and turns His eye, not to search for a diamond, but to look for a tear.

O wondrous mercy of God! How strange that the King of kings should go to the top of His castle to look for a poor, wretched soul!

Yet, dear friends, after this manner do the benevolent of the earth, who are most like their God, act.

See the man whose duty it is to watch the coast. Observe him going up and down the seashore and the cliff, walking to and fro with his telescope under his arm. There is a pleasure yacht yonder, but he does not specially notice that. There is a steamer ploughing the deep, but he does not notice that. Here are little rowing or sailing boats flitting about, but he does not notice them.

Now it is night, and presently a rocket flies up into the air. Ah! he is all attention now. There is another rocket. He calls his fellows and soon they will be off with the lifeboat in answer to the signals of distress at sea.

Just so is it with God. He is looking for signals of distress.

Some of you are bent on pleasure, but He does not take special note of you. Some of you are full of pride; you are rich and increased in goods; you have all your canvas spread, and all your flags flying; but the Lord does not notice you, except in sorrow and anger. But if there is a signal of distress anywhere about, or a poor anxious soul is crying,

"O God, have mercy upon me!" or one who cannot get as far as that, but whose moan is too suffocating to become an articulate prayer (for that is what is implied in the word *groaning* here), God is sure to notice that and to hear the groaning and mark the falling tear of the penitent.

To my mind it is very wonderful that, while God is omniscient and so sees everything, there should be some special objects of His omniscient regard.

Think for a moment what concentrated omniscience must be, each individual as closely looked upon by God as if there were not another person for Him to look upon, as if he were as much the sole object of the thought of the Most High as if He had forgotten the whole universe besides. That is really the purport of what we are here taught.

God is reading you through and through, poor soul—watching you as if He had nobody else to watch, understanding you as fully as if there were nobody else to be understood—leaning over you that He may get the better view of you, bringing all His infinite faculties to bear upon your case, searching it from top to bottom. The origin of your sorrow, the ramifications of your grief, planning the outcome of the whole matter—what balms and what catholicons you need to heal your wounds and charm away your distresses!

Why, it is really worthwhile to be a prisoner to have God looking upon one like this. It is worthwhile to feel the sentence of death in one's soul in order to know, by the testimony of inspiration, that God is looking upon one out of Heaven in this special and peculiar sense. He never can forget His children anywhere; but if there is one place where He remembers them more specially than anywhere else, it is in the place of their sorrow.

I wonder whether you, good mother, have been specially thinking of anyone at home while I have been preaching. I should not wonder if it is so, and I can guess which member of your family you have thought of more than of all the rest. Of course you have been thinking of the little one whom you left so ill. You were scarcely sure whether you might venture to steal out this evening, but you said, "I think I must go, and bow before the Lord in His house." And while you have been here, you have been wondering whether the nurse has been properly caring for your sick child.

Why have you not been concerned about your big boy John who is away at school, or about your daughter Mary who is well and strong? Ah, no! you have been able to keep your thoughts away from them, but you could not keep your thoughts away from the little sick one.

Now, like as a father and a mother of a family pity their children, so the Lord pitieth them that fear Him, and He specially pities His poor tried and troubled ones.

Thirdly, keeping to the same strain, we see

Misery Relieved

God looks down from Heaven to hear the groaning of the prisoner and to loose those who are appointed to death. God's thoughts do not end in thoughts, nor do His words end in words. David wrote truly, "How precious also are thy thoughts unto me, O God!" So they are; but how precious also must His actions be!

Our text is one of the many proofs that *God does really hear prayer.* My dear brethren and sisters in Christ, I should be greatly grieved if any of you were moved in the slightest degree by the assertion that is made in these evil days that our prayers are really not heard by God. The persons who make that assertion do not know anything at all about the matter. They do not themselves pray to God, so what can they know about it?

If I were to contradict one of these philosophers concerning certain natural phenomena which I have never observed, he would at once say that I was out of court. If I said that I did not believe in the result which he said he had attained, he would say, "But I have proved it, therefore, I am able to speak so positively concerning it." If I were to say, "I have not tried it, and so do not believe it," he would say to me, "Negative evidence is of no use in such a case as this."

I cannot help using this simple illustration concerning a man who was charged with theft. They brought five persons to prove that he stole the goods, and they all saw him do it. "But," said he, "that is nothing. I can bring fifty people who *did not* see me steal the goods." But the magistrate knew that there was nothing in the evidence of the fifty people who did not see the theft; the evidence of the five people who did see it was much stronger.

So, if there is but a very small number of us who have really proved the power of prayer and who know that we have obtained answers to our petitions, the evidence of the small number who have tested the matter is worth far more than the evidence of any number who have not tried it and who, therefore, cannot say anything about it.

Some of us have been to God about great things and little things, temporal things and spiritual things; we are in the habit of going to Him all day long. There is scarcely an hour in the day in which we do not ask Him for something or other. And for us to receive answers to our prayers is as common a thing for us as breathing the air, or seeing the sun shine by day or the stars by night. It has become such an ordinary, common occurrence with us that we cannot doubt it.

Our text also reminds us that *God hears the very poorest prayers*, those which are the poorest in the judgment of men—the groanings of the prisoners.

I do not think them the poorest prayers; I consider that they are really the most powerful prayers. The prayers of the heart are often the most prevalent with God when they cannot be expressed in words, for the weight of meaning would break the backs of the words, and human language would stagger beneath the crushing load. Then it is that we often pray best of all.

If a man gets up from his knees, groans and says, "I cannot pray," he need not fret about not finding suitable words, for he *has* prayed.

Our wordy prayers, whether in our private devotions or in public prayer meetings are often so much chaff and nothing more. God does not need our words, yet we sometimes string them together as if we were displaying our oratory before the Eternal. This must not be. God loves the heart of the suppliant to be poured out before Him.

The best prayer is when a man can take his heart and turn it bottom upwards and let all that is in it run out. That is the style praying that has most influence with God.

He does "hear the groaning of the prisoner" and *with God, to hear means to answer.* We need not say, as many do, that "He is a prayer-hearing and prayer-answering God," for prayer-hearing involves prayer-answering.

O mourners, still mourn before your God, but mourn with this mixture of hope, that God will not suffer the groanings that arise from your heart, in the name of Jesus, to be like the mere whisperings of the wind. He will hear them ere long.

It is also said, in our text, that the Lord will *"loose those that are appointed to death."* Is it not wonderful that God should deliver men just when it seems as if all is over with them?

I remember lying in the condemned cell—I mean, spiritually. I thought I heard the bell tolling out my doom. I expected soon to be taken away to execution. But it was just then that God came and loosed my bonds.

I had tugged hard at them, trying to untie the knots that Moses had tied, and seeing if I could break the iron fetters of conviction and condemnation which were riveted upon me; but I could not. But the sight of Jesus Christ and Him crucified and the omnipotent might of His atoning sacrifice broke every bond from off my soul in a single moment, and I leaped into ecstatic liberty.

This is how God will deal with every soul that will but turn to Jesus on the cross and leave himself in the hands of Infinite Love.

Sinner, even if thou art on the very verge of Hell, if thou believest on the Lord Jesus Christ, He will loose thy bonds and set thee at liberty. Even though thy death warrant seems to be signed and sealed, the prey shall be taken from the mighty and the lawful captive shall be delivered, for the Lord, thy Redeemer, is almighty and none can withstand Him when He resolves to bring up His children even from their prison houses. Only trust in Jesus, rest your soul upon Him, and God will yet come to your deliverance.

The last thing in our text is

Gratitude Eloquent

"To declare the name of the Lord in Zion, and his praise in Jerusalem; when the people are gathered together, and the kingdoms, to serve the Lord."

One of the most powerful preachers who ever lived was the Prophet Jonah. I believe that Jonah learned to preach by going in the whale's belly to the bottom of the Mediterranean. That voyage was better than a university education for him. He said, "Salvation is of the Lord," before the Lord told the fish to give him up. And I have no doubt that he often preached that doctrine afterwards.

And if some preachers whom I know, instead of having lessons in elocution, were sent for a little while down into the depths of soul-despair, if they were tried and plagued and vexed and chastened every morning, they would learn a way of speaking which would reach the people's hearts far better than any that can be learned by human teaching.

If we are to speak aright for God, we need to know something of our soul's need, and the depths of it, then something of the grace of God and the height of it in bringing us out of our distresses. Hence, according to our text, *those who are set free declare or publish the name of the Lord.*

You cannot keep a man quiet if he has been, spiritually, in prison and has been brought out by God. If he has been condemned to die and has had his sentence cancelled at the last moment, you cannot make him hold his tongue. You may tell him that he must keep his religion to himself, but it is impossible. He is so overjoyed about it, it has so charmed him that he must begin to tell somebody about it.

John Bunyan said that he wanted to tell the crows on the ploughed land all about his conversion. It was quite natural that he should feel like that. He did tell a great many besides the crows about it.

There is something in a man who gets joy and peace in believing that will not be quiet.

Perhaps some of you have been very ill. A certain medicine has been recommended to you and it has restored you. Now, do you not always feel, when you meet anybody who is ill as you were, that you must tell him about the remedy that cured you? You say, "You should try so-and-so; see what it has done for me." Why do you want to tell him? You do not know why; you do not claim any very great measure of benevolence for doing it, for you cannot help communicating the good news to others.

So is it with the man who is really saved by the grace of God. He wants to communicate it, and he is the fit man to communicate it, because he who speaks from the heart speaks to the heart, and he who speaks experimentally is the man by whom the Holy Spirit is most likely to speak to those who are in a similar experience.

Perhaps, my dear friends, some of you are now suffering on purpose that God may afterwards fit you the better to speak to others in a similar case. I believe it is often so, and trust that it may turn out to be so in your case.

These people declared the goodness of God among the saints. So ought we to do. Some Christians cannot tell their experience very readily, but I think they should try to do so. Tell your brethren and sisters in Christ what the Lord has done for you. If there were more commerce among Christians with their experience, they would be mutually the more enriched.

But *these people also declared the name of the Lord among the nations* when they were gathered together. And soul, if God has suffered you to go down into the deeps of the prison house and to lie in the condemned cell, then has brought you out to life and liberty, you will surely not blush to tell to all what great things God hath done for you.

I think you must sometimes feel in your heart as if you wished you had a whole universe for an audience—the devils in Hell and the angels in Heaven, the saints above and the saints below, and the sinners too. You would like to say to them, "I sought the Lord, and he heard me, and delivered me from all my fears. This poor man cried, and the Lord heard him, and saved him out of all his troubles."

You cannot have quite so large an audience as that just yet; so, meanwhile, make use of the audience you can have and—

**Tell to sinners round
What a dear Saviour you have found.**

It is in part for this purpose that this great blessing has been given to you that you might tell all you can about it to others. I pray you not to rob God of the revenue of glory which His grace deserves at your hands.

Brethren and sisters, the gist of what I have said to you is just this: Are we rejoicing in the Lord? Then, let us turn our joy into praise of Him! Are we very much cast down? Then, let us look up to Him who looks down upon us, and let us rest in the Lord and wait patiently for Him, for He will yet bring us out of our prison house.

Are we as yet unsaved? Then, let us catch at those words in the text that tell us that God looks down from Heaven "to hear the groaning of the prisoner."

Will you not groan, poor prisoner? The Devil tempted you never to do so anymore. You yourself said, "It is no use; I have been to the Tabernacle so long, and I have been to other places of worship, but I cannot get any comfort; I will give up trying." Oh, do not so, I pray you.

Have you come to the end of yourself? Well, then, now you have come to the beginning of God. It is when the last farthing of creature-merit is gone that God comes to us with the boundless treasures of His grace. If you have one moldy crust of your own homemade bread left, you shall not have the Bread of Heaven. But when you are starved, when you have no goodness in you, nor any hope of goodness, no merit, nor hope of merit, no reliance, nor shadow of reliance upon anything that you are, or ever can be, then is the time to cast yourself upon the all-sufficient mercy of God in Christ Jesus.

Everything that you can spin, God will unravel. Everything that you can do for yourself, He will throw down. Your spider's webs He will break. You think to spin them into silken robes, but He will strip you and He will slay you, for it is written, "I wound, and I heal, I kill, and I make alive."

Blessed is the man who is wounded by God, for He will afterwards heal him! Blessed is the man who is slain by God in this sense, for He will make him alive! Blessed is the man who is empty, for God will fill him.

That was the theme of the Virgin's song, and let it be ours as I close my discourse, "He hath filled the hungry with good things; and the rich he hath sent empty away. He hath put down the mighty from their seats, and exalted them of low degree."

So may He do now, for His dear Son's sake! Amen.

CLARENCE EDWARD MACARTNEY
1879-1957

ABOUT THE MAN:

During his long and distinguished career, Dr. Macartney served three great Presbyterian churches: First Church in Paterson, New Jersey; Arch Street Church in Philadelphia, Pennsylvania; and First Church of Pittsburgh, Pennsylvania. After his retirement from the active ministry he devoted his time to writing, lecturing and preaching.

Though Macartney remained conservative in theology, he never separated himself from his apostate denomination.

Famous for his powerful biographical sermons about Bible characters, yet his best work was his own autobiography, *The Making of a Minister.* Some others of his many books are: *The Parables of the O. T., The Wisest Fool,* and *The Woman of Tekoah.*

His books reflect the keen mind of a scholar, the proficiency of a master of the English language, a genuine student of Scripture, and the sympathetic heart of a true pastor.

Dr. Macartney died in 1957.

XIX.

The Man Who Forgot:
The Chief Butler

CLARENCE E. MACARTNEY

"Yet did not the chief butler remember Joseph, but forgat him." —
Gen. 40:23.

The miserable ingrate! When the butler was a criminal in the jail, not
knowing what a day would bring to him—liberty or bondage, life or
death—he did not forget Joseph.

The chief butler and the chief baker had offended their lord, and
Pharaoh had committed them to the dungeon. The captain of the guard
gave them into the keeping of the young Hebrew captive, Joseph, who
was in prison because of the hatred of a wicked woman whose advances
he had scorned. Everybody down in Egypt seems to have had the habit
of dreaming, from the king on his throne to the baker who made his
bread. Both the chief butler and the chief baker dreamed during that
first night in the prison, and their dreams left them filled with sadness
and apprehension. Joseph himself was an exile from his home, sold
by his brothers into Egypt and now in prison charged with a crime he
did not commit. One would think it was he who needed comfort. But
he was kindhearted, this Hebrew exile; and when he saw the two
prisoners looking so sad in the morning, his heart went out to them
in sympathy. His own problem made him only the more sympathetic
with others in their troubles, instead of hardening and souring him and
making him look with suspicion upon all mankind.

One of the best ways to cure your own sorrow is to take an interest
in the sorrows of others. Joseph "sat where they sat," and therefore
he was able to meet them on a common footing and give them what
cheer he could. But Joseph, while not boasting that he could tell them

what they wished to know, said that with the help of God he would interpret their dreams. "Do not interpretations belong to God? tell me them, I pray you."

First, the chief butler told his dream:

"In my dream, behold, a vine was before me; And in the vine were three branches: and it was as though it budded, and her blossoms shot forth; and the clusters thereof brought forth ripe grapes: And Pharaoh's cup was in my hand: and I took the grapes, and pressed them into Pharaoh's cup, and I gave the cup into Pharaoh's hand. And Joseph said unto him, This is the interpretation of it: The three branches are three days: Yet within three days shall Pharaoh lift up thine head, and restore thee unto thy place: and thou shalt deliver Pharaoh's cup into his hand, after the former manner when thou wast his butler. But think on me when it shall be well with thee and shew kindness, I pray thee, unto me, and make mention of me unto Pharaoh, and bring me out of this house: For indeed I was stolen away out of the land of the Hebrews: and here also have I done nothing that they should put me into the dungeon."—Gen. 40:9-15.

Then the chief baker related his dream:

"I also was in my dream, and, behold, I had three white baskets on my head: And in the uppermost basket there was of all manner of bakemeats for Pharaoh; and the birds did eat them out of the basket upon my head. And Joseph answered and said, This is the interpretation thereof: The three baskets are three days: Yet within three days shall Pharaoh lift up thy head from off thee, and shall hang thee on a tree; and the birds shall eat thy flesh from off thee."—Gen. 40:16-19.

On the third day the interpretation of the dreams came true. Both of the men were taken out of the jail and brought to the court of Pharaoh. There the chief butler was restored to his office and held again the cup of Pharaoh, but the chief baker was hanged. I fancy I can see Joseph at the dungeon door watching those two men go out. He heard the sad farewell of the baker and the effusive gratitude of the butler who vowed that the first thing he would do when he was restored to his place would be to put in a word for the Hebrew lad who had interpreted his dream.

Joseph's heart beat high with hope, for now he was sure that he had a friend at court who would state his case to Pharaoh. But the days and the weeks and the months passed by, and still no word from the chief butler. He cannot completely have forgotten Joseph. For a few weeks at least he must have thought of him the last thing before he went to sleep and the first thing when he arose in the morning. But it was difficult to bring the matter before Pharaoh. Pharaoh might be in a bad humor and commit him again to that dungeon. Then he had fine friends, this butler, and they might wonder at his intimacy with a Hebrew slave. If he did get Joseph out of the dungeon, the youth might be on his hands.

Thus day by day it became easier for him to postpone that word with Pharaoh in behalf of Joseph, until at length, in the cares and pleasures of his office, Joseph and the promise made to him were completely forgotten. "Yet did not the chief butler remember Joseph, but forgat him." At the end of two years, when Pharaoh had his dreams about the ears of corn and the kine, the butler suddenly remembered Joseph, not out of gratitude, but hoping to win the favor of the king by bringing in a man who could tell him his dream.

Joseph was making rapid progress in the experimental knowledge of the depravity of the human heart. He knew what jealousy could move men to do, for his brothers had sold him into Egypt. He had learned from Potiphar's wife what lust and lying could do. Now he was to discover how one can forget a benefactor. If Joseph had injured this chief butler, the man would not have forgotten him to his dying day; but because Joseph had helped him in the day of trouble, he quickly forgot. "Yet did not the chief butler remember Joseph, but forgat him." O thou most human butler!

Filial Ingratitude

This most popular sin, like all sin, takes many forms and wears many different garments. It appears sometimes in the form of filial ingratitude. 'Honour thy father and mother, for this is right in the sight of the Lord.' Happy the son who can honor a mother and a father who were all to him that parents ought to be. But even when this has not been the case, children still owe a debt to the sacred relationship of father and mother, no matter how sinned against or how abused that relationship has been. It is hardly necessary to speak of extreme cases of filial neglect, for this is not respectable with either man or God. When you hear an infant crying and see its mother go to take it up in her arms and rock it and soothe it with songs and mother-talk, does it remind you that someone

must have done likewise to you, in season and out of season? When
you see anxious, careworn, sleep-robbed mothers, do you realize the
hours of anxious watching and waiting, toil and labor, playing and singing, which you yourself once cost your parents?

I went one summer in Edinburgh to visit Alison Cunningham, the
aged nurse of Robert Louis Stevenson, to whom he dedicates his book
of verse with the following lines:

> **For the long nights you lay awake**
> **And watched for my unworthy sake:**
> **For your most comfortable hand**
> **That led me through the uneven land:**
> **For all the story-books you read:**
> **For all the pains you comforted:**
> **For all you pitied, all you bore,**
> **In sad and happy days of yore: —**
> **My second Mother, my first Wife,**
> **. . . . .**
> **From the sick child, now well and old,**
> **Take, nurse, the little book you hold!**

Those are lines that every mother's son might well frame and hang
upon the walls of his room and upon the walls of the chamber of
memory.

Some think that Shakespeare sounded the depths of mortal sorrow
and suffering in that tremendous scene in *King Lear*, where the aged
king and father, cast out by his unnatural daughters, wanders on the
gloomy heath at night and utters his apostrophe to wind and rain,
thunder and lightning. He had learned how "sharper than a serpent's
tooth it is to have a thankless child." Ingratitude in all its degrees is an
ugly thing, but most loathsome when it shows itself in a child.

> **Ingratitude, thou marble-hearted fiend,**
> **More hideous, when thou show'st thee in a child,**
> **Than the sea-monster!**

It is always pleasant to look on the other side of this relationship between parents and children and to behold the beauty of gratitude. Thaddeus Stevens, one of America's most powerful and influential statesmen
before, during and after the Civil War, had a devout mother who toiled
for her lame son that he might secure an education. When he had
achieved success as a lawyer, he told how it was his delight to give every
week a gold piece to his mother so that she might put it in the collection box of the Baptist church which she attended. Every spring and

summer, in a cemetery in Lancaster you will find roses and other pleasant flowers beginning to bloom, for in his will Thaddeus Stevens provided that such flowers be planted to keep his mother's grave ever bright and fresh.

In a churchyard at Hamilton, Scotland, is the stone erected by David Livingstone and his brothers and sisters to their godly parents. It bears this inscription:

> **To show the resting place of**
> **Neil Livingstone**
> **And Agnes Hunter, his wife,**
> **And to express the thankfulness to God**
> **Of their children**
> **For poor and pious parents.**

Ingratitude to Friends and Benefactors

On one occasion Tallyrand, being told that a certain public officer was saying evil things against him, exclaimed: "That surprises me; I have never done him a favor!"

When the ministry of Robert Walpole fell and a hostile vote was being taken in the House of Commons, Walpole, watching those who voted against him, said to the one who sat near him: "Young man, I will tell you the history of all these men as they come in. That fellow I saved from the gallows. And that one, from starvation. That other one's son I promoted."

When Jesus healed the ten lepers and sent them off to the priest to declare themselves and get a certificate of health, only one returned to give thanks. Jesus was amazed, "Were there not ten cleansed?" He exclaimed, "Where are the nine?" How tenacious are our memories of occasional injuries or slights we receive, but how careless as to benefits!

> **Blow, blow, thou winter wind,**
> **Thou art not so unkind**
> **As man's ingratitude;**
> **Thy tooth is not so keen,**
> **Because thou art not seen,**
> **Although thy breath be rude.**
>
> **Freeze, freeze, thou bitter sky,**
> **That dost not bite so nigh**
> **As benefits forgot:**
> **Though thou the waters warp,**
> **Thy sting is not so sharp**
> **As friend remember'd not.**
> **Shakespeare, *As You Like It*, II. 7.**

In *Gulliver's Travels* Jonathan Swift gives us his opinion of ingratitude to friends and benefactors when he thus describes the laws of the Lilliputians:

Ingratitude is among them a capital crime . . . for they reason thus, that whoever makes ill returns to his benefactor, must needs be a common enemy to the rest of mankind, from whom he hath received no obligation, and therefore such a man is not fit to live.

In the laws of the Spartans, however, it was different. When Lycurgus was asked why his laws provided no penalty for ingratitude, he said, "I have left the punishment of that crime to the gods."

David knew the bitterness of ingratitude. Some friend or counselor had returned evil for good, treachery for confidence and to this David refers in the fifty-fifth Psalm. He says he could have stood it if it had been the work of one who hated him or some open enemy or a stranger; but what hurt him deeply was that it was by a former friend.

"For it was not an enemy that reproached me; then I could have borne it: neither was it he that hated me that did magnify himself against me; then I would have hid myself from him: But it was thou, a man mine equal, my guide, and mine acquaintance. We took sweet counsel together, and walked unto the house of God in company." —Ps. 55:12-14.

The wounds that hurt most are not those inflicted by the enemy or the stranger, but those which we have received in the house of our friend. "I was wounded in the house of my friends." It was not the dagger of Brutus, but the changed heart of Brutus which slew Caesar.

> **For when the noble Caesar saw him stab,**
> **Ingratitude, more strong than traitor's arms,**
> **Quite vanquish'd him: then burst his mighty heart;**
> **And, in his mantle muffling up his face,**
> **Even at the base of Pompey's statue,**
> **Which all the while ran blood, great Caesar fell.**
>
> *Julius Caesar*, III, 2.

On the other side, beautiful are the instances of gratitude on the part of those who did not forget their benefactors. General Grant arrived in New York in 1854 after he had resigned, under a cloud, from the army in California; he was without funds and still far from his Ohio home. In this difficulty he went to call on a West Point friend and comrade in the Mexican War, Simon Bolivar Buckner. Buckner generously supplied him with funds so that he could reach his home in Ohio. Eight years afterward when Grant captured Fort Donelson in February, 1862, the surrender was made by General Buckner, the other officers having fled. In a speech delivered long after at a Grant birthday dinner, Buckner told what had happened there at Fort Donelson:

> Under these circumstances I surrendered to General Grant. I had at a previous time befriended him, and it has been justly said that he never forgot an act of kindness. I met him on the boat [Grant's headquarters boat], and he followed me when I went to my quarters. He left the officers of his own army and followed me, with that modest manner peculiar to him, into the shadow, and there he tendered me his purse. It seems to me that in the modesty of his nature he was afraid the light would witness that act of generosity, and sought to hide it from the world.

One of the charming things about the letters of Paul is the way in which he makes mention of the different friends who have done him a kindness: "Greet Priscilla and Aquila my helpers in Christ Jesus: who for my life laid down their own necks." "Greet Amplias my beloved in the Lord." "Salute Rufus chosen in the Lord, and his mother and mine." "The Lord give mercy unto the house of Onesiphorus; for he oft refreshed me, and was not ashamed of my chains." And so down the long list of those who had shown him any kindness. The last message for Onesiphorus was given when Paul was "ready to be offered up" and his own death was at hand. Yet in that hour the memory of a friend refreshed him.

Like a sudden glow of sunlight appearing through the black clouds at the close of a stormy winter's day, is that last act in the tragedy of King Saul. When Saul had fallen on Gilboa's mount, the Philistines cut off his head and stripped the armor from the body, sending the armor to different parts of the Philistine country as monuments to the victory over their great foe. His body they nailed to the wall of Bethshan. The news soon spread throughout Israel of the defeat and the death of Saul and his sons. At length the tidings came to Jabesh-gilead, away across the Jordan, the town that Saul had saved out of the hand of the Ammonites when first he became king. No other city in all Israel raised a finger to save the body of Saul from desecration. But these men of Jabesh-gilead remembered the kindness he had done them years before. In gratitude for that deed, these men, taking their lives in their hands, "went all night" to the Philistine stronghold. Removing the body of Saul and the bodies of his sons from the wall of Bethshan, they brought them to Jabesh and burned them there, burying the ashes under the tamarisk tree. This was followed by seven days of fasting.

Can you think now of anyone who has helped you, strengthened you, guided you, supported you when you were weak, warned you when you were tempted, lifted you up when you were falling? Then crown yourself with the beauty of gratitude. Write the letter, send the greeting, say the word that can cheer a soul around whom winter's gloom may be gathering. Like the Jabeshites, you can honor the relics of the dead; but still better, you can cheer the living.

Ingratitude to God

All ingratitude is a sin against God. In his terrible, but true, arraignment of fallen human nature, Paul, in the first chapter of the letter to the Romans, describes man's sin and corruption in the terms of ingratitude:

"When they knew God, they glorified him not as God, neither were thankful; but became vain in their imaginations, and their foolish heart was darkened. . . . [They] changed the truth of God into a lie, and worshipped and served the creature more than the Creator."—Rom. 1:21-25.

For the common blessings of our life, how little thought we take and how little thanks we give! As certain birds do not reveal the brilliance of their plumage until they spread their wings in flight, so many of our blessings are not appreciated until they have departed. "Have you given any thanks to God today for your reason?" said one man to another as he stopped him on the street. Somewhat startled by the solemn look of the man, the other answered, "I confess that I have not." "Go then, and do so instantly," replied the man, "for I have lost mine!"

A popular lecturer of the last quarter of the nineteenth century had a lecture on "Sunshine" which he gave all over the country. Having arrived at a city where he was to give his lecture, he was passing through the station with a member of the lecture committee who had met him, when he saw a stretcher being carried by on which lay a paralyzed man. Pausing, he looked at the man on the stretcher and said to the young man who had met him: "Whenever I see anything like that, I say to myself, 'Every misery missed is a new blessing.'"

When that celebrated mariner and philosopher, Robinson Crusoe, was wrecked on his lonely isle, he drew up two columns which he called "the evil and the good," and set over against the evil, the good. He was cast on a desolate island; but he was alive, and not drowned, as were all his ship's company. He was divided from mankind and banished from human society; but he was not starving. He had no clothes; but the climate was so hot he did not need them. He was without means of defense; but he saw no wild beasts such as he had seen on the coast of Africa. He had not a soul to speak to; but God had sent the ship so near the shore that he could get from it all things necessary for his wants. Hence, he concluded that there was no condition in the world so miserable but there was something negative or something positive in it to be thankful for.

Paul was the man who said, "In every thing give thanks," and was himself able to do so. Even on that storm-driven vessel, tossing in the night off the shore of Malta, with the waves breaking in thunderous roars against the granite cliffs a few ship-lengths off, Paul persuaded the ship's company to take some food. But first of all, before partaking of it himself, he gave thanks unto God.

David is spoken of in the Bible as a man "after God's own heart." One reason no doubt is that David, although he sinned so deeply, confessed his sin, repented and sought after God. But another reason was his unfailing thankfulness, even in the midst of his sorrows and adversities. In David's hour of triumph, when after all his trials he became king, he did not celebrate his victory by taking vengeance upon his enemies. Instead, he wondered if there were any left of the house of Saul, that he might show the "kindness of God" unto him.

He was thinking, of course, of Saul's son Jonathan—Jonathan whose love to him was "wonderful, passing the love of women" and who had protected him against the murderous vengeance of Saul. When the king learned that there was a lame son of Jonathan still alive, Mephibosheth, David sent for him and established him in the palace, saying to him, "Fear not: for I will surely shew thee kindness for Jonathan thy father's sake." David thus remembered the kindness of Jonathan; and especially did he recall that night in the wood of Ziph when, with his fortunes at their lowest ebb and his faith in God shaken, Jonathan came to him and "strengthened his hand in God."

Show, then, your gratitude to God in deeds of kindness and goodness to others, as David did to the son of Jonathan, and by your belief and trust in God—that God from whom all blessings flow. Forget not all

His benefits! Paul had a vast vocabulary, but when he came to speak of the kindness of God to man in Christ his vocabulary failed him. All he could say was, "Thanks be unto God for his unspeakable gift"! The only thing you can give to God is your thanks.

(From *The Man Who Forgot,* copyright 1956 by Pierce & Washabaugh, used by permission of Abingdon Press.)

XX.

The Occasions of Thanksgiving

W. B. RILEY

Read Psalm 147

Thanksgiving is one of the most ancient of customs. In fact, it is altogether probable that Adam and Eve were not unmindful of the favor of God, nor silent in the autumn season when the fruits of the earth so eloquently proclaimed His grace.

Americans may imagine that the custom of Thanksgiving Day originated with the Plymouth Pilgrims in 1621; that it was made official when George Washington proclaimed Thursday, November 26, 1789, as a day of national thanksgiving, and perennial when in 1863 Abraham Lincoln established the last Thursday in November as the date on which the people should assemble in their churches and acknowledge the "grace of God" as manifested in the abundant fruits of field and forest.

But all this is modern enough! We know that an oriental custom of Thanksgiving existed even back of Israel's day and throughout the Old Testament. This custom is referred to again and again, and the feast of tabernacles became its official and annual recognition. It is not improbable that some of these later Psalms were written by David as the songs of praise expressing the thankfulness of the people in these annual occasions. If so, they were certainly well-adapted and combined in one production all that now belongs to both sermon and anthem, characterizing the same occasion. The almost infinite variety revealed in the grace of God is shown in the various objects treated in these anthems of praise.

There is a similarity between Psalms 145 to 150 inclusive; but there is also extensive variety due to the fact that no one of them was sufficient in length to voice the multiplied favors from above. In this 147th, David does what the energetic director of music often voices. He calls, as if to a choir, once, twice, thrice, "Sing! sing! sing!" He sings of God's great power! He sings of God's abundant provision! He sings of God's universal providence!

GOD'S GREAT POWER

"Praise ye the Lord: for it is good to sing praises unto our God." —vs. 1.

It certainly is! He is worthy! Few things give greater joy than praise when it comes from a heart happy in the Lord, and deserved praise is comely. The first portion of the hymn is based on what follows in verses 3 to 6.

His power is revealed in His exceeding grace.

"The Lord doth build up Jerusalem: he gathereth together the outcasts of Israel. He healeth the broken in heart, and bindeth up their wounds." — Vss. 2, 3.

The first favor from the Lord is not material prosperity. Due to men's shortsightedness and selfishness, they often so imagine, but experience proves the contrary. "Grace" is better than gifts. "Mercy" exceeds favor. "Healing" is above riches. And the binding of "the broken heart" is more to be desired than big harvests.

In fact, it is doubtful if any man or woman has ever come into the truest favor from the Lord who falls short of experiencing a sense of His care, the deep consciousness of His grace. The poet put first things first when he wrote:

> What can it mean? Is it ought to Him
> That the nights are long and the days are dim?
> Can He be touched by the griefs I bear,
> Which sadden the heart and whiten the hair?
> Around His throne are eternal calms,
> And strong, glad music of happy psalms,
> And bliss unruffled by any strife,
> How can He care for my life?

> Oh, wonderful story of deathless love!
> Each child is dear to that heart above;
> He fights for me when I cannot fight,
> He comforts me in the gloom of night.
> He lifts the burden, for He is strong,
> He stills the sigh and awakens the song;
> The sorrow that bowed me down He bears,
> And loves and pardons because He cares.

> Let all who are sad take heart again.
> We are not alone in our hour of pain;
> Our Father stoops from His throne above

To soothe and quiet us with His love:
He leaves us not when the storm is high,
And we have safety, for He is nigh.
Can it be trouble which He doth share?
Oh, rest in peace, for the Lord does care.

His power is also shown in His matchless wisdom. The study of astronomy is adding to the significance of the sentence,

"He telleth the number of the stars; he calleth them all by their names. Great is our Lord, and of great power: his understanding is infinite."— Vss. 4, 5.

Once we imagined that they amounted to a few hundred. Now we know that the sidereal systems amount to millions on millions; and we have little reason to doubt that beyond the possible reach of the mightiest instrument yet conceived by man, infinite additional sidereal systems swing through endless space. Truly did the psalmist speak, "The heavens declare the glory of God."

He calleth them by their names. How interesting it would be to know what God's names for these stars are; how surely they would exceed in suggestiveness the appellations of men!

We marvel at the wisdom of Adam when it is written:

"The Lord God formed every beast of the field, and every fowl of the air; and brought them unto Adam to see what he would call them: and whatsoever Adam called every living creature, that was the name thereof. And Adam gave names to all cattle, and to the fowl of the air, and to every beast of the field."—Gen. 2:19, 20.

Some years since, I inquired who gave names to all the pullman cars that moved by the thousands across our mighty country, and was told that an individual was paid a very high salary to do nothing else. The number and variety of them, and the necessity of no repetition, requires real ingenuity.

But Adam's task and that of the pullman car employee is trivial beside the wisdom that called the stars by name.

No wonder it is followed by the phrase, "Great is our Lord, and of great power: his understanding is infinite."

Before passing from these verses, it is well to remark the juxtaposition of the "grace of God" and the "power of God"—grace revealed in gathering "together the outcasts of Israel," healing "the broken-hearted," and binding "up their wounds," and the power exhibited in telling "the number of the stars," calling "them all by their names," which is truly interpreted as "commanding their courses."

In God, gentleness and greatness perfectly combined! How marvelous that He who framed the worlds by His Word, "so that things which are seen were not made of things which do appear" (Heb. 11:3), is the very same "who sitteth beside every sparrow" that falls to the street and flutters in dying, resting the same in the hollow of His hand till breath goes from the tiny and seemingly worthless body. That is God, and therein is His greatness!

It is further revealed in His judgments.

"The Lord lifteth up the meek: he casteth the wicked down to the ground." — Vs. 6.

There are those who would object to this because there are those who hate judgment. There are those who want no discernment between righteousness and wickedness, who would have no favor shown to the first and who would certainly have no adjudication exercised against the second. But if God did not do both, He would not be God and the very world in which we live would shortly become a moral chaos.

Illinois once had a governor who set free hundreds and thousands of her criminals. Texas had a woman governor who did the same. At first, this unmerited favor is popular. It commonly results in a re-election of such governors, but they seldom get beyond two short terms when the reeking state of society demands reform.

On the contrary, God who lifts "up the meek," and casts "the wicked down to the ground," justifies Himself in that righteous judgment, and gives men everywhere to know that the right will triumph and the wrong will go to defeat.

George Lorimer once said:

> As we look backward and comprehensively grasp all that has fallen out, both of good and bad, and observe their bearing and results, we are constrained to recognize a guiding intelligence that is not of earth, and a benevolence that has never failed to bring light out of darkness. Why then should we, who have been thus taught, falter in our faith or yield to the dismay of doubt? Though we see Him not, we have sufficient reason for trust; and though error may for the time being seem to prevail against truth, and the hearts of His children fail them for fear, unless the centuries have lied to us, He will yet remember the kingdom of His dear Son, will enlarge its borders, establish its authority, and bring forth its righteousness as the noonday.

Careless seems the Great Avenger:
History's pages but record
One death-struggle in the darkness
'Twixt false systems and the Word;

Truth forever on the scaffold,
Wrong forever on the throne;
But that scaffold sways the future,
And behind the dim unknown

Standeth God within the shadow,
Keeping watch above His own.

But we come to our second appeal for a further burst of praise, and the occasion is:

AN ABUNDANT PROVISION

"Sing unto the Lord with thanksgiving; sing praise upon the harp unto our God: Who covereth the heaven with clouds, who prepareth rain for the earth, who maketh grass to grow upon the mountains. He giveth to the beast his food, and to the young ravens which cry. He delighteth not in the strength of the horse: he taketh not pleasure in the legs of a man. The Lord taketh pleasure in them that fear him, in those that hope in his mercy."—Vss. 7-11.

Let us return to the study of these verses and see what they suggest.

God regards and provides nature's real necessities. There are those who imagine that clouds are independent of God, that rains are subject only to natural laws, that grass on the mountains to give to the beast his food, and by his carcass in turn to silence the cry of young ravens, is all by fixed and eternal laws of unconscious nature. But our Bible does not so teach, and true believers do not so hold. They entertain rather the conviction that as the stars in their courses execute the divine command, so the clouds come at the divine will; and the rain pours on earth to express the divine pleasure, and that no grass ever grew apart from the active will of God.

Robertson Nicoll has well said,

The yearly miracle which brings from some invisible storehouse the clouds to fill the sky and drop down fatness, the answer of the brown earth which mysteriously shoots forth the tender green spikelets away up on the mountain flanks, where no man has sown and no man will reap, the loving care which thereby provides food for the wild creatures, owned by no one, and answers the hoarse croak of the callow fledglings in the raven's nest—these are manifestations of God's power and revelations of His character worthy to be woven into a hymn which celebrates His restoring grace, and to be set beside the apocalypse of His greatness in the nightly heavens.

California, in America, with a climate close akin to that of Palestine, profoundly impresses these truths; and in its long, hot summer season, vegetation perishes from wide fields. The forests themselves grow brown, the grass on the mountainsides dries up and dies, and the inhabitants of the mountainsides grown lean and long for the rainy season; and lo, when it comes, what instant change!

I have seen brown fields and even mountainsides change to green overnight; and one could readily imagine the famished hart feeling a sense of gratitude to the God who thus gives the tender, luscious grass to fatten the very food on which young ravens, in a later season, shall feed.

The verses that follow sound like an abrupt and illogical change, but no so. They only teach a converse truth.

God delights in human affection, not in animal strength.

"He delighteth not in the strength of the horse: he taketh not pleasure in the legs of a man. The Lord taketh pleasure in them that fear him, in those that hope in his mercy."—Vss. 10, 11.

The time was when the strength of the horse was consummate, when the legs of a man were a synonymn for swiftness. But, alas, for miracle inventions! They have both lost their meaning. That may be why God never took delight in them. He knew how puny and poor they were, as compared with the multiplied forces at His command yet to be discovered by men.

God never rests in the ephemeral thing, but rather in the eternal. That is why He taketh pleasure in "them that fear him," in "those that hope in his mercy." "The fear of the Lord is the beginning of wisdom." Hope in God is the prophecy of its consummation.

Lot and Abraham were perfect illustrations of these converse truths. Lot believed in temporal power expressed by the strength in the horse. Lot trusted in his business sagacity, voiced by the swiftness of man's feet. Consequently, he lifted up his eyes and made choice of the rich plains of Sodom, and counted himself a farseeing man, as all conscience-less businessmen so suppose themselves.

Abraham waited for the Word of the Lord; and when it was spoken, it was this: "Lift up now thine eyes and look from the place where thou art northward, and southward, and eastward, and westward: For all the land which thou seest, to thee will I give . . . ." The truth is, then, that what Lot had chosen was finally to fall out as belonging also to Abraham and to his seed after him. Even so, and it is commonly so, the man who chooses God's will, fearing Him and "hoping in his mercy," that man will know God's pleasure and enjoy a prosperity of divine appointment.

God is not like nature — indifferent to moral rules. Henry Van Dyke writes:

> If we regarded nature as impersonal and the universe as a material mechanism, we should find no difficulty in it. For then this shining of the sun and falling of the rain upon the evil and the good, this procession of the seasons, this interflow of forces and influences which work together in productiveness, this germinating of the seed and unfolding of the blade and forming of the ear and ripening of the full corn in the ear—the same for every child of man who toils and waits—all this would be to us only the proof and illustration of what we should call the large indifference of nature. . . .
>
> But the moment we see God behind the face of nature, the moment we believe that this vast and marvelous procession of seasons and causes and changes, this array of interworking forces, is directed and controlled by a supreme, omniscient Holy Spirit, whose will is manifest in the springing of the seed, the ripening of the fruit, the fading of the leaf, the shining of the sun, and the falling of the rain—this indifference becomes incomprehensible and impossible. . . . You tell me that nature is indifferent. I say, Not if God is behind nature.
>
> You tell me that it matters not whether the hand that guides the plow be pure and clean, or wicked and defiled. Nature feels alike and will do alike for both. I say, Not if God is behind nature; not if nature is the expression of His will. He may do alike, but He does not feel alike. As well say that He who made light and darkness cannot distinguish between them, as that He whose will is the moral law ever forgets it, ignores it, casts it aside, in any sphere or mode of His action. Evermore He loves the good, the true, the noble. Evermore He hates the base, the false, the evil. Evermore iniquity is an abomination unto Him and righteousness is His delight.

But we come to the third appeal of this choir director. Once more, he calls upon the singers to unite their voices in loudest paeans.

"Praise the Lord, O Jerusalem; praise thy God, O Zion. For he hath strengthened the bars of thy gates; he hath blessed thy children within

thee. He maketh peace in thy borders, and filleth thee with the finest of the wheat. He sendeth forth his commandment upon earth: his word runneth very swiftly. He giveth snow like wool: he scattereth the hoar-frost like ashes. He casteth forth his ice like morsels: who can stand *before his cold? He sendeth out his word, and melteth them: he causeth his wind to blow, and the waters flow. He sheweth his word unto Jacob, his statutes and his judgments unto Israel. He hath not dealt so with any nation: and as for his judgments, they have not known them. Praise ye the Lord.*"—Vss. 12-20.

What does it mean? Several things! First,
God's providence is peculiar over His own people.

"Praise the Lord, O Jerusalem; praise thy God, O Zion. For he hath strengthened the bars of thy gates; he hath blessed thy children within thee."—Vss. 12, 13.

There are comely leaders among singers. A great soprano, noble alto, a high tenor, a mighty bass. They sound the note loudest and clearest. Other voices unite to swell the praise.

Why should not Jerusalem lead? Why should not Zion be first in song? These are God's own! They know Him! They love Him! They can sing from grateful hearts. Their voices express conscious favor. Such are the first singers always!

To review the divine favors is to find the lips filled with song. God is ever revealing a special grace toward His own. This single fact gave birth to more of the Psalms than all other influences combined. Take the 106th Psalm with its 48 verses, and the 107th Psalm with its 43 verses; and they are a review of God's favor to Israel and voice the psalmist's earnest plea for "praise" unto "the Lord for his goodness, and for his wonderful works to the children of men" (Ps. 107:8).

But the descendants of Jacob are not the lone children of God. Through all the centuries, His favor has been upon them that feared Him, His blessing upon believers.

Read the book of the Acts. Regard the divine inference and rejoice that God "careth for his own." Look into so-called secular history! See it made doubly sacred by the defeat of the Duke of Alva's intention against the Christians in Holland through a tide that refused to turn in twelve long hours. Look into the history of England, and recall how the fierce wind scattered the Armada of Spain over the north and spared the people of God. Or do what David is constantly doing—reduce it to individual preservation.

Remember how John Knox felt strangely moved to give up his seat in front of a window and take another. You see that impulse proven to have been of God when, a little later, a musket ball crashed past the very place where he sat and buried itself in an opposite wall. No wonder the psalmist concludes a great Psalm, written in review of such incidents, by saying, "Whoso is wise, and will observe these things, even they shall understand the lovingkindness of the Lord" (Ps. 107:43).

In the providence of God is both peace and prosperity.

*"He maketh peace in thy borders, and filleth thee with the finest of the wheat."—*Vs.14.

These two commonly walk hand in hand, just as war and want were almost always co-workers. People seldom appreciate the prosperity that belongs to a time of peace until lands are war-swept and impoverished. Germany, Russia, Austria, Rumania, Poland, Italy, Belgium, France, England—these all now appreciate the days back of 1914 when "peace was in their borders." When will the nations learn that war and want walk together, and, turning with believers hearts to the Prince of Peace, implore His presence and His administration of life—personal, national, international!

Poverty of nations and individuals will end only when God is taken into partnership, or rather is accepted in leadership. Campbell Morgan, in one of his books, tells the story of the Scotch lord who called his faithful servant into his presence and said, "Donald, I have decided to give you that farm that you may work it for yourself, own it, and spend the rest of your days on your own property."

But Donald, with all the canniness that characterized his nationality, looked up into the face of his lord and said, "It is nae gude to gie me the farm; I have nae capital to stock it."

His lordship was touched, and so he answered, "Oh, Donald, I think I can manage to stock it also."

Whereupon Donald replied, "Oh, well, if it is you and me for it, I think we will manage."

And then Morgan applied his story, "Jesus, Master, if it be Thee and me for it, we can manage." God with us, who can be against us!

His providence is over all the earth.

"He giveth snow like wool: he scattereth the hoarfrost like ashes. He

casteth forth his ice like morsels: who can stand before his cold?"—
Vss. 16, 17.

A strange expression of providence, you say! These are curses! Pardon me; not at all! Snow, frost, ice—these are as absolutely essential to the seasons' success as is spring or summer themselves. Is it not written, "As the rain cometh down, and the snow from heaven, and returneth not thither, but watereth the earth, and maketh it bring forth and bud, that is may give seed to the sower and bread to the eater"? (Isa. 55:10).

Certainly! The winter season is not a time of fruitfulness in itself, but it is an essential preparation of the earth for the same. God is not cursing man with cold! God is blessing him! By the cold, he is resting nature, refreshing her to make her more fruitful; and by the cold, He is toning up the blood, enlarging the veins, quickening the arteries, adding zest to life. These are the inheritance of all men!

Nature's pageant in the recurring seasons is only an expression of God's care for all His creatures. In fact, winter is perhaps God's own appointment for bringing men to appreciate the spring and summer and autumn. But for the very contrast, spiritual carelessness and spiritual ingratitude of a deeper and baser sort might characterize men.

It was some such thought that Robert Louis Stevenson voiced in verse:

> **If I have faltered more or less**
> **In my great track of happiness:**
> **If I have moved among my race,**
> **And shown no glorious morning face;**
> **If beams from happy human eyes**
> **Have moved me not; if morning skies,**
> **Books, and my food, and summer rain,**
> **Knocked on my sullen heart in vain,**
> **Lord, Thy most pointed pleasure take,**
> **And stab my spirit broad awake.**

And it was this same thought that David himself evidently had, for he concludes his anthem of praise with this expression:

*"He sendeth out his word, and melteth them: he causeth his wind to blow, and the waters flow. He sheweth his word into Jacob, his statutes and his judgments unto Israel. He hath not dealt so with any nation: and as for his judgments, they have not known them. Praise ye the Lord."—*Vss. 18-20.

(From the book, *The Bible of the Expositor and the Evangelist,* volume ten of a 40-volume commentary by Dr. W. B. Riley.)

ROBERT REYNOLDS JONES, SR.
1883-1968

ABOUT THE MAN:

Called the greatest evangelist of all time by Billy Sunday, Robert Reynolds Jones, better known as Dr. Bob Jones, Sr., was born October 30, 1883, in Shipperville, Alabama, the eleventh of twelve children. He was converted at age 11, a Sunday school superintendent at 12 and ordained at 15 by a Methodist church.

"Dr. Bob" was a Christ-exalting, sin-condemning preacher who preached in the cotton fields, in country churches and in brush arbors. Later he held huge campaigns in American cities large and small, and preached around the world.

Billy Sunday once said of him: "He has the wit of Sam Jones, the homely philosophy of George Stuart, the eloquence of Sam Small, and the spiritual fervency of Dwight L. Moody."

He saw crowds up to 10,000 in his meetings, with many thousands finding Christ in one single campaign.

But Dr. Bob was more than an evangelist. He was also an educator—a pioneer in the field of Christian education, founding Bob Jones University some 57 years ago.

Behind every man's ministry is a philosophy. Dr. Bob's was spelled out in the sentence sermons to his "preacher boys" in BJU chapels. Who has not heard or read some of these: "Duties never conflict!" "It is a sin to do less than your best." "The greatest ability is dependability." "The test of your character is what it takes to stop you." "It is never right to do wrong in order to get a chance to do right."

"DO RIGHT!" That was the philosophy that motivated his ministry, saturated his sermons, and spearheaded his school.

His voice was silenced by death January 16, 1968, but his influence will forever live on and Christians will be challenged to "DO RIGHT IF THE STARS FALL!"

XXI.

"Bless the Lord"

BOB JONES, SR.

(Message given at Sword of the Lord Conference on Evangelism, Chicago, Illinois, Thanksgiving week, 1948.)

"Bless the Lord, O my soul: and all that is within me, bless his holy name. Bless the Lord, O my soul, and forget not all his benefits: Who forgiveth all thine iniquities; who healeth all thy diseases; Who redeemeth thy life from destruction; who crowneth thee with lovingkindness and tender mercies; Who satisfieth thy mouth with good things; so that thy youth is renewed like the eagle's. The Lord executeth righteousness and judgment for all that are oppressed. He made known his ways unto Moses, his acts unto the children of Israel. The Lord is merciful and gracious, slow to anger, and plenteous in mercy. He will not always chide: neither will he keep his anger for ever. He hath not dealt with us after our sins; nor rewarded us according to our iniquities. For as the heaven is high above the earth, so great is his mercy toward them that fear him. As far as the east is from the west, so far hath he removed our transgressions from us. Like as a father pitieth his children, so the Lord pitieth them that fear him. For he knoweth our frame; he remembereth that we are dust. As for man, his days are as grass: as a flower of the field, so he flourisheth. For the wind passeth over it, and it is gone; and the place thereof shall know it no more. But the mercy of the Lord is from everlasting to everlasting upon them that fear him, and his righteousness unto children's children; To such as keep his covenant, and to those that remember his commandments to do them. The Lord hath prepared his throne in the heavens; and his kingdom ruleth over all. Bless the Lord, ye his angels, that excel in strength, that do his commandments, hearkening unto the voice of his word. Bless ye the Lord, all ye his hosts; ye ministers of his, that do

his pleasure. Bless the Lord, all his works in all places of his dominion: bless the Lord, O my soul."—Ps. 103.

A hobbyist is a man who plays on the same note all the time. He has the best time of any man on earth, but he is a pest! This 103rd Psalm hits all the notes. You cannot find a spiritual note that it does not hit.

Paul played on all the notes. You remember he said, "Ye turned to God from idols [that is conversion] to serve the living and true God [that is Christian service]. . . to wait for his Son from heaven [that is the Christian hope]" (I Thess. 1:9, 10).

The worst hobbyists in this country are modernists, not fundamentalists. We are bad enough, but we are not as bad as they are. Hobbyists!

Once in a while I hear a pianist who goes away over and hits a note that ought to be hit just once in a while. What would you think about a fellow who hit that note all the time? It is a nice note, but it is not to be played all the time. There are a few fundamental notes.

Brother, there is one note you cannot overplay, and that is the Jesus note. The blood note, the resurrection note, the regeneration note, the salvation-by-grace-through-faith-in-the-atoning-blood note—you cannot overplay those. But there are some notes that need to be hit just once in a while.

You can overplay the Hell note. You can overplay the Heaven note. I do not want to shock you, but you can overplay the Second-Coming note. I am a premillennial, pretribulation rapturist Christian. Don't misunderstand me! But listen, we are neglecting the fundamental notes in this country. You can overplay the church notes. You can overplay the body-of-Christ note. But you cannot overplay the evangelism note. God has only one program in this age and that is the program of evangelism. Everything is evangelism. That is the only program God has.

But I started out to say that this Psalm plays on all the notes.

"All That Is Within Me"

"Bless the Lord, O my soul: and all that is within me, bless his holy name. . . ."

God does not ask you to get something out that is not there. Some folks do not have much in them. Some folks are awfully shallow. "All that is within me"!

I used to have a sister just older than myself. She had a good husband. His business failed and he died and left her with nine children. I helped to take care of her children, educated all of her children. She was the sweetest thing you ever saw in your life. She had the keenest sense of gratitude of anybody I ever knew. I would just have to make her take money. Did you ever have any relatives that you had to take care of—the kind that wanted something every time they saw you! I had a relative like that. I never saw him any oftener than I had to!

Some of us go to God and say, "Give me, give me, give me." All you want is a handout! It is a wonder that God does not get disgusted with us. Did you ever go to God and God said, "What do you want?" and you answered, "God, I just want to be near You; I don't want anything—I just like to be near You"?

One day I was at my sister's house. I said, "Here is some money for you."

"Oh," she said, "Bob, I don't need a thing."

I said, "Yes, you do; shut up!"

"No, I don't. You've already done too much for me!"

Oh, say, brother, you would give a person like that just anything. Some folks have such a sense of gratitude! 'All that is within me says hallelujah!' You know, God does not ask you for anything you do not have. If you are a little, shallow fellow, He knows it.

"Forget Not All His Benefits"

"Bless the Lord, O my soul, and forget not all his benefits."

It is very easy to forget, isn't it? God has been so good to us. He has been good to me. I wonder if you would think me immodest if I told you this?

Twenty-three years ago my son and his mother and I stayed down here at the LaSalle Hotel. This time while I am in town I am staying over there just for old-time's sake. (I had not stayed there since the fire.) I sat here and heard my son preach the other day and I said, "Isn't God good to me? Suppose my boy were in a drunkard's ditch. Suppose he were in jail." It is so easy for us to take God for granted and our blessings for granted!

You take your wife for granted. You take your friends for granted. (My wife and I had an anniversary the other day. We had been married forty years. She has great big black eyes and white hair. They go together so well!) We just take so much for granted! We should not forget all His benefits. Say, aren't you glad you live in this country where you have the privilege of hearing the Gospel?

"Who Redeemeth Thy Life From Destruction"

"Who forgiveth all thy iniquities; who healeth all thy diseases; Who redeemeth thy life from destruction."

He has done that for me. I stayed in the Winecoff Hotel in Atlanta, Georgia, the night before the fire. I was in that hotel and planned to stay the night the fire came. I finished my business in Atlanta. I was due in Mobile, Alabama, the next day; had reservations at the hotel there. I called up the hotel and said, "Say, I can get a train reservation out of here. I will come down to Mobile tonight. Can you take care of me?"

They said, "Dr. Jones, we are sorry. There is a convention here. We haven't a bed. There are cots all over the place. We have a reservation for you tomorrow, but we can't take care of you until then."

I said, "All right, I'll just stay here." But something kept saying, "Get out of here!" I cannot describe the feeling.

I called another hotel in Mobile. It happened that a friend of mine was at the desk. He said, "Yes, Dr. Bob, I have a room for you; come on." I caught the train and went on down.

That night the Winecoff fire came. When the fire came, my phone began to ring and folks said, "Oh, we just heard over the radio about the fire in the Winecoff at Atlanta and thought you were there!" Now, what took me out? Listen!

When you get to Heaven you will find that there were ten thousand deliverances in your life that you never even knew about. I would have been dead and in eternity had I stayed in that hotel that night. Everybody on that side of the building on the floor I was on burned to death.

"Who Crowneth Thee With Lovingkindness and Tender Mercies"

I would like to preach a sermon on those words, "lovingkindness and tender mercies." If a man comes to your house and says, "I am hungry," and you give him something to eat; that is kindness. But it is not necessarily lovingkindness. Lovingkindness is handing him something to eat and saying, "God bless you, I am sorry you are up against it," and then telling him good-by when he has eaten.

"Tender mercies." If a judge in a courtroom should say to me, "I'll be merciful to you! Get out of here!"—I would be glad to get out. But if the judge should say, "I'm going to be merciful to you. I am sorry you got in trouble. Be a good boy now"—that would be tender mercy. I think we Christian people could learn something about that. We need lessons in this matter.

"Who Satisfieth Thy Mouth With Good Things..."

I am so glad I have a sense of taste. I would never eat if I did not have; honest, I wouldn't. It is my sense of taste that makes me eat. I would not stop to eat if I did not get hungry. Did you ever thank God for your sense of taste? Suppose you did not know sugar from quinine?

"The Lord executeth righteousness and judgment for all that are oppressed."

We need today to get a new conception of God Almighty's justice. "Vengeance is mine; I will repay, saith the Lord" (Rom. 12:19). Almighty God knows how to take care of your enemies. Thank God, you have Him on your side.

"He made known his ways unto Moses, his acts unto the children of Israel. The Lord is merciful and gracious, slow to anger, and plenteous in mercy. He will not always chide: neither will he keep his anger for ever. He hath not dealt with us after our sins; nor rewarded us according to our iniquities."

Suppose you got what you deserved. You would be in Hell. Every one of us would be there!

"For as the heaven is high above the earth, so great is his mercy toward them that fear him. As far as the east is from the west, so far hath he removed our transgressions from us."

I do not know how far that is, God; but if there is any distance further than that, take mine on further. I do not know how far that is, but You can't get mine too far to suit me!

"Like as a father pitieth his children, so the Lord pitieth them that fear him."

Do you know what comfort is? Comfort is the hand of pity pulling you out of the ditch, brushing the dirt off you and telling you to be careful. Isn't that good? Pity!

"For He Knoweth Our Frame; He Remembereth That We Are Dust"

I am surely glad He knows my frame. I am Irish. If I were dealing with a God who did not know the Irish blood, I would be up against it.

A fellow once said about me, "If you fuss long enough and give him time, he will eventually do right. He will come around after a while." "He knoweth our frame." He looks down and says, "Look what he is made out of. He is nothing but dirt, anyhow." He *remembers* that we are dust.

You know, the wonderful thing to me is that God loved me and sent Jesus to die for me. The most wonderful thing is that the thing works. I have often thought of that day when He is going to present me faultless in the presence of His glory. One day I am going to be put on exhibition. You watch me! I am going to be a model. I am going to walk by the throne of God. God will look me over. Jesus will say, "What do You think of him?" God will say, "He is perfect, absolutely flawless!" Brother, that is going some for me! "Present us faultless"!

Wait a minute. Let me say to you by way of parenthesis that we ought to try to be blameless now. We cannot be faultless but we ought to be blameless down here in this world.

"As for man, his days are as grass: as a flower of the field, so he flourisheth. For the wind passeth over it, and it is gone; and the place thereof shall know it no more. But the mercy of the Lord is from everlasting to everlasting upon them that fear him, and his righteousness unto children's children; To such as keep his covenant, and to those that remember his commandments to do them. The Lord hath prepared his throne in the heavens; and his kingdom ruleth over all. Bless the Lord, ye his angels, that excel in strength, that do his commandments, hearkening unto the voice of his word. Bless ye the Lord, all ye his hosts; ye ministers of his, that do his pleasure. Bless the Lord, all his works in all places of his dominion: bless the Lord, O my soul"!

> **All hail the pow'r of Jesus' name!**
> **Let angels prostrate fall:**
> **Bring forth the royal diadem,**
> **And crown Him Lord of all.**
> **Bring forth the royal diadem,**
> **And crown Him Lord of all!**

Let ev'ry kindred, ev'ry tribe
On this terrestrial ball,
To Him all majesty ascribe,
And crown Him Lord of all.
To Him all majesty ascribe,
And crown Him Lord of all!

O that with yonder sacred throng
We at His feet may fall!
We'll join the everlasting song,
And crown Him Lord of all.
We'll join the everlasting song,
And crown Him Lord of all!

George Washington's Thanksgiving Proclamation

Whereas it is the duty of all nations to acknowledge the providence of Almighty God, to obey His will, to be grateful for His benefits, and humbly to implore His protection and favor: and

Whereas, both houses of Congress have, by their joint committee, requested me "to recommend to the people of the United States a day of public thanksgiving and prayer, to be observed by acknowledging with grateful hearts the many and signal favors of Almighty God, especially by affording them an opportunity peacefully to establish a form of government for their safety and happiness";

Now, therefore, I do recommend and assign Thursday, the 26th day of November, next, to be devoted by the people of these states to the service of that great and glorious Being who is the beneficent author of all the good that was, that is or that will be; that we may then all unite in rendering unto Him our sincere and humble thanks for His kind care and protection of the people of this country previous to their becoming a nation, for the signal and manifold mercies and the favorable interpositions of His providence in the course and conclusion of the late war, for the great degree of tranquility, union, and plenty which we have since enjoyed; for the peaceable and rational manner in which we have been enabled to establish constitutions of government for our safety and happiness, and particularly the national one now lately instituted; for the civil and religious liberty with which we are blessed, and the means we have of acquiring and diffusing useful knowledge; and, in general, for all the great and various favors which He has been pleased to confer upon us.

And also that we may then unite in most humbly offering our prayers and supplications to the great Lord and Ruler of nations, and beseech Him to pardon our national and other transgressions; to enable us all, whether in public or private stations, to perform our several and relative duties properly and punctually; to render our national government a blessing to all the people by constantly being a government of wise, just and constitutional laws, discreetly and faithfully executed and obeyed; to protect and guide all sovereigns and nations (especially such as have shown kindness to us), and to bless them with good government, peace and concord; to promote the knowledge and practice of true religion and virtue, and the increase of science among them and us; and, generally, to grant unto all mankind such a degree of temporal prosperity as He alone knows to be best.

Given under my hand, at the city of New York, the third day of October, A.D. 1789.

G. WASHINGTON

In Everything Give Thanks

When clouds of sorrow sweep across my sky of brilliant hue,
  When grey and somber, warlike, fierce they hide away the blue,
I am not bidden to despair or mope with clouded brow;
  God's Word comes shining—'tis His Sun, my courage to endow,
    "In Everything Give Thanks!"

When faced with dire calamity, when driven to despair,
  When tempted to cry out, "My God! Thy dealings are unfair!"
He shows me One whose awful grief made Heaven hide its face;
  And then His Word comes shining through to give sustaining grace—
    "In Everything Give Thanks!"

When bounties rich and plentiful are lavished from His hand,
  When all my needs are met by Him on whom my life depends,
'Tis then of all times, I am tempted to forget His Love,
  Forget to offer praise to Him, to lift mine eyes above—
    "In Everything Give Thanks!"

God grant that I may learn to walk so humbly with my Lord,
  So keep in fellowship with Him, abiding in His Word,
That not one day but every day may be Thanksgiving Day,
  That life and lips, and all I am—may all of me, alway,
    "In Everything Give Thanks!"

—Paul Hutchens

"My Cup Runneth Over"

There is always something over
   When we trust our gracious Lord,
Every cup He fills o'erfloweth,
   His great rivers all are broad.
Nothing narrow, nothing stinted,
   Ever issues from His store;
To His own He gives full measure,
   Running over, evermore.

There is always something over
   When we, from the Father's hand,
Take our portion with thanksgiving,
   Praising for the path He planned.
Satisfaction, full and deepening,
   Fills the soul, and lights the eye,
When the heart has trusted Jesus,
   All its need to satisfy.

There is always something over
   When we tell of all His love;
Unplumbed depths still lie beneath us,
   Unscaled heights rise far above:
Human lips can never utter
   All His wondrous tenderness,
We can only praise and wonder,
   And His name forever bless.

             —Margaret E. Barber

Thanksgiving

Once again our glad thanksgivings
  Rise before our Father's throne,
As we try to count the blessings
  Of the year so swiftly flown;
As we trace the wondrous workings
  Of His wisdom, power, and love
And unite our "Holy! Holy!"
  With the seraphim above.

As we gather round our firesides
  On this new Thanksgiving Day
Time would fail to count the blessings
  That have followed all our way.
Grace sufficient, help and healing,
  Prayer oft answered at our call;
And the best of all our blessings,
  Christ Himself, our All in all.

He has blessed our favored country
  With a free and bounteous hand;
Peace and plenty in our borders,
  Liberty through all our land.
And although our sins and follies
  Oft provoked Him to His face,
Mercy still restrains His judgments,
  And prolongs our day of grace.

While we love to count the blessings,
  Grateful for the year that's gone,
Faith would sweep a wider vision,
  Hope would gaze yet farther on.
For the signals all around us
  Seem with one accord to say,
"Christ is coming soon to bring us
  Earth's last, best, Thanksgiving Day!"

—A. B. Simpson

In Everything

In everything? In sorrow, pain, and loss?
  When some hard lesson racks the weary mind?
When, just before, there looms the threat'ning cross?
  When nights are long, and morn brings day unkind?

In everything! Each sorrow and each pain
  Is known by One who measures every day;
And lessons hard, well mastered, will make plain
  The faithful Teacher planning all the way.

Dost know the cross must come before the crown?
  And seed unburied must abide alone?
Dost know the cloud that spreads its sullen frown
  Harms not the sun, whose power must be shown?

Then waiting not for that which shall make clear
  The tender love in what seems harsh and stern,
O Soul redeemed, look up! Dismiss thy fear!
  Now is the time when thanks thou shouldst return!

                    —Author Unknown

'MID PLEASURE, PLENTY, AND SUCCESS,
  FREELY WE TAKE FROM HIM WHO LENDS:
WE BOAST THE BLESSING WE POSSESS,
  YET SCARCELY THANK THE ONE WHO SENDS.

BUT LET AFFLICTION POUR ITS SMART,
  HOW SOON WE QUAIL BENEATH THE ROD!
WITH SHATTERED PRIDE, AND PROSTRATE HEART,
  WE SEEK THE LONG FORGOTTEN GOD.

                    —Eliza Cook.